MW00653241

How To Compile Your Own Handicap

by

David Dickinson

©David Dickinson/Raceform Ltd
Compton, Newbury, Berkshire, RG20 6NL
Tel: 01635 578080 Fax: 01635 578101
INTERNET: http://www.raceform.co.uk

To Sonia

Without her hard work
and encouragement, this book would not have seen
the light of day.

With many thanks to Graham Wheldon, Richard
Lowther, Steven Clarke and everyone else who has
helped along the way.

CONTENTS

INTRODUCTION

Why do people handicap? To those of you like myself who are married, this will be an all too familiar question. After all, our other halves do have a point. Why should any sane person spend hours each day looking up the form of horses, compiling figures etc. and still not be guaranteed to come up with the race winner? Maybe it's the 'Del Boy' philosophy, "This time next year we'll be millionaires!" More likely it is the thrill of pitting your judgement against the Bookmakers'. Whatever the reason, you will probably find handicapping addictive, and ultimately your pocket ought to benefit.

Be warned, one of the great attractions of our wonderful sport can also become its great frustration, as no amount of work can guarantee success. As someone who has spent a considerable part of his life compiling a handicap, firstly as a hobby but latterly for a living, I write this in the hope that it will offer others a short cut past the many pitfalls and blind alleys that I have encountered over the years.

In my experience, the punters who do best without resorting to ratings are those who visit the track almost every day. A wonderful life I'm sure, but for most of us a pipe-dream. In general these people are wealthy and/or professional punters. A professional punter will use the evidence of his own eyes to decide whether or not a horse has done its best to win. Some horses have retained their pack instinct and are not natural leaders. These are rarely winners.

A pre-race talk to regular racegoers will elicit such terms as 'dog' or 'ungenuine' to describe a horse who does his best not to win. Another term sometimes heard is a 'no-race', this being a race that took so little winning that the form should be ignored. In the Handicapper's world there is no such thing as a no-race, every performance can be given a rating if the scale is taken low enough. In practice such effort would be a monumental waste of time as there are plenty of horses around who rarely merit a rating and would be rank outsiders in even the most dire of contests.

The majority of racing fans still regard handicapping in the same way that walkers regard golf, a pleasure spoiled. Lesson one is among the hardest to learn, keep an open mind. If running your own ratings do not ignore the possibility (probability, in truth) that you will make mistakes, it is impossible not too. Ratings have great merit, but are not the be all and end all.

CHAPTER 1

THE THEORY BEHIND HANDICAPPING

Since early times, handicapping and Handicappers have been as much at the core of racing as training and betting. However, in recent years, interest and press coverage of the subject have really begun to blossom. When I first started to read racing publications as a boy, the results sections of the old *Sporting Chronicle Handicap Book* and the *Sporting Life Guide* consisted of facts and not figures, certainly not figures to describe horses' ability anyway.

Over the years, many things have changed, including the quality of racing papers. *Raceform Update,* formerly the *Sporting Chronicle Handicap Book,* has greatly increased the amount of information provided to punters, not least in the area of handicapping. As well as the "Split Second" time ratings which have appeared in the paper for many a long year, there are also official handicap and private handicap marks for every horse in every race. But why do we need all of this information, you may well ask? Are we in danger of information overload? Before we get lost in the mountain of figures available, we should go back to basics and see why handicapping came about.

Men have always liked to boast, or so my wife tells me!, so it's not too surprising that in the earliest days of racing, the Lords of the Manor often boasted that their prize steed was the fastest horse around. As with all such boasts, there comes a day of reckoning. Jump racing apparently began with matches being made by the local gentry, to be run between the steeples of churches in adjacent villages (hence the term steeplechasing), Flat racing having started considerably earlier in a similar way. Now put yourself in the shoes of a landed gent whose horse had just suffered a defeat at the hands of his local rival. Beaten once, you would probably want a rematch. Beaten over and over again, you would surely call it a day. The obvious consequence of this being the death of racing.

However, with hindsight, there were three ways out of such a situation. The first is quite simple, buy another horse and start the process all over again, or choose one of the other two options - betting and handicapping. The owner of the beaten horse may be more willing to try again if, in the unlikely event that his horse should win, his financial gain would be greater than his rival's. So, by not having an equal stake from each participant, your opponent's horse would effectively become odds-on.

The other alternative is to slow down your opponent's horse with extra weight to even up their chances of victory, in short 'handicap' his horse.

Handicapping really started to flower in the mid-1800s, courtesy of a veteran of both the Navy and the Houses of Parliament, Admiral Henry Rous. He was appointed as public Handicapper rather late in life and, by the time of his death some twenty years later, racing was a good deal closer to the industry we know today. One of his most famous quotes is that, "every great handicap offers a premium to fraud, for horses are constantly started without any intention of winning, merely to hoodwink the Handicapper".

More than a hundred years on and how things have changed depends on how cynical your view of life. We know that when a travel agent says of a destination that it has a "lively nightlife", what he really means is that, because of the noise, we are unlikely to get any sleep before four in the morning! It's the same in all walks of life, for example Estate Agents are renowned for their creative use of the English language. Let's face it, to describe a property as 'compact and bijou' really means not much bigger than your average toilet. Horseracing is no different. The cynics amongst you might think that to say a trainer has a "shrewd ability to land big handicaps" is merely racing journalese for something not entirely dissimilar to the practices of the last century.

There are a number of assumptions which need to be made and acknowledged before handicapping can be taken seriously. Firstly, that a graph plotting any horse's completion time at any distance, against the increase in poundage on its back, will be linear. This does assume the same course and ground conditions.

For any distance,

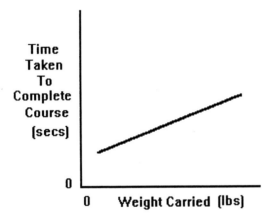

In theory, the above graph is correct but, as with most things, it is not completely true. I'm sure some of you are thinking, there must be some point where the horse is carrying so much weight that it would be unable to complete the course, whereas carrying just 1lb less it would be capable of the task. You are right, it would be naive to think that you can keep adding weight to a horse and it would still complete the course. How many of us have backed horses that have pulled up in a race because they just couldn't continue?

However, the reason that the graph can be justified is that the weights horses carry vary comparatively little once the horse's own body weight is included in the equation. The variation between the highest and the lowest weight an animal is ever likely to carry under any particular code (i.e. Flat or jumps), is around three stone (3st). OK, 3st excess baggage for a human is a lot to carry, but to a horse it represents only 2 or 3% of the entire load.

This assumption allows us to conclude that, if a horse is slowed by, for example, a fifth of a second in a specific type of race by the raising of his weight from 8st to 8st 1lb, then the same deterioration in performance would occur by raising his weight from 9st to 9st 1lb.

Another assumption that Handicappers make is that the level of deterioration in performance as weight is increased is the same for every horse. That is to say that if a horse is one length slower in a specific race carrying an extra pound, then all others will slow in the same way given the same set of circumstances. This is not entirely true, a fully mature seventeen-hand horse will be less inconvenienced by extra weight than a lightly-built two-year-old. After all, the extra weight will be a larger percentage of the youngster's total burden.

The performance of a horse will improve as it progresses towards full maturity; to allow for this an official weight-for-age table exists. This table makes the assumption that, over any given distance at any given time of year, if one horse of a certain age is, for example, 10lb short of full maturity, then all others of the same age will be as well. Horses, like humans, do not all grow and mature at the same time. Therefore, even the most perfect weight-for-age table could only represent the average shortfall from full maturity.

So far, in handicapping terms, I appear to be setting out the case for the non-believers. I know and respect plenty of racing people who set little or no store by ratings. The trainer of a recent Classic winner, when asked by a colleague about the placing of his horses and how much time he spent analysing the form replied, "If I have a Group Three horse in my yard, I run it in a Group Three race".

In the days of the *Sporting Chronicle*, I used to take a keen interest in horses tipped by Dick Adderley. When I became a journalist and met the man, I got quite a shock for, far from studying form, Dick took much more interest in the horses themselves. By noting horses in-form, those about to strike form, and those running below their class, Dick provided his followers with a steady stream of winners. He had little time for the figures compiled by the so-called private Handicappers like myself, figures which a few of my colleagues still make fun of. It is quite common to hear one particular Press Room wag shout to me those immortal words, "top on my figures, old boy", as soon as some nag with no possible hope on form has romped home. Such is a Handicapper's lot.

However, I firmly believe in handicapping, but don't hold with the sort of blinkered approach which says, "this has to win, I've got it 10lb clear". Racing is about so much more than that.

Handicapping is not about being right all the time, it is about being least wrong all the time. This is the most important lesson to learn, whether compiling your own handicap ratings or using those compiled by someone else from a newspaper or tipping sheet. The figures are not carved in stone - if they were it would add plenty to the postage cost of *Raceform Private Handicap* - and plenty of other factors come into play to decide the winner of any race - state of the ground, skill of the jockey, distance of the race, or even if the horse is just having an off-day. The list could go on and on. The figures you use just tell you what a horse has appeared able to achieve in the past, not for certain what he will prove capable of in the future. Try not to learn this lesson through your pocket.

The aim of what follows is to give you a deeper understanding of both private and official handicapping, and to offer some advice on their benefits and pitfalls. I hope to show you how to use your own skills so you will be placed in a much better position to form your own opinions on the rights and wrongs of handicapping. At the end of the day, why should you trust a complete stranger to advise you on which horse to back when you can make up your own mind. Be the master of your own destiny. There's no better feeling than backing a long-priced winner that you've found and the bookies haven't!

This book sets itself the rather ambitious task of being all things to all men (and to avoid the wrath of female readers, women!). Such a target is unattainable unless I rival the Encyclopedia Brittanica for space on your library shelf. However, I have set out to detail the ideas behind handicapping for the raw novice, but still in the hope that the occasional piece of information in these pages may aid even the most experienced Handicappers.

CHAPTER 2

THE RULES A HANDICAPPER FOLLOWS

In the previous chapter we looked at the reasoning behind the rules to handicapping. Now we are ready to establish a framework for our handicapping by applying numeric values to the rules.

What we need are answers to questions. Using the minimum race distance of five furlongs, the most basic question is "just how many extra pounds on a horse's back will slow it by a length". In feet, the distance of such a race is 3,300 and, as the weight of the average horse and the average jockey combined is roughly 1,100lb, it essentially follows that each pound slows a horse by three feet. As the average length of a horse is around nine feet, our first conclusion is that one length (nine feet) is worth roughly 3lb in a five furlong race.

From the other conclusions we drew in the last chapter, we can deduce that if 3lb is worth one length in a five furlong race, then it is worth two lengths in a ten furlong race, three lengths in a fifteen furlong race and so on. From this we can derive the following chart:-

Race Distance in Furlongs	Pound value of One Length
5	3
6	2.5
7	2.14
8	1.875
9	1.67
10	1.5
11	1.36
12	1.25
13	1.15
14	1.07
15	1
16	0.94

Another way of expressing this is that,

Furlongs in race x Pounds per length = 15

That is to say that, in a six furlong race for example, one length would be worth 2½lb, because 6 multiplied by 2.5 is equal to 15.

The parts of a length

When a race finishes, the official Judge places each horse in finishing order, which is then reported in the Racing Papers and *the Form Book*. His other task is to give the distance each horse finished behind the one immediately in front. Most of the distances that he uses are self explanatory, but some are not.

The largest distance a Judge can return is a distance. This means that two of the horses were split by more than thirty lengths at the finish. Unfortunately, from a Handicapper's point of view, this could mean thirty-one or 131 lengths.

It is therefore advisable to stop assessing the horses in a race once you get to one that has been beaten a distance.

At the other end of the scale, distances under half a length could also cause confusion. A few years back I sat down and measured side-on pictures of galloping horses with a ruler to establish what percentage of a length each distance represented. To the best of my knowledge the following are correct:-

a neck	0.4 of a length
a head	0.25 of a length
a short Head	0.1 of a length

The one that gives most concern is a short-head. This is because it is the minimum distance that a Judge can use to split horses, or at least it is in the UK. Whether the horses are divided by a tenth of a length or a tenth of an inch, the Judge will use a short-head. My advice is to treat short-head margins as dead-heats.

The race shown over is a good example of the mixture of distances that can occur.

2037-ASCOT (R-H) (Good to firm)
Wednesday June 19th
WEATHER: warm WIND: almost nil

2050   JERSEY STKS (Gp 3) (3-Y.O) (Class A)
2-30 (2-31) 7f £34,400.00 (£13,032.50: £6,391.25: £2,926.25) Stalls: Centre GOING minus 0.25 sec per fur (GF)

	SP	RR	SF
1495² **Lucayan Prince (USA) (97)** (DRLoder) 3-8-10b RHughes(2) (dwlt: gd hdwy on bit over 1f out: n.m.r & squeezed thro: led wl ins fnl f: r.o wl) — 1	50/1	114	55
1796· **Ramooz (USA) (106)** (BHanbury) 3-8-10 PatEddery(4) (nt clr run, swtchd lft & bmpd 2f out: hdwy over 1f out: led ins fnl f: sn hdd: unable qckn) 1½ 2	4/1¹	111	52
1639· **Bewitching (USA) (102)** (JARToller) 3-8-7 SSanders(14) (hld up: rdn over 2f out: one pce) ¾ 3	25/1	106	47
1796³ **Almushtarak (IRE) (99)** (MissGayKelleway) 3-8-10 WJO'Connor(12) (b.hind: lw: a.p: led over 2f out tl ins fnl f: one pce) s.h 4	20/1	109	50
1151· **Ali-Royal (IRE) (114)** (HRACecil) 3-8-13 WRyan(10) (swtg: nt clr run 3f out to 1f out: gd hdwy fnl f: fin wl) 2 5	9/2²	107	48
1329⁸ **General Academy (IRE)** (PAKelleway) 3-8-10 KFallon(16) (lw: rdn over 4f out: hdwy over 1f out: nvr nrr) s.h 6	66/1	104	45
Helsingor (IRE) (TStack,Ireland) 3-8-10 MRoberts(17) (hld up: rdn over 2f out: one pce) 2½ 7	66/1	98	39
1567a³ **My Branch (112)** (BWHills) 3-8-10 MHills(11) (hdwy over 2f out: wknd 1f out) ½ 8	4/1¹	97	38
1493· **King of The East (IRE) (105)** (MRStoute) 3-8-10 KDarley(6) (hdwy over 3f out: wkng whn hmpd ins fnl f) 1 9	20/1	95	36
1574a⁸ **Musick House (IRE) (98)** (PWChapple-Hyam) 3-8-10 JReid(8) (hld up: n.m.r 2f out: wknd over 1f out) nk 10	33/1	94	35
1574a⁷ **Russian Revival (USA)** (SbinSuroor) 3-8-10 OPeslier(7) (lw: plld hrd: hdwy over 5f out: led 4f out tl over 2f out: wknd over 1f out) ½ 11	14/1	93	34
966· **Please Suzanne (100)** (RHannon) 3-8-7 CAsmussen(3) (bmpd 2f out: hdwy over 1f out: sn wknd) hd 12	20/1	90	31
1435· **Sandhill (IRE) (90)** (JHMGosden) 3-8-7 WCarson(15) (led 3f: wknd wl over 1f out) 3½ 13	25/1	82	23
1187⁴ **Tamhid (USA) (104)** (HThomsonJones) 3-8-10 RHills(9) (prom 5f) ¾ 14	25/1	83	24
Requin Bleu (IRE) (APO'Brien,Ireland) 3-8-10v¹ CRoche(1) (leggy: a bhd) 15	16/1	83	24
926⁹ **Leonine (IRE) (105)** (PFICole) 3-8-10 MJKinane(13) (prom 5f) 1¾ 16	11/1³	79	20

(SP 112.8%) **16 Rn**

1m 28.35 (1.15) CSF £208.20 TOTE £56.20: £11.80 £1.40 £4.90 (£100.40) Trio £752.40 OWNER Lucayan Stud (NEWMARKET) BRED Airdrie

Ramooz has finished one and a half lengths behind the winner Lucayan Prince. Bewitching in third, is three-quarters of a length behind Ramooz, and a total of two and a quarter lengths behind the winner. By using the percentages of a length from the neck, head and short-head we can establish a 'lengths beaten by winner' table for all the runners in the race.

Ramooz	1.5	lengths
Bewitching	2.25	lengths
Almushtarak	2.35	lengths
Ali-Royal	4.35	lengths
General Academy	4.45	lengths

11

Helsingor	6.95	lengths
My Branch	7.45	lengths
King of The East	8.45	lengths
Musick House	8.85	lengths
Russian Revival	9.35	lengths
Please Suzanne	9.6	lengths
Sandhill	13.1	lengths
Tamhid	13.85	lengths
Requin Bleu	14.25	lengths
Leonine	16	lengths

This one exercise allows us to establish how many pounds inferior to Lucayan Prince at today's weights each of his rivals were. We have already calculated that a length is worth 2.14lb in a seven furlong race.

Horse	Lengths Behind Winner		Pounds Per Length		Exact Poundage Value		Pounds Rounded
Ramooz	1.5	x	2.14	=	3.21	=	3
Bewitching	2.25	x	2.14	=	4.81	=	5
Almushtarak	2.35	x	2.14	=	5.03	=	5
Ali-Royal	4.35	x	2.14	=	9.29	=	9
General Academy	4.45	x	2.14	=	9.52	=	10
Helsingor	6.95	x	2.14	=	14.87	=	15
My Branch	7.45	x	2.14	=	15.94	=	16
King of The East	8.45	x	2.14	=	18.08	=	18
Musick House	8.85	x	2.14	=	18.94	=	19
Russian Revival	9.35	x	2.14	=	20.01	=	20
Please Suzanne	9.6	x	2.14	=	20.54	=	21
Sandhill	13.1	x	2.14	=	28.03	=	28
Tamhid	13.85	x	2.14	=	29.64	=	30
Requin Bleu	14.25	x	2.14	=	30.49	=	30
Leonine	16	x	2.14	=	34.24	=	34

Most Handicappers keep their ratings in whole numbers, and I suggest that you do the same. Therefore, the rounded figure on the right is the one to use. What this effectively means is that, whatever rating you allot Lucayan Prince, if Leonine re-opposes on 34lb better terms, then we will have the two horses rated equally (that is, we anticipate a dead-heat). A 35lb pull in Leonine's favour and we would have him top-rated (precluding the pitfalls of falsely-run races which are covered later).

Depending on how your ratings are to be calculated and stored, there is a quicker and easier method of converting the distances to pounds, namely a conversion table. This needs to be established only once for each race distance and is then kept in a safe place for reference. The procedure is to turn every beaten distance into a number of pounds. To do this, multiply the pounds per length for that race distance by the number of lengths the beaten distance represents, rounding the answer up or down to the nearest whole number.

e.g. The calculation for being beaten a neck in a seven furlong race would be:-
   0.4 x 2.14 = 0.856, which rounds up to 1
This gives us the table below for a seven furlong race.

Beaten Distance	Value in Pounds	Beaten Distance	Value in Pounds
Short-head	0	10 lengths	21
Head	1	11 lengths	24
Neck	1	12 lengths	26
½ length	1	13 lengths	28
¾ length	2	14 lengths	30
1 length	2	15 lengths	32
1¼ lengths	3	16 lengths	34
1½ lengths	3	17 lengths	36
1¾ lengths	4	18 lengths	39
2 lengths	4	19 lengths	41
2¼ lengths	5	20 lengths	43
2½ lengths	5	21 lengths	45
2¾ lengths	6	22 lengths	47
3 lengths	6	23 lengths	49
3½ lengths	7	24 lengths	51
4 lengths	9	25 lengths	54
4½ lengths	10	26 lengths	56
5 lengths	11	27 lengths	58
6 lengths	13	28 lengths	60
7 lengths	15	29 lengths	62
8 lengths	17	30 lengths	64
9 lengths	19		

The only time such tables need any attention is if the British Horseracing Board (BHB) decide to allow new beaten distances, which has happened a couple of times in recent years.

Let us now return to the Jersey Stakes and again assess the pounds each horse was beaten, but this time using the conversion table. Look up each distance on the table and add it to the figure for the horse in front. You should get this result.

Ramooz	3
Bewitching	5
Almushtarak	5
Ali-Royal	9
General Academy	9
Helsingor	14
My Branch	15
King of The East	17
Musick House	18
Russian Revival	19
Please Suzanne	20
Sandhill	27
Tamhid	29

| Requin Bleu | 30 |
| Leonine | 34 |

The outcome is similar, although not exactly the same as our initial calculations. These results will be good enough for most people, generating figures that differ from the original by a maximum of 1lb in the example shown. Remember, you are going to need a conversion table for every distance your handicap will cover.

There are flaws in this system with regard to odd race distances, but use common sense. The 5f 218y course at Leicester and the 6f 3y course at Yarmouth can both be treated as six furlongs whilst, for distances more in the mid-range such as Epsom's 1m 114y, you can look at both the eight and nine furlongs tables if you keep them on cards, as I used to.

Allowing for weight carried

Our calculation of the inferiority in pounds of each horse in the Jersey Stakes to the winner, Lucayan Prince, has ignored weight carried. To rectify this situation we need to adjust the figures for the pounds carried more or less than the winner. With 8st 7lb on her back, the third horse Bewitching was carrying 3lb less than the winner and she is therefore another 3lb inferior to the winner. This is normally referred to as receiving 3lb from the winner. The situation is reversed for the fifth home, Ali-Royal, whose performance is 3lb nearer to the winner's than our initial table implied because of his weight concession.

Obviously, there is 14lb to a stone. However, to save time you may prefer to keep a poundage table like the one below.

Poundage Table

Weight in Stones and Pounds	Weight in Pounds
12st 7lb	175
12st 6lb	174
12st 5lb	173
12st 4lb	172
12st 3lb	171
12st 2lb	170
12st 1lb	169
12st	168
11st 13lb	167
11st 12lb	166
11st 11lb	165
11st 10lb	164
11st 9lb	163
11st 8lb	162
11st 7lb	161
11st 6lb	160
11st 5lb	159
11st 4lb	158
11st 3lb	157
11st 2lb	156
11st 1lb	155
11st	154

10st 13lb	153
10st 12lb	152
10st 11lb	151
10st 10lb	150
10st 9lb	149
10st 8lb	148
10st 7lb	147
10st 6lb	146
10st 5lb	145
10st 4lb	144
10st 3lb	143
10st 2lb	142
10st 1lb	141
10st	140
9st 13lb	139
9st 12lb	138
9st 11lb	137
9st 10lb	136
9st 9lb	135
9st 8lb	134
9st 7lb	133
9st 6lb	132
9st 5lb	131
9st 4lb	130
9st 3lb	129
9st 2lb	128
9st 1lb	127
9st	126
8st 13lb	125
8st 12lb	124
8st 11lb	123
8st 10lb	122
8st 9lb	121
8st 8lb	120
8st 7lb	119
8st 6lb	118
8st 5lb	117
8st 4lb	116
8st 3lb	115
8st 2lb	114
8st 1lb	113
8st	112
7st 13lb	111
7st 12lb	110
7st 11lb	109
7st 10lb	108

Weight-For-Age Tables

If all horses that met in all races were of the same age, weight-for-age tables would not be needed, but that is not the case. The theory goes that most Flat horses do not reach full maturity until some time either late in their three-year-old or early in their four-year-old careers. Allowance is also made for the fact that younger horses do better against their elders in the shorter distance races sooner than they do in longer distance events.

Having laid down the principle that if *horse A* dead-heats with *horse B* at one distance then he ought to at any distance, we are forced to qualify the statement. The weight-for-age implies that if a fully mature and an immature horse dead-heat over five furlongs then, once the distance is extended, the older horse will win with no alteration in the weights carried.

You may or may not agree with this. It is these assumptions made by the weight-for-age table about average improvement that put so many people off using them. Don't be too hasty to abandon them, for if you do you will lose the chance to compare your findings with both official and the easily-available *Raceform Private Handicap* ratings like my own, unless of course you confine your activities to horses of a single age group.

My advice would be to use the BHB tables shown in this book, not necessarily because you trust them with your life, but because it makes your ratings much easier to compare with others, and any discrepancies will be easier to spot. Remember, just because your ratings differ from other people's, it does not make them wrong. However, using other people's as a quick way of checking which races you may have assessed too high or too low has to be a good idea.

SCALE OF WEIGHT-FOR-AGE (JUMPING)

HURDLE RACES

ALLOWANCE, ASSESSED IN LBS WHICH 3 YEAR OLDS AND 4 YEAR OLDS WILL RECEIVE FROM 5 YEAR OLDS AND UPWARDS

		J	**F**	**M**	**A**	**M**	**J**	**J**	**A**	**S**	**O**	**N**	**D**
2M	3							20	20	18	17	16	14
	4	12	10	8	6	5	5	3	3	2	1	-	-
2½M	3							21	21	19	18	17	15
	4	13	11	9	7	6	6	3	3	2	1	-	-
3M	3							23	23	21	19	18	16
	4	14	12	10	8	7	7	4	4	3	2	1	-

STEEPLECHASES

ALLOWANCE, ASSESSED IN LBS WHICH 4 YEAR OLDS AND 5 YEAR OLDS WILL RECEIVE FROM 6 YEAR OLDS AND UPWARDS

		J	**F**	**M**	**A**	**M**	**J**	**J**	**A**	**S**	**O**	**N**	**D**
2M	4							15	15	14	13	12	11
	5	10	9	8	7	6	6	3	3	2	1	-	-
2½M	4							16	16	15	14	13	12
	5	11	10	9	8	7	7	4	4	3	2	1	-
3M	4							17	17	16	15	14	13
	5	12	11	10	9	8	8	5	5	4	3	2	1

The letters in **bold** along the top relate to the month of the race.

A 4-y.o running in a two-mile hurdle is considered 3lb less mature than a horse of 5-y.o or above. Were this 4-y.o to run in a steeplechase it would be considered 15lb less mature than any horse of 6-y.o and above.

THE OFFICIAL SCALE OF WEIGHT, AGE & DISTANCE (Flat)

The following scale of weight-for-age should be used only in conjunction with the Official ratings published in this book. Use of any other scale will introduce errors into calculations. The allowances are expressed as the number of pounds that is deemed the average horse in each group falls short of maturity at different dates and distances.

Distance Furlongs	Age	JAN 1/15	JAN 16/31	FEB 1/14	FEB 15/28	MAR 1/15	MAR 16/31	APR 1/15	APR 16/30	MAY 1/15	MAY 16/31	JUN 1/15	JUN 16/30	JUL 1/15	JUL 16/31	AUG 1/15	AUG 16/31	SEP 1/15	SEP 16/30	OCT 1/15	OCT 16/31	NOV 1/15	NOV 16/30	DEC 1/15	DEC 16/31
5	2	-	-	-	-	-	47	44	41	38	36	34	32	30	28	26	24	22	20	19	18	17	17	16	16
	3	15	15	14	14	13	12	11	10	9	8	7	6	5	4	3	2	1	1	-	-	-	-	-	-
6	2	-	-	-	-	-	-	-	-	44	41	38	36	33	31	28	26	24	22	21	20	19	18	17	17
	3	16	16	15	15	14	13	12	11	10	9	8	7	6	5	4	3	2	2	1	1	-	-	-	-
7	2	-	-	-	-	-	-	-	-	-	-	44	41	38	35	32	30	27	25	23	22	21	20	19	19
	3	18	18	17	17	16	15	14	13	12	11	10	9	8	7	6	5	4	3	2	1	-	-	-	-
8	2	-	-	-	-	-	-	-	-	-	-	-	-	44	41	37	34	31	28	26	24	23	22	21	20
	3	20	20	19	19	18	17	16	15	14	13	12	11	10	9	8	7	6	5	4	3	2	1	-	-
9	3	22	22	21	21	20	19	18	17	16	15	14	13	12	11	10	9	8	7	6	5	4	3	2	1
	4	1	1	-	-	-	-	-	-	-	-	-	-	-	-	-	-	-	-	-	-	-	-	-	-
10	3	23	23	22	22	21	20	19	18	17	16	15	14	13	12	11	10	9	8	7	6	5	4	3	2
	4	2	2	1	1	-	-	-	-	-	-	-	-	-	-	-	-	-	-	-	-	-	-	-	-
11	3	24	24	23	23	22	21	20	19	18	17	16	15	14	13	12	11	10	9	8	7	6	5	4	3
	4	3	3	2	2	1	-	-	-	-	-	-	-	-	-	-	-	-	-	-	-	-	-	-	-
12	3	25	25	24	24	23	22	21	20	19	18	17	16	15	14	13	12	11	10	9	8	7	6	5	4
	4	4	4	3	3	2	1	-	-	-	-	-	-	-	-	-	-	-	-	-	-	-	-	-	-
13	3	26	26	25	25	24	23	22	21	20	19	18	17	16	15	14	13	12	11	10	9	8	7	6	5
	4	5	5	4	4	3	2	1	-	-	-	-	-	-	-	-	-	-	-	-	-	-	-	-	-
14	3	27	27	26	26	25	24	23	22	21	20	19	18	17	16	15	14	13	12	11	10	9	8	7	6
	4	6	6	5	5	4	3	2	1	-	-	-	-	-	-	-	-	-	-	-	-	-	-	-	-
15	3	28	28	27	27	26	25	24	23	22	21	20	19	18	17	16	15	14	13	12	11	10	9	8	7
	4	6	6	5	5	4	3	2	1	-	-	-	-	-	-	-	-	-	-	-	-	-	-	-	-
16	3	29	29	28	28	27	26	25	24	23	22	21	20	19	18	17	16	15	14	13	12	11	10	9	8
	4	7	7	6	6	5	4	3	2	1	-	-	-	-	-	-	-	-	-	-	-	-	-	-	-
18	3	31	31	30	30	29	28	27	26	25	24	23	22	21	20	19	18	17	16	15	14	13	12	11	10
	4	8	8	7	7	6	5	4	3	2	1	-	-	-	-	-	-	-	-	-	-	-	-	-	-
20	3	33	33	32	32	31	30	29	28	27	26	25	24	23	22	21	20	19	18	17	16	15	14	13	12
	4	9	9	8	8	7	6	5	4	3	2	1	-	-	-	-	-	-	-	-	-	-	-	-	1

Flat explanation

To use this table first turn the distance of the race into furlongs, look along until you find the date range into which the race falls. For instance, in a mile and a half race (12 furlongs) on 20th July a 3-y.o is considered 12lb less mature than a horse who is 4-y.o or older.

<u>What is a length?</u>

This may sound like a silly question, but the BHB has issued Judges with different guidelines for their calculations in the last year or two. When asked to describe what it means to be beaten a 'length', most people would say it occurs when, as one horse's head meets the line, the one behind has its nose immediately behind its rival's quarters (so to speak).

There has always been a problem of sorts which is clear if you understand the way the photofinish equipment works. A photofinish print is not like a polaroid snap of horses passing the finish with the middle of the course car park shown in all its glory. No, a photofinish is a large number of very slim vertical prints placed side by side to give a comprehensive view of how the horses passed the finish. Traditionally, the official Judge would hold a pencil against each horse on the developed strip and count the number of lengths back to the following horse. A very logical approach, but not foolproof. Horses that were easing up caused major problems for the Judges.

A heavily-eased horse that is going slowly as it passes the line will appear deformed on the photofinish print. It will look as if it has a very long back because it has taken longer to go through the line than the equipment has allowed for, and it therefore appeared on more vertical prints than it should.

The BHB now use a method suggested by former jockey and now-Judge Simon Cowley. Winning a Flat race by one second will now result in a winning margin of five lengths, but winning a jump race by one second will result in a margin of only four lengths. This is a considerable improvement on what went before, but it still has its problems. The method appears based on the assumption that Flat races are run one and a quarter times as fast as jump races. This could well be derived from the fact that Flat race standard times for the minimum five furlong trip are roughly one minute. To put it another way, each of the five furlongs should take twelve seconds. The minimum trip over jumps of two miles has a standard time of roughly four minutes, or fifteen seconds per furlong.

However, no method is perfect. This formula ignores the fact that, even under the same code, different races can be run at vastly different speeds. Taking this to its extreme, a one second victory on fast ground in the Champion Hurdle would be worth only a four-length margin, whereas a one second victory in a two mile five furlong-plus slog around Pontefract on soft ground would be worth an additional length.

A further flaw, regarding small fields, was highlighted by my colleague David Smalley in *Raceform Update* some time back. He picked on a two-runner race at Ascot during November 1996, in which the two competitors crossed the line roughly twelve to fifteen lengths apart to the naked eye. Once the winner, Strong Promise, had passed the line, the runner-up Minor Key was eased to a walk by jockey Graham Bradley. Because of the extra time taken to complete the course, the Cowley Conversion Chart came up with a winning margin of twenty-seven lengths. So much for betting on winning distances!

I am reluctant to use the distances to generate a completion time for each horse which, when used in tandem with the lengths per second explained later on, could prove the most accurate measurement we have, as I feel the formula will not last forever. My advice is to stick to the conversion tables.

And so the groundwork is done and, armed with conversion tables, poundage charts and weight-for-age tables, we are ready to compile our first ratings.

Furlongs × 1B length = 15.

15 / Furlongs = LB Length.

1 Danseuse Argentine
2 Hadega
3 Bôlder Alexander
4 Shipbing Moon.
5 Crach on Cheryl
6 Atahya
7 Rocket Man
8 Romancer
9 Jade Tiger
~~(Atahja's sister)~~
10 Saint Ciel
11 Donruma
12 Denel Lady
13 Loch Tully
14 Premier Foulee.

CHAPTER 3

DIFFERENT TYPES AND STYLES OF HANDICAP

We've all seen or heard horses being described as 'well handicapped' when reading the papers or watching racing on the TV. All too often the idea has been formed on the basis of a single form line, e.g. *A* beat *B* last time, *B* had beaten *C* the time before, therefore *A* must be a good thing to beat *C* today. Collateral lines like these tend to come from people who have spent a few minutes flicking through *The Form Book*, studying a race and coming to the conclusion that one form line is enough. It rarely is.

There are many reasons why our form line may not work out. For example, a trainer or jockey is out of form, a horse is in season, the ground is unsuitable, the horse could be a course specialist, etc. The list would go on and on.

The idea is that the running of a 'collateral form handicap' allows you to work around the inconsistencies of horses and establish a mark for a given race, using the most reliable benchmarks the result has to offer.

The Official Handicapper

The job of the official Handicapper is to provide a numeric assessment of each horse's ability. These ratings are used as the basis for the weights horses are set to carry in handicap races. They are also used to form the British part of the International Classification. The International Classifications are fast becoming the accepted guide to the quality of the best horses world-wide.

Until the early seventies, Handicappers were employed by each racecourse to set the weights for that venue's handicap races. As no two Handicappers' figures are ever exactly the same, this gave owners and trainers the opportunity to look for courses where their charges were particularly well treated. Once handicapping was centralised, first under the wing of the Jockey Club, and more recently by the BHB, such opportunities disappeared overnight.

The BHB handicapping team consists of several Handicappers, all of whom have their specialist areas. The overall task is split into Flat, All-Weather, chase and hurdle before being further divided in areas which feature the most racing. For Instance, Flat racing on Turf is divided into nine different areas which are shared amongst five Handicappers. These areas are two-year-olds, five and six furlongs, seven and eight furlongs (Class E to G only), seven and eight furlongs (Class A to D only), nine furlongs, ten furlongs (Class E to G only), ten to twelve furlongs (Class A to D), eleven to twelve furlongs (Class E to G), and thirteen furlongs and upwards. This lets the official Handicappers specialise in a particular area, and therefore allows them to give a more informed assessment of the horses they rate.

In 1987, the official Handicappers changed their rating scale from 0-100 to 0-140 for Flat racing, and from 0-140 to 0-175 for jumping, the upper figure being based on the normal maximum weight in pounds under each code. Horse entries for handicaps used to be made three weeks in advance of the race. Late in 1988, the BHB introduced the five-day entry system, and owners and trainers found their horses' handicap marks moving more quickly to allow for recent performances. As it stands at present, official handicap marks are updated every Saturday, having been published on the previous Wednesday. These take into account the form up to the previous weekend.

Gone are the days when horses like Chaplins Club could take advantage of an out-of-date handicap mark and win seven handicaps in nineteen days. Trainers do complain that the current system can give too much power to one individual, as a handicap mark that is too high can do much to sour a horse and ruin its career.

Even if a horse wins on a Monday, it still has only until the following Friday, just eleven days, to take advantage of any leniency in its old mark. A victory on a Saturday will see a revised mark come into use only seven days later.

Master and Performance ratings

In order to make sense of what follows, we need to be clear about the difference between master and performance ratings. Different terms may be used for these elsewhere but these are the ones that I use throughout this book.

A performance rating is the figure given to a horse for one run. Therefore, a horse who has raced twenty times will have twenty separate, but not necessarily different, performance ratings.

The master rating is the one figure which identifies a horse's ability under any particular code. A horse can therefore have separate master ratings for chase, hurdle, Turf Flat and All-Weather Flat.

The Private Handicapper

The term Private Handicapper is becoming rather a misnomer for people like myself. When I began as a *Raceform* Handicapper, my ratings were held on index cards and disguised before they were published in *Raceform Private Handicap* by conversion to a different scale (-2 to +5 for handicaps and -7 to +99 for all other races).

Less than fifteen years on and those methods seem prehistoric. Not only is *Raceform Private Handicap* far more informative about the assessments these days, but *the Form Book* has moved on as well. *Raceform Note-Book* began including the Master Rating of all horses in its index in 1987, four years later each performance in the book received a Performance Rating. *Raceform, The Official Form Book* did not contain even official handicap marks until 1991. By 1994, it was showing both *Raceform* performance and master ratings for all races. This publication merged with *Raceform Note-Book* the following year.

At *Raceform*, Private Handicapper is hardly the appropriate term when public Handicapper seems closer to the truth. Normally, a Private Handicapper is a person who runs their handicap alongside the official handicap and, by compiling their own figures, forms judgements concerning which horses have been let in lightly in any particular race. Trainers may employ such people to advise them on the placement of their horses.

Ratings of various types appear in all sorts of different publications, but mine are based on the same 0-140 scale that the BHB Handicappers use. It certainly will make getting started easier if you do the same.

The Time Handicapper

A time Handicapper is someone who puts all his faith in the clock, come what may. The basis of the argument is that two horses who have completed the same course in the same conditions, carrying the same weight, on the same day, are of equal ability. If it were a perfect world where all races are run at a true gallop to bring the best out of each competitor, this would be true.

Unfortunately life isn't that simple. In this country, you are more likely to see slowly-run and tactical races than truly-run ones. Therefore, it is not hard to see why most people regard time handicapping in the UK as little more than a page filler.

As someone who compiles time ratings (speed figures) as part of my job, I think they are just as important as the collateral form that is the basis for all other types of rating. However, it is important to be aware of the limitations of time ratings. Done properly, they should tell the compiler what has the best chance of winning were the race truly-run. But what if there are no confirmed front-runners in the field? Even worse, what if every horse in the race seems best coming from behind? In these cases, a punt on a Time Rating may prove rather less effective than trying to sell the Arabs sand. Quite frankly, finding a candidate who already has good form in a slowly-run race is a much better option.

The Amateur Handicapper

The basic difference between amateur and professional is the time available to each to devote to the task. Having kept a handicap for many years prior to it becoming my career, I know how hard it can be to find the time. The racing programme is hardly laid out with the handicapping enthusiast in mind. Long periods of frozen ground with little or no work to do mingled in with the Bank Holidays - Easter Monday normally has sixteen meetings. Harder still is trying to convince those around you that it is time well spent, when they have other pastimes for you to concentrate on such as gardening and decorating.

The way to keep abreast of your handicap is to pick an area to specialise in. Take on too much of a task and you will be struggling to keep up during busy spells. The advice has to be to set yourself the sort of task that you can achieve easily when racing is just ticking over with two or three meetings a day. For instance, concentrate on two-year-old races, or just races on the All-Weather.

Formats for holding Ratings

With 0 to 140 (or 0-140) on the Flat and 0-175 over jumps so universally used, it seems unlikely that you would choose to hold your ratings in any other manner.

However, I have come across other systems over the years. As I said before, the official Handicappers used the 0-100 system until the late 1980s and *Raceform*'s "Split Second" speed figures are still shown on that scale.

The third method was the one I came across first, namely holding ratings in stones and pounds. This is a system I still like and one I found easy to run once getting started. The mathematics involved in converting an animal rated at 9st 3lb carrying 10st in a race to a rating of minus 11 is not too complicated.

The adjustment of Master Ratings

Ask ten different handicap compilers how to turn performance ratings into master ratings and you are liable to get ten different answers.

To illustrate, here is a fictitious example of extreme variation in the last six performance ratings for a certain horse, with the most recent shown on the right.

30   60   90   60   50   10

What should the master rating be? If using its most recent effort as the sole guide, the master rating would be 10. This would appear to not do the horse justice. An average of the last three performance ratings would be 40. Now that is all very well but the horse has never run to 40 in its life. The average rating is 50 and an average of the best three of its last six performance ratings would be 70, again a figure the horse has never run to. The most common performance rating is 60 and also a possible master rating.

My point in showing you this example is that this is the point where your own judgement takes over. I know that some Handicappers do average a horse's better ratings (although they probably would not in such an extreme example). However, I remain unconvinced as to the merits of the practice. The *Raceform* master rating in such a circumstance would probably be 90d, with the 'd' denoting that the horse has become disappointing in its most recent outings. Our theory is that a horse should keep its master rating until we are pretty sure it is unlikely to reproduce it. The line has eased over the last few years, but four or five poor runs will probably see a high master rating go - fewer if the high performance rating was gained in dubious circumstances.

I am not asking you to follow exactly the same policy, merely to consider how you are going to tackle the problem. One thing you can be sure of is that you will find inconsistencies in your performance ratings. How you go about solving the problem with regard to establishing master ratings is up to you. After all, two horses at the same weights will reverse form, and it will show as a variation in the performance ratings of these horses.

The running of a handicap for Turf and All-Weather races

Since the demise of All-Weather hurdle racing, this has been a problem purely for Flat Handicappers. The facts are irrefutable. At the start of each Turf season many horses who have improved on the artificial surfaces over the winter try their luck on grass. Some transfer their improvement to the different surface, others don't. I have never conducted a study of the percentages both ways, but I have handicapped enough races to know that the ones who fail to reproduce their improvement on the new surface are significantly in the majority.

I run two separate handicaps, one for Turf, one for All-Weather, which take no account of form on the other surface, although a quick glance at the performance ratings will tell you how they stand. However, most rating services mix the ratings in some way.

The BHB Handicappers are put in a very tricky position by the two surfaces and adopt what can only be described as a 'fudge' approach. Take the example of a horse called Mischief Star who, on her All-Weather debut in a handicap, was understandably asked to run off her Turf handicap mark of 56. She took well to the surface at Lingfield and swept clear in the home straight to win the two mile race by five lengths. What should happen to her handicap mark for All-Weather and Turf racing? On this occasion the Handicappers involved decided to raise her All-Weather handicap mark 8lb to 64, but they neither left her Turf mark untouched nor raised it a similar 8lb. No, her mark was raised 3lb to 59, presumably to allow for the fact that she had won a race, but also to allow for the fact that the race in question was on a different surface.

If officialdom does not have a satisfactory answer, the problem is clearly not an easy one to solve.

Non-weight allowed

There is a theory expressed in some quarters that weight on a horse's back has no bearing on the race result. Most traditional Handicappers would discount such an idea out of hand and, whilst not agreeing with the view, I do understand that some of you may wish to follow this route. It certainly makes the mathematics a bit easier.

CHAPTER 4

STARTING A HANDICAP FROM SCRATCH

A two-year-old handicap was the first one I ever tried, and the writing of this book is due in no small measure to the success of Pseudonym at Ascot in 1967. She was top-rated that day by an experimenting eleven-year-old schoolboy during his spare time. The satisfaction gained from her victory spurred him on to further efforts.

To me, the fact that there is no form in the book when the stalls open for Doncaster's Brocklesby adds to the attraction of the two-year-old game, as all Handicappers start on equal terms. The only edge that can be reasonably gained is the attempts some make to assess the unraced animals on their pedigree. Recent advances in technology have helped here, with *Computer Raceform* listing an average handicap rating for each sire, as well as details of win-to-runs ratios at various distances, shown by age. Another thing that makes a two-year-old handicap ideal is the lack of need for a weight-for-age table.

However, those methods are way beyond the basics and arguably misleading as well. The method shown here is much more straightforward. Wait until about twenty-five two-year-old races have been run, and then begin to use horses who have run more than once to tie the form together. What you need to start is a race where most of the runners have appeared elsewhere, within the twenty-five races you have chosen.

This is where *the Form Book* or the results pull-outs from one of the weekly papers come into their own. The back reference numbers (showing the number of the race in which the horse last ran) quickly allow you to find the previous races for horses you are considering. When rating your very first race, you are going to have to make a guess at the rating of the winner. As a guide, the average selling race winner rates roughly 60, the average claimer winner 65, and average maiden auction winner 70. A maiden winner is worth on average 85 and conditions races featuring previous winners will rate about 95. I suggest you use these as your start point, but employ common sense if the first four in your chosen maiden auction won next time out, because then you are looking at a well above-average race of its type.

DONCASTER (L-H) (Good becoming Good to soft)
Thursday March 21st
WEATHER: misty & raining WIND: mod half bhd

441 CONSTANT SECURITY BROCKLESBY CONDITIONS STKS (2-Y.O) (Class C)
2-35 (2-37) **5f** £4,710.00 (£1,740.00: £832.50: £337.50: £131.25: £48.75) Stalls: High GOING: 0.13 sec per fur (G)
SP

Indian Spark (WGMTurner) 2-8-11 TSprake(7) (w'like: mde all: edgd lft 1f out: r.o wl: readily) ....— 1 100/30 [2]
Joint Venture (IRE) (BJMeehan) 2-8-11 MTebbutt(3) (cmpt: trckd ldrs: chal 1f out: unable qckn) 4 2 5/1
Muchea (MRChannon) 2-8-11 RHughes(1) (leggy: unf: dwlt: sn trckng ldrs: effrt on ins & ev ch 1f out: sn
wknd)..3½ 3 100/30 [2]
Fredrik The Fierce (IRE) (JBerry) 2-8-11 JCarroll(4) (leggy: scope: sn w ldrs: rdn 2f out: sn wknd) ....5 4 5/2 [1]
Mr Fortywinks (IRE) (JLEyre) 2-8-11 RLappin(5) (lt-f: unf: b.hind: sn rdn & outpcd) ....s.h 5 14/1
Mujova (IRE) (RHollinshead) 2-8-11 KDarley(2) (w'like: bit bkwd: s.i.s: o outpcd) ....½ 6 9/1
M T Vessel (JRJenkins) 2-8-11 LDettori(6) (leggy: scope: w ldrs to ½-wy: sn wl outpcd & bhd)..................10 7 9/2 [3]
(SP 126.2%) **7 Rn**

62.03 secs (3.63) CSF £20.98 TOTE £3.70: £2.20 2.00 (£21.40) OWNER Mr Frank Brady (SHERBORNE) BRED H. Young

In most seasons the Brocklesby, as well as being the first two-year-old race of the season, is a really good guide to the weeks ahead. It is, therefore, an excellent start point for a handicap. However, 1996 proved the exception and this is why. What we are looking for with our early links in race ratings are lines of form that can be trusted. We have little information to go on, and so things like the close-up running descriptions become vital in deciding if horses have run two similar races.

CATTERICK (L-H) (Good to soft, Good patches, Soft patches home bnd)
Wednesday March 27th
WEATHER: cloudy WIND: fresh across

481   TOYTOP CONDITIONS STKS (2-Y.O) (Class D)
4-00 (4-02) **5f** £3,125.50 (£934.00: £447.00: £203.50) Stalls: Low GOING: 0.73 sec per fur (S)

				SP
441[3]	**Muchea** (MRChannon) 2-8-11 RHughes(5) (lw: led after 1½f: qcknd clr over 1f out: easily) ....—	1	4/9 [1]
	Red Garter (IRE) (KMcAuliffe) 2-8-6 KDarley(3) (neat: unf: chsd ldrs: rdn ½-wy: styd on: no ch w wnr) 10	2	3/1 [2]
	Perfect Bliss (PDEvans) 2-8-6 SSanders(2) (lt-f: unf: led 1½f: outpcd fr ½-wy) 1	3	7/1 [3]
	Silver Raj (WTKemp) 2-8-11 KFallon(4) (lt-f: unf: s.s: a wl bhd) 10	4	33/1
	Chilled Wine (NBycroft) 2-8-6 LCharnock(1) (neat: bkwd: prom to ½-wy: wknd qckly) 5	5	66/1

(SP 111.2%) **5 Rn**
64.7 secs (7.20) CSF £2.22 TOTE £1.50: £1.10 £1.50 (£1.70) OWNER Albion Investments (UPPER LAMBOURN) BRED Lady Richard Wellesley

In 1996, the first horse to reappear after the Brocklesby was Muchea, who landed the odds at Catterick by a very wide margin. Hardly the best of starts as, with 3lb per length, every length counts. The other thing which sets me against the form is the fact that Muchea missed the break at Doncaster, only to recover, then weaken. At Catterick, he hit the front inside the first two furlongs.

This wasn't good, but a bigger setback was to follow.

NOTTINGHAM (L-H) (Good, Good to soft patches)
Tuesday April 2nd
WEATHER: cloudy WIND: almost nil

523   E.B.F. CINDERHILL MAIDEN STKS (2-Y.O) (Class D)
2-30 (2-35) **5f 13y** £3,175.75 (£946.00: £450.50: £202.75) Stalls: High GOING: 0.32 sec per fur (G)

				SP
	Weet Ees Girl (IRE) (PDEvans) 2-8-9 LDettori(3) (chsd ldrs: rdn 2f out: chal fnl f: styd on to ld wl ins fnl f) ....—	1	14/1 [3]
452[6]	**Nervous Rex** (WRMuir) 2-9-0 JReid(5) (led: rdn over 1f out: chal fnl f: edgd lft & hdd wl ins fnl: no ex) ....½	2	4/1 [2]
441[6]	**Mujova (IRE)** (RHollinshead) 2-9-0 KDarley(4) (w ldr: rdn 2f out: no ex ins fnl f) 3½	3	16/1
441[2]	**Joint Venture (IRE)** (BJMeehan) 2-9-0 BDoyle(1) (swvd bdly lft s: sn pushed along: hdwy ½-wy: prom 2f out: btn over 1f out: eased) 10	4	4/11 [1]
	Bold Welcome (JWharton) 2-9-0 JQuinn(2) (s.i.s & wnt lft s: hdwy & in tch ½-wy: sn outpcd: wknd qckly appr fnl f) 12	5	14/1 [3]

(SP 112.5%) **5 Rn**
66.1 secs (7.50) CSF £59.53 TOTE £10.50: £3.50 £1.50 (£21.00) OWNER Ed Weetman (Haulage & Storage) Ltd (WELSHPOOL) BRED Mrs Catherine Flanagan

It terms of getting the handicap started, this rates as little less than a disaster. Joint Venture, confidently expected to win if the market was taken as a guide, swerves his chance away at the start and is eased towards the finish. He came home ten lengths behind Mujova, whom he had beaten over nine lengths at Doncaster. Can Mujova be taken as a yardstick? Not with confidence, as the Doncaster close-up suggests that the horse weakened, whereas the Nottingham report gives no such indication.

Friday April 12th
WEATHER: overcast WIND: str bhd

624 SCARBOROUGH (S) STKS (2-Y.O) (Class F)
2-20 (2-32) **5f** £2,616.00 (£726.00: £348.00) Stalls: Low GOING minus 0.44 sec per fur (F)

			SP
533²	Contravene (IRE) (JBerry) 2-8-6 JCarroll(6) (trckd ldrs: led ins fnl f: r.o) ....—	1	6/4¹
506³	Small Risk (CADwyer) 2-8-6 JTate(3) (lw: led tl hdd & no ex ins fnl f) 1½	2	13/8²
533³	Abstone Queen (PDEvans) 2-8-6 KFallon(4) (a chsng ldrs: hdwy over 1f out: no imp)................................1¼	3	6/1³
590³	Chilled Wine (NBycroft) 2-8-6 GBardwell(2) (chsd ldrs: rdn ½-wy: nvr able to chal)................................¾	4	10/1
538⁴	Mill End Girl (MWEasterby) 2-8-6 MBirch(1) (unruly leaving paddock & led to s: cl up tl rdn & btn 1f out)................................1½	5	10/1
	Flood's Flyer (IRE) (NTinkler) 2-8-6 LCharnock(5) (small: str: bkwd: sn outpcd & bhd)................................13	6	14/1

(SP 117.2%) 6

64.2 secs (2.70) CSF £4.50 TOTE £2.30: £1.30 £1.60 (£1.90) OWNER Mr William Burns (COCKERHAM) BRED E. O'Leary

Neither of the other races for two-year-olds at the opening Doncaster meeting gave us much to go on, and we needed to be patient. The wait for a decent starting race was finally rewarded with this selling race at Beverley. All of the first five had made the frame previously in four different races. Those who were meeting for a second time went close to reproducing their previous efforts, with the exception of Chilled Wine, who had missed the break badly that day. As the Beverley winner Contravene may not have been fully extended, the fact that she had a couple of lengths extra to spare over Abstone Queen suggests that the latter is the one to take at face value.

So, with our five furlong conversion table to hand, we are ready to begin.

Five furlong conversion table

Beaten Distance	Value in Pounds	Beaten Distance	Value in Pounds
Short-head	0	3½ lengths	11
Head	1	4 lengths	12
Neck	1	5 lengths	15
½ length	2	6 lengths	18
¾ length	2	7 lengths	21
1 length	3	8 lengths	24
1¼ lengths	4	9 lengths	27
1½ lengths	5	10 lengths	30
1¾ lengths	5	11 lengths	33
2 lengths	6	12 lengths	36
2¼ lengths	7	13 lengths	39
2½ lengths	8	14 lengths	42
2¾ lengths	8	15 lengths	45 etc.
3 lengths	9		

The Beverley race looks a perfectly reasonable, but not outstanding, seller, so start by rating the winner 60. Using the conversion table to establish ratings for the other horses, we get:-

Contravene	60
Small Risk	55
Abstone Queen	51
Chilled Wine	49
Mill End Girl	44
Flood's Flyer	5

You may decide to take the sensible course of only rating horses to have finished within ten lengths on the winner, in which case Flood's Flyer would remain unrated. Using Abstone Queen as our yardstick for the Wolverhampton race, we get ratings of:-

Lawful Find	75
Contravene	66
Abstone Queen	51
Dancing Star	40
D-Day-Smoke	34
Chilled Wine	27

This result brings us onto the subject of jockeys' allowances. I prefer to add them back into the weight before doing the calculations. This is to allow for the fact that the replacement of a top pilot by a 7lb claimer does not increase a horse's chance, certainly not by 7lb. Conversely, the replacement of a 7lb claimer by a top jockey would be considered a bonus by most of us. People who keep their handicap based on weight carried alone found themselves misled in these areas. Judge jockey changes from run to run, purely on their merits.

HAMILTON (R-H) (Good to soft)
Wednesday April 3rd
WEATHER: overcast WIND: almost nil

538 RUTHERGLEN MEDIAN AUCTION MAIDEN STKS (2-Y.O F) (Class E)
2-55 (2-57) **5f 4y** £2,831.85 (£856.80: £417.90: £198.45) Stalls: High GOING: 0.02 sec per fur (G)
SP

Northern Sal (JBerry) 2-8-11 JCarroll(3) (unf: cl up: led 2f out: rn green: hld on wl) ....—	1	Evens [1]
Tazibari (DMoffatt) 2-8-8(3) DarrenMoffatt(5) (cmpt: a.p: disp ld over 1f out: no ex towards fin) ....nk	2	5/2 [2]
465 6 Face It (WGMTurner) 2-8-11 TSprake(2) (led 3f: sn outpcd) 3	3	14/1
Mill End Girl (MWEasterby) 2-8-11 DaleGibson(4) (neat: bit bkwd: nvr wnt pce) 5	4	20/1
Epaulette (MRChannon) 2-8-11 KDarley(1) (neat: sn drvn along & bhd) ....s.h	5	4/1 [3]

(SP 110.0%) **5 Rn**

64.7 secs (6.40) CSF £2.36 TOTE £1.70: £1.10 £1.70 (£1.60) OWNER Mr A. R. Breeze (COCKERHAM) BRED Mrs V. E. Hughes

Using Mill End Girl as the link to this race, we get ratings of:-

Northern Sal	69
Tazibari	68
Face It	59
Mill End Girl	44
Epaulette	44

From this Hamilton race, Face It had run previously in the race that follows at Folkestone.

465 HEADCORN MAIDEN AUCTION STKS (2-Y.O F) (Class F)
1-50 (1-55) **5f** £2,381.00 (£656.00: £311.00) Stalls: Low GOING: 0.75 sec per fur (S)
SP

Jennelle (CADwyer) 2-7-13 JQuinn(9) (neat: a.p: led over 2f out: clr over 1f out: r.o wl) ....—	1	5/2 [1]
Swift Refusal (MJHaynes) 2-8-0 CRutter(7) (unf: rdn over 2f out: hdwy over 1f out: r.o one pce)........6	2	11/4 [2]
Caviar And Candy (DJSCosgrove) 2-7-12(5)ow4 FLynch(3) (small: led over 2f: one pce)..............¾	3	25/1
Molly Music (GGMargarson) 2-7-10(5) MBaird(4) (neat: bkwd: a.p: ev ch 2f out: wknd fnl f) 1½	4	25/1
Summer Risotto (DJSffrenchDavis) 2-7-8(5) CAdamson(5) (neat: a.p: rdn over 2f out: sn wknd) ....½	5	25/1
Face It (WGMTurner) 2-7-10(5)ow3 ADaly(11) (neat: a.p: hrd rdn over 2f out: sn wknd) 5	6	100/30 [3]
Dozen Roses (TMJones) 2-7-13(3)ow3 AWhelan(8) (neat: bkwd: a bhd) 2	7	20/1
Burberry Quest (BRMillman) 2-7-12 JFanning(6) (small: a.p: rdn over 2f out: sn wknd) 4	8	25/1
Anatomic (MRChannon) 2-7-12 AGorman(10) (small: bhd fnl 3f: t.o: sddle slipped) ....dist	9	11/2
Sylvania Lights (WRMuir) 2-7-12(5) MHenry(2) (Withdrawn not under Starter's orders: uns rdr & bolted bef s)	W	12/1

(SP 121.5%) **9 Rn**

66.7 secs (9.10) CSF £8.71 TOTE £2.40: £1.10 £1.40 £4.80 (£4.70) Trio £107.90 OWNER Mrs J. A. Cornwell (NEWMARKET) BRED Mrs A. J. Owen

Although well beaten on both occasions, Face It initially seems to have run a similar race, using the close-up as a guide. If we use her to assess the race, we get:-

Jennelle	99
Swift Refusal	82
Caviar And Candy	83
Molly Music	76
Summer Risotto	72
Face It	59
Dozen Roses	54
Burberry Quest	38
Anatomic	Do not rate horses beaten a distance, or those behind them.

You will notice that, for the three horses which carried overweight, Caviar And Candy, Face It and Dozen Roses, I have included this in their weight carried.

Of the three horses from this race that reappeared in the twenty-five races studied, Caviar And Candy was hampered in running at Musselburgh, and Dozen Roses tried making the running when finishing last at Nottingham. However, Molly Music stepped up to maiden company to finish third at Lingfield.

0498·LINGFIELD (L-H) (Turf Good to soft, Soft patches, AWT Standard)
Thursday April 4th
WEATHER: sunny WIND: almost nil

551 E.B.F. TANDRIDGE MAIDEN STKS (2-Y.O) (Class D)
2-00 (2-00) **5f** £3,146.50 (£937.00: £446.00: £200.50) Stalls: High GOING: 0.29 sec per fur (G)

				SP
	Bilko (GLewis) 2-9-0 PatEddery(5) (str: w ldr: led over 1f out: rdn out) ....—	1	4/6 [1]
490[2]	**Irish Fiction (IRE)** (MRChannon) 2-9-0 JWeaver(4) (hld up: swtchd lft over 1f out: ev ch ins fnl f: r.o) 1¼	2	9/4 [2]
465[4]	**Molly Music** (GGMargarson) 2-8-9 PBloomfield(1) (led over 3f: wknd fnl f) 5	3	20/1
	Salome (NAGraham) 2-8-9 AMcGlone(2) (small: bhd fnl 3f) 9	4	25/1
	Impulsion (IRE) (RHannon) 2-8-9(5) DaneO'Neill(3) (cmpt: bit bkwd: s.s: a bhd) 13	5	6/1 [3]

(SP 113.7%) 5

63.71 secs (6.71) CSF £2.66 TOTE £1.40: £1.10 £2.10 (£1.10) OWNER Mr John Manley (EPSOM) BRED Roldvale Ltd

This performance gives us ratings of:-

Bilko	100
Irish Fiction	96
Molly Music	76
Salome	49
Impulsion	15

Irish Fiction had run previously at Leicester and looks to have shown a similar level of ability.

LEICESTER (R-H) (Soft, Heavy patches)
Thursday March 28th
WEATHER: overcast & cold, hail-storm race 1 WIND: mod against

490 KNIGHTON MEDIAN AUCTION MAIDEN STKS (2-Y.O) (Class F)
2-25 (2-27) 5f 2y £2,642.80 (£730.80: £348.40) Stalls: High GOING: 0.56 sec per fur (GS)

			SP
Iechyd-Da (IRE) (MBell) 2-9-0 MFenton(3) (leggy: unf: outpcd & pushed along: str run fnl f: led nr fin) ....—	1	5/1 [2]
Irish Fiction (IRE) (MRChannon) 2-9-0 RHughes(5) (leggy: sn pushed along: hdwy over 1f out: kpt on nr fin) ....¾	2	6/4 [1]
Swino (PDEvans) 2-9-0 SSanders(6) (leggy: lt-f: w ldr: led ins fnl f: hdd & no ex nr fin) ....s.h	3	12/1
Foot Battalion (IRE) (RHollinshead) 2-9-0 LDettori(2) (lt-f: unf: chsd ldrs: no ex appr fnl f) 2½	4	10/1
Corinchili (GGMargarson) 2-8-9 PRobinson(7) (cmpt: bit bkwd: led tl ins fnl f: wknd)..................................1¼	5	7/1 [3]
Gresatre (CADwyer) 2-9-0 CDwyer(1) (w'like: bkwd: bhd: hdwy & nt clr run ins fnl f: nvr nrr)................½	6	5/1 [2]
Tinker's Surprise (IRE) (BJMeehan) 2-9-0 MTebbutt(4) (unf: trckd ldrs: rdn over 2f out: wknd over 1f out) 1¼	7	5/1 [2]

(SP 119.3%) **7 Rn**

67.3 secs (8.80) CSF £13.24 TOTE £6.80: £3.60 £1.20 (£17.20) OWNER Mr & Mrs K Mercer, Mr & Mrs H Ceredig (NEWMARKET) BRED W. Powell-Harris

This generates the following ratings:-

Iechyd-Da	98
Irish Fiction	96
Swino	96
Foot Battalion	88
Corinchili	79
Gresatre	82
Tinker's Surprise	78

By now, you may realise, we have a problem. A median auction race with the winner rated 98? The last three races seem to be correct in relation to each other, a fact confirmed by this race at Musselburgh.

MUSSELBURGH (R-H) (Good)
Thursday April 4th
WEATHER: sunny WIND: almost nil

557 CARLYLE PLACE MAIDEN AUCTION STKS (2-Y.O) (Class F)
2-20 (2-20) 5f £2,540.80 (£713.80: £348.40) Stalls: High GOING minus 0.05 sec per fur (G)

			SP
Sweet Emmaline (WGMTurner) 2-8-0 TSprake(4) (w'like: scope: lw: mde most: shkn up & qcknd 2f out: eased fnl f) ....—	1	4/1 [2]
490³ Swino (PDEvans) 2-8-7 RLappin(6) (lw: chsd ldrs: hung rt fr ½-wy: styd on one pce) 5	2	3/1 [1]
Tribal Mischief (DMoffatt) 2-7-13(3) DarrenMoffatt(3) (unf: scope: in tch: styd on fnl 2f: nvr able to chal) ....¾	3	7/1
465³ Caviar And Candy (DJSCosgrove) 2-7-7(5) PFessey(7) (chsd ldrs: nt clr run & swtchd 2f out: styd on towards fin) ....½	4	8/1
Bolero Boy (MWEasterby) 2-8-7 KDarley(9) (cmpt: scope: bit bkwd: disp ld to ½-wy: grad wknd) 3	5	3/1 [1]
Super Saint (TDBarron) 2-8-7 JFortune(8) (leggy: unf: chsd ldrs to ½-wy: sn btn)..................................4	6	5/1 [3]
506⁵ Ramsey Pride (CWFairhurst) 2-8-7 NKennedy(1) (racd centre: in tch: effrt ½-wy: no imp)................s.h	7	14/1
Midyans Song (JJO'Neill) 2-8-0 DaleGibson(2) (lt-f: dwlt: a bhd) ....¾	8	10/1
481⁴ Silver Raj (WTKemp) 2-8-3 JCarroll(5) (sn outpcd & wl bhd) 9	9	50/1

(SP 128.0%) **9 Rn**

61.1 secs (3.40) CSF £17.52 TOTE £6.80: £2.20 £1.10 £5.80 (£7.90) Trio £36.90 OWNER Mr G. L. Barker (SHERBORNE) BRED Mrs P. J. McCreery

Here, Swino has given Caviar And Candy a 13lb beating, exactly as we anticipated. It looks as if the ratings got too high once we used Face It as a guide. This is confirmed by a look at a subsequent run by one of the other horses in that Folkestone race, Dozen Roses.

Monday April 8th
WEATHER: overcast WIND: slt against

590 EASTER EGG (S) STKS (2-Y.O) (Class G)
2-20 (2-20) **5f 13y** £1,932.00 (£532.00: £252.00) Stalls: High GOING: 0.22 sec per fur (G)

SP

Folly Foot Fred (BRMillman) 2-8-8(3) SDrowne(8) (leggy: lt-f: bhd & outpcd: hdwy & wnt lft 2f out: rdn & veered rt ent fnl f: str run to ld cl home)	—	**1**	8/1
533⁴ **Dancing Star (IRE)** (PDEvans) 2-8-6 JFortune(1) (a.p: led 2f out tl wl ins fnl f)	1	**2**	9/1
533⁶ **Chilled Wine** (NBycroft) 2-8-6 PRobinson(2) (prom: ev ch 1f out: one pce ins fnl f)	1¾	**3**	33/1
446⁷ **Nattie** (AGNewcombe) 2-8-11 JQuinn(6) (lw: hdwy 2f out: nvr nr to chal)	¾	**4**	8/1
I Can't Remember (JBerry) 2-8-11 JWeaver(5) (neat: swvd lft s: w ldrs: rdn 2f out: btn whn hmpd appr fnl f)	2½	**5**	7/4 ¹
Emmas Breeze (CADwyer) 2-8-6 KRutter(7) (lt-f: wl bhd tl sme late hdwy)	hd	**6**	7/2 ³
533* **Lawful Find (IRE)** (RHollinshead) 2-8-11(5) FLynch(3) (prom: ev ch 2f out: sn rdn & wknd)	1¼	**7**	3/1 ²
465⁷ **Dozen Roses** (TMJones) 2-8-3(3) AWhelan(9) (b: led 3f: sn rdn & outpcd)	4	**8**	16/1

(SP 124.6%)

66.2 secs (7.60) CSF £72.36 TOTE £12.40: £1.90 £1.90 £3.90 (£80.40) Trio £64.00; £72.21 to Uttoxeter 9/4/96 OWNER Mr Derek Dymond (CULLOMPTON) BRED B. Byford

Here, Dozen Roses, who we rated 54 at Folkestone, finishes last, behind Chilled Wine, who rated 49 in our very first race. Granted, Dozen Roses may have gone too fast early on, but to have her 5lb above Chilled Wine is clearly wrong. Things do not always go according to plan and this is where a bit of intelligent judgement comes into play.

When we used Face It to rate the Folkestone race, he finished five lengths behind the horse in front. We gave this five lengths the full 15lb from the conversion table, but what if he were eased when his chance had gone. After all, it was his debut. It may be better to value the gap to the horse in front as one length or 3lb. You may be wondering why I have chosen to use one length. To choose anything less would not represent a clear beating, even at five furlongs. I take the view that to use anything more would leave the ratings too high. This looks to make a great deal more sense in terms of our ratings and we are left with:-

Raceform Race 624
Contravene	60
Small Risk	55
Abstone Queen	51
Chilled Wine	49
Mill End Girl	44
Flood's Flyer	5

Raceform Race 533
Lawful Find	75
Contravene	66
Abstone Queen	51
Dancing Star	40
D-Day-Smoke	34
Chilled Wine	27

Raceform Race 538
Northern Sal	69
Tazibari	68
Face It	59

Mill End Girl	44
Epaulette	44

Raceform Race 465
Jennelle	87
Swift Refusal	70
Caviar And Candy	71
Molly Music	64
Summer Risotto	60
Face It	47
Dozen Roses	42
Burberry Quest	26

Raceform Race 551
Bilko	88
Irish Fiction	84
Molly Music	64
Salome	37
Impulsion	3

Raceform Race 490
Iechyd-Da	86
Irish Fiction	84
Swino	84
Foot Battalion	76
Corinchili	67
Gresatre	70
Tinker's Surprise	66

As a consequence, we can put a sensible figures on the Musselburgh meeting of Caviar And Candy and Swino.

Raceform Race 557
Sweet Emmaline	92
Swino	84
Tribal Mischief	77
Caviar And Candy	71
Bolero Boy	71
Super Saint	59
Ramsey Pride	54
Midyans Song	50
Silver Raj	26

Even now, our handicap could be rather on the high side with a maiden auction winner rated 92. However, the problem is now more likely to lie with our earliest assumption of Contravene as a 60 horse.

With seven of our twenty-five races now assessed, our options for rating more races continue. The final two races of our sample are rateable without any further work.

NOTTINGHAM (L-H) (Good, Good to soft patches becoming Good to soft)
Friday April 12th
WEATHER: raining WIND: fresh across

639
TROWELL MAIDEN AUCTION STKS (2-Y.O) (Class F)
3-00 (3-02) **5f 13y** £2,381.00 (£656.00: £311.00) Stalls: High GOING: 0.69 sec per fur (GS)

				SP	
	Superior Premium (RAFahey) 2-8-5 ACulhane(8) (unf: scope: lw: dwlt: led after 2f: qcknd clr fnl f)............—	1	4/1 [1]		
	Castle House (JAkehurst) 2-8-5 TQuinn(7) (leggy: unf: bit bkwd: plld hrd: chsd ldrs: kpt on one pce fnl f) 5	2	11/5 [2]		
557[4]	Caviar And Candy (DJSCosgrove) 2-7-12 JQuinn(9) (led 2f: kpt on ins fnl f)............¾	3	6/1 [3]		
	Legend of Aragon (JAGlover) 2-8-3[ow1] PRobinson(5) (w'like: unf: a.p: rdn & one pce fnl 2f) ....½	4	12/1		
	Chopin (IRE) (RFJohnsonHoughton) 2-8-7 AMcGlone(1) (narrow: bit bkwd: mid div: effrt & wnt rt over 2f out: no imp)............5	5	10/1		
	Hever Golf Lily (TJNaughton) 2-8-5 PatEddery(3) (w'like: lengthy: bkwd: s.i.s: nvr gng pce of ldrs)............½	6	6/1 [3]		
490[6]	Gresatre (CADwyer) 2-8-10 CDwyer(2) (chsd ldrs 3f: sn outpcd)............nk	7	6/1 [3]		
	Scarrots (SCWilliams) 2-8-10 RHughes(10) (cmpt: bkwd: dwlt: a bhd & outpcd) 1	8	4/1 [1]		
	Radar O'Reilly (RJRWilliams) 2-8-7 DBiggs(4) (leggy: unf: bit bkwd: spd centre 3f) 1¼	9	14/1		
568[3]	C-Harry (IRE) (RHollinshead) 2-8-0[(5)] FLynch(6) (spd 3f: sn wknd) 5	10	7/1		

(SP 134.2%) **10**

65.8 secs (7.20) CSF £28.60 TOTE £6.00: £1.30 £1.90 £2.20 (£9.90) Trio £32.20 OWNER Mr J. C. Parsons (MALTON) BRED Giles W. Pritchard-Gordon

WARWICK (L-H) (Good to soft)
Saturday April 13th
WEATHER: fine WIND: slt across

643
HATTON MAIDEN STKS (2-Y.O F) (Class D)
1-50 (1-56) **5f** £3,333.50 (£998.00: £479.00: £219.50) Stalls: Low GOING: 0.38 sec per fur (GS)

				SP	
	Bettynouche (RHannon) 2-8-11 RHughes(6) (lt-f: unf: a.p: c wd over 2f out: rdn over 1f out: led ins fnl f. r.o wl)............—	1	9/4 [2]		
	Woman of Wit (IRE) (APJarvis) 2-8-11 JTate(1) (unf: scope: bit bkwd: chsd ldr: led over 2f out tl ins fnl f)............2½	2	2/1 [1]		
551[3]	Molly Music (GGMargarson) 2-8-11 PBloomfield(3) (led over 2f: rdn & hung rt wl over 1f out: r.o one pce)....½	3	11/2		
	Muppet (MissGayKelleway) 2-8-11 KFallon(5) (leggy: unf: bkwd: s.s: rdn 3f out: nvr trbld ldrs) 4	4	7/2 [3]		
	Emilyjill (JGMO'Shea) 2-8-11 JQuinn(2) (leggy: unf: s.i.s: no hdwy fnl 2f) 1	5	8/1		

(SP 112.8%) **5**

66.5 secs (8.50) CSF £7.02 TOTE £2.40: £1.60 £1.60 (£4.10) OWNER Mr Hubert Honore (MARLBOROUGH) BRED The Sussex Stud

Taking Caviar And Candy as having run to his form, we get:-

Raceform Race 639
Superior Premium	95
Castle House	80
Caviar And Candy	71
Legend of Aragon	74
Chopin	63
Hever Golf Lily	59
Gresatre	63
Scarrots	60
Radar O'Reilly	53
C-Harry	36

And Molly Music makes the final race:-

Raceform Race 643
Bettynouche	74
Woman of Wit	66
Molly Music	64
Muppet	52
Emilyjill	49

Small Risk and Ramsey Pride, for whom we have ratings, both made their debuts at Beverley.

BEVERLEY (R-H) (Good)
Saturday March 30th
WEATHER: Cloudy

506 CHAIR MAIDEN AUCTION STKS (2-Y.O F) (Class F)
3-35 (3-36) **5f** £2,693.00 (£748.00: £359.00) Stalls: Low GOING: 0.10 sec per fur (G)

			SP
	Enchanting Eve (CNAllen) 2-7-8(5) MHenry(1) (leggy: mde all: pushed out) ....—	1	3/1 2
	Full Traceability (IRE) (JBerry) 2-7-9(5) PFessey(6) (neat: chsd ldrs: hung rt ½-wy: kpt on fnl f) 3	2	9/2 3
	Small Risk (CADwyer) 2-7-13 JQuinn(3) (cmpt: trckd ldrs: rn green & edgd rt ½-wy: wknd appr fnl f) 5	3	13/8 1
	Run For Us (IRE) (CADwyer) 2-7-6(7) RMullen(2) (leggy: unf: unruly s: sn outpcd & bhd: kpt on fnl f) 1	4	8/1
	Ramsey Pride (CWFairhurst) 2-8-3 NKennedy(5) (w ldrs to ½-wy: sn wknd) 2	5	13/2
	Morritt Magic (CWThornton) 2-8-0 LCharnock(4) (cmpt: unf: s.s: bhd tl sme late hdwy) ....hd	6	12/1
446 3	Rahona (IRE) (BSRothwell) 2-8-2 MFenton(7) (chsd ldrs: drvn along & wl outpcd ½-wy: sn bhd) 18	7	9/2 3

(SP 131.6%) **7 Rn**

66.5 secs (5.00) CSF £18.50 TOTE £4.50: £2.00 1.90 (£13.80) OWNER Mr Alexander MacGillivray (NEWMARKET) BRED P. Young

It seems reasonable to assume that neither went backwards from their debut. The market on their second start suggests that both ran up to expectation. However, to use Ramsey Pride's mark of 54, Small Risk would have deteriorated. Therefore, use Small Risk to rate the race:-

Raceform Race 506

Enchanting Eve	79
Full Traceability	71
Small Risk	55
Run For Us	52
Ramsey Pride	50
Morritt Magic	46
Rahona	No Rating (below zero)

Run For Us is not an ideal yardstick, having given trouble at the start on both occasions, but if we use her to rate this second start at Brighton, we get:-

BRIGHTON (L-H) (Firm)
Friday April 12th
WEATHER: very cold WIND: str half bhd

630 E.B.F. SOUTHWICK MEDIAN AUCTION MAIDEN STKS (2-Y.O) (Class F)
2-10 (2-10) **5f 59y** £2,761.80 (£764.80: £365.40) Stalls: Low GOING minus 0.45 sec per fur (F)

			SP
569 3	Masterstroke (BJMeehan) 2-9-0 BDoyle(1) (mde all: pushed out) ....—	1	4/6 1
	Royal Emblem (AGFoster) 2-8-2(7) RWaterfield(2) (b: neat: chsd wnr: rdn over 2f out: no imp) 2	2	8/1 3
	Nightingale Song (MartynMeade) 2-8-9 JReid(5) (neat: bit bkwd: a.p: rdn over 2f out: one pce) ....s.h	3	4/1 2
	Our Kevin (KMcAuliffe) 2-9-0 SSanders(3) (neat: no hdwy fnl 2f) 1½	4	10/1
506 4	Run For Us (IRE) (CADwyer) 2-8-2(7) RMullen(7) (s.s: hdwy on ins over 3f out: wknd fnl f) 2	5	8/1 3
	Singforyoursupper (GGMargarson) 2-8-9 PBloomfield(6) (str: scope: bit bkwd: no hdwy fnl 2f) ....hd	6	16/1
	Mollily (MRChannon) 2-8-9 CandyMorris(8) (cmpt: a bhd) 10	7	8/1 3

(SP 128.3%) **7 Rn**

62.1 secs (2.10) CSF £8.05 TOTE £1.60: £1.10 3.30 (£7.70) OWNER Mr N. B. Attenborough (UPPER LAMBOURN) BRED G. C. Morley

Masterstroke	74
Royal Emblem	63
Nightingale Song	63
Our Kevin	63
Run For Us	52

Singforyoursupper 51
Mollily 21

Always try to avoid using winners of races as yardsticks, as they often win with something in hand, but a little work on these two races suggest that Masterstroke is the exception.

KEMPTON (R-H) (Good)
Saturday April 6th
WEATHER: overcast WIND: almost nil

569 E.B.F. REDFERN MAIDEN STKS (2-Y.O) (Class D)
1-45 (1-46) 5f £3,473.50 (£1,048.00: £509.00: £239.50) Stalls: High GOING: 0.16 sec per fur (G)

					SP
Herecomestheknight (MartynMeade) 2-8-9(5) RHavlin(7) (unf: bit bkwd: s.s: hdwy over 2f out: led ins fnl f: pushed out)	—	1			25/1
Rude Awakening (GLewis) 2-9-0 PatEddery(6) (str: scope: lw: led 1f: led wl out over 1f out tl ins fnl f: r.o)	½	2			4/6 [1]
Masterstroke (BJMeehan) 2-9-0 BDoyle(3) (neat: bit bkwd: lost pl 3f out: rallied 2f out: unable qckn fnl f)	2	3			6/1 [2]
Dowry (RHannon) 2-8-4(5) DaneO'Neill(4) (neat: a.p: rdn 2f out: one pce)	2½	4			9/1 [3]
Don't Forget Shoka (IRE) (JSMoore) 2-8-9 JFEgan(8) (led 4f out tl wl over 1f out: sn wknd)	2½	5			33/1
Bapsford (GLMoore) 2-9-0 SWhitworth(5) (neat: nvr nr to chal)	1¾	6			16/1
Rebuke (RFJohnsonHoughton) 2-9-0 JReid(2) (neat: a bhd)	s.h	7			10/1
Countless Times (WRMuir) 2-9-0 Jean-PierreLopez(1) (neat: bit bkwd: bhd fnl 3f)	2½	8			12/1

446 5 (before Don't Forget Shoka line)

(SP 113.7%)

64.15 secs (5.95) CSF £41.14 TOTE £21.00: £2.90 £1.10 £1.70 (£14.40) OWNER Mr Derek Clee (MALMESBURY) BRED Derek D. Clee

Herecomestheknight	82
Rude Awakening	80
Masterstroke	74
Dowry	61
Don't Forget Shoka	53
Bapsford	53
Rebuke	53
Countless Times	45

This looks reasonable once we put Don't Forget Shoka's rating into this Doncaster seller.

0439·DONCASTER (L-H) (Good to soft, Soft patches)
Friday March 22nd
WEATHER: overcast, misty WIND: almost nil

446 CYSTIC FIBROSIS MAIDEN (S) STKS (2-Y.O) (Class F)
1-30 (1-35) 5f £2,560.00 (£760.00: £360.00: £160.00) Stalls: High GOING: 0.50 sec per fur (GS)

					SP
Hit Or Miss (MRChannon) 2-8-9 TQuinn(5) (neat: chsd ldrs: led 2f out: rdn out)	—	1			11/4 [1]
Hello Dolly (IRE) (KTIvory) 2-8-2(7) CScally(6) (cmpt: hdwy ½-wy: rdn & r.o wl ins fnl f)	¾	2			8/1
Rahona (IRE) (BSRothwell) 2-8-9 MFenton(2) (cmpt: w ldr tl wknd ins fnl f)	5	3			6/1 [3] =
Contravene (IRE) (JBerry) 2-8-9 JCarroll(3) (leggy: lt-f: unf: led 3f: sn drvn along: wknd over 1f out)	2	4			4/1 [2]
Don't Forget Shoka (IRE) (JSMoore) 2-8-9 JFEgan(7) (leggy: unf: s.s: hdwy ½-wy: wknd wl over 1f out)	¾	5			6/1 [3]
Skyers Flyer (IRE) (RonaldThompson) 2-8-9 TWilliams(4) (unf: s.s: rn green: a bhd)	½	6			10/1
Nattie (AGNewcombe) 2-9-0 LDettori(1) (unf: bkwd: racd alone centre: sn drvn along: eased whn btn wl over 1f out)	6	7			4/1 [2]

(SP 115.4%) 7 P

65.74 secs (7.34) CSF £22.47 TOTE £2.60: £1.70 £3.60 (£13.50) OWNER Mr Brian Lovrey (UPPER LAMBOURN) BRED B. Lovrey

Hit or Miss	78
Hello Dolly	76
Rahona	61
Contravene	55
Don't Forget Shoka	53
Skyers Flyer	51
Nattie	38

This suggests that Contravene, by leading and then weakening on her debut, has run 5lb below her win at Beverley. However, according to our ratings, she has achieved her correct finishing position, and we look to have found another sensible line of form.

Armed with this, we can use Hello Dolly to rate the following auction race:-

WARWICK (L-H) (Good)
Monday April 8th
WEATHER: cloudy WIND: mod half bhd

596   LIONS CLUB INTERNATIONAL MEDIAN AUCTION MAIDEN STKS (2-Y.O F) (Class E)
2-35 (2-37) 5f £3,015.60 (£898.80: £428.40: £193.20) Stalls: Low GOING minus 0.40 sec per fur (F)

			SP	
Connemara (IRE) (CADwyer) 2-8-8(3) JStack(10) (leggy: a.p: led over 1f out: easily)	—	1	7/4 [1]	:
Wait For Rosie (MRChannon) 2-8-11 RHughes(1) (leggy: a.p: led over 2f out tl over 1f out: no ch w wnr) 6		2	7/2 [2]	
446[2] Hello Dolly (IRE) (KTIvory) 2-8-4(7) CScally(4) (reard s: hdwy over 1f out: rn green: r.o one pce fnl f) 3		3	15/2	
Enchantica (JBerry) 2-8-11 JCarroll(3) (w'like: a.p: edgd rt over 1f out: one pce) ......¾		4	4/1 [3]	
Will To Win (PGMurphy) 2-8-11 MFenton(6) (lt-f: led over 2f: wknd over 1f out) ......s.h		5	33/1	
Windborn (KMcAuliffe) 2-8-6(5) MHenry(5) (unf: s.s: hdwy over 1f out: nrst fin) 2		6	33/1	
Heavenly Miss (IRE) (BPalling) 2-8-11 TSprake(8) (unf: chsd ldrs over 3f: btn whn edgd lft ins fnl f) ......½		7	16/1	
Northern Girl (IRE) (BJMeehan) 2-8-11 DeclanO'Shea(7) (bit bkwd: bhd fnl 2f) 2		8	12/1	
Sea Mist (IRE) (PWChapple-Hyam) 2-8-4(7) RCody-Boutcher(9) (cmpt: outpcd: t.o) 15		9	13/2	
Belle Dancer (TWall) 2-8-11 NAdams(2) (wl grwn: bit bkwd: s.s: a bhd: t.o) 2½		10	20/1	
		(SP 127.9%)	**10 Rn**	

59.8 secs (1.80) CSF £9.12 TOTE £4.40: £1.80 £1.80 £1.50 (£10.60) Trio £20.90 OWNER Dr A. Haloute (NEWMARKET) BRED Rathasker Stud

Connemara	103
Wait For Rosie	85
Hello Dolly	76
Enchantica	74
Will To Win	74
Windborn	68
Heavenly Miss	66
Northern Girl	60
Sea Mist	15
Belle Dancer	7

As a result of rating the Doncaster seller, we now have ratings on all horses who have run elsewhere from the Nottingham race below. At first glance, this form looks to make very little sense.

522-NOTTINGHAM (L-H) (Good to firm, Good patches)
Monday April 8th
WEATHER: overcast WIND: slt against

590   EASTER EGG (S) STKS (2-Y.O) (Class G)
2-20 (2-20) 5f 13y £1,932.00 (£532.00: £252.00) Stalls: High GOING: 0.22 sec per fur (G)

			SP	
Folly Foot Fred (BRMillman) 2-8-8(3) SDrowne(8) (leggy: lt-f: bhd & outpcd: hdwy & wnt lft 2f out: rdn & veered rt ent fnl f: str run to ld cl home)	—	1	8/1	=
533[4] Dancing Star (IRE) (PDEvans) 2-8-6 JFortune(1) (a.p: led 2f out tl wl ins fnl f) 1		2	9/1	
533[6] Chilled Wine (NBycroft) 2-8-6 PRobinson(2) (prom: ev ch 1f out: one pce ins fnl f) 1¾		3	33/1	
446[7] Nattie (AGNewcombe) 2-8-11 JQuinn(6) (lw: hdwy 2f out: nvr nr to chal) ......¾		4	8/1	
I Can't Remember (JBerry) 2-8-11 JWeaver(5) (neat: swvd lft s: w ldrs: rdn 2f out: btn whn hmpd appr fnl f) 2½		5	7/4 [1]	
Emmas Breeze (CADwyer) 2-8-6 KRutter(4) (lt-f: wl bhd tl sme late hdwy) ......hd		6	7/2 [3]	
533* Lawful Find (IRE) (RHollinshead) 2-8-11(5) FLynch(3) (prom: ev ch 2f out: sn rdn & wknd) 1¼		7	3/1 [2]	
465[7] Dozen Roses (TMJones) 2-8-3(3) AWhelan(9) (b: led 3f: sn rdn & outpcd) 4		8	16/1	
		(SP 124.6%)	**8 Rn**	

36.2 secs (7.60) CSF £72.36 TOTE £12.40: £1.90 £1.90 £3.90 (£80.40) Trio £64.00; £72.21 to Uttoxeter 9/4/96 OWNER Mr Derek Dymond (CULLOMPTON) BRED B. Byford

We have Dancing Star at 40, Chilled Wine at 49, Nattie at 38, Lawful Find at 75 and Dozen Roses at 42.

According to the weights and the conversion table, these five horses are inferior to the winner as follows:-

Dancing Star	8	(as she is receiving 5lb and is beaten a total of one
Chilled Wine	13	length, which is worth 3lb)
Nattie	10	
Lawful Find	18	
Dozen Roses	40	

When added to the ratings we currently have on each of these horses, these inferiorities will generate a suggested mark for the winner, giving:-

Dancing Star	48
Chilled Wine	62
Nattie	48
Lawful Find	93
Dozen Roses	82

In an effort to keep our error-margin to a minimum, we could average all of these. However, it does appear certain that Lawful Find has failed to reproduce his All-Weather form. Both Dancing Star and Chilled Wine, who were behind him at Wolverhampton, have comprehensively reversed the form. Therefore, we total the others and divide.

```
      48
  +   62
  +   48
  +   82
      ==
     240,   which, divided by 4, gives us a winner's rating of 60
```

Folly Foot Fred	60
Dancing Star	52
Chilled Wine	47
Nattie	50
I Can't Remember	42
Emmas Breeze	36
Lawful Find	42
Dozen Roses	20

Our assessment of Irish Fiction some time back gives us the chance to rate this race.

0537·HAMILTON (R-H) (Good to soft, Good patches)
Thursday April 11th
WEATHER: cloudy WIND: almost nil

618 DUNWAN MEDIAN AUCTION MAIDEN STKS (2-Y.O) (Class F)
4-05 (4-05) 5f 4y £2,507.00 (£702.00: £341.00) Stalls: Low GOING: 0.06 sec per fur (G)

				SP
	Express Girl (DMoffatt) 2-8-6[3] DarrenMoffatt(2) (neat: lw: unruly in paddock: mde all: kpt on wl fnl f).........—	1	25/1	
476[2]	I'm Still Here (JBerry) 2-9-0 JCarroll(4) (lw: trckd ldrs: hdwy to chal over 1f out: rdn & nt qckn) 1¾	2	11/10[1]	
551[2]	Irish Fiction (IRE) (MRChannon) 2-9-0 RHughes(1) (lw: s.s: hdwy over 1f out: nvr nr to chal)...........2½	3	6/4[2]	
	Our Future (IRE) (MJohnston) 2-9-0 JWeaver(3) (w'like: str: bit bkwd: gd spd over 3f: sn btn).......5	4	4/1[3]	

(SP 111.5%) **4 R**

64.6 secs (6.30) CSF £50.96 TOTE £12.20 (£8.80) OWNER Mr P. G. Airey (CARTMEL) BRED P. G. Airey and R. R. Whitton

Express Girl	92
I'm Still Here	92
Irish Fiction	84
Our Future	59

Leading to rating this race, via I'm Still Here.

NEWCASTLE (L-H) (Good to soft, Soft st)
Tuesday March 26th
Race 1: hand-timed
WEATHER: overcast WIND: fresh across

476   E.B.F. BACKWORTH MAIDEN STKS (2-Y.O) (Class D)
4-40 (4-40) **5f** £3,176.25 (£960.00: £467.50: £221.25) Stalls: High GOING: 0.96 sec per fur (S)

		SP
Blue Movie (MBell) 2-9-0 MFenton(3) (cmpt: trckd ldrs: led wl over 1f out: r.o) .... —	**1**	1/2 [1]
I'm Still Here (JBerry) 2-8-9(5) PFessey(1) (leggy: cl up: disp ld over 1f out: nt qckn towards fin) .... ½	**2**	5/1 [3]
Wagga Moon (IRE) (JJO'Neill) 2-9-0 SDWilliams(4) (unf: hld up: effrt 2f out: sn btn) 9	**3**	9/2 [2]
C-Harry (IRE) (RHollinshead) 2-9-0 KDarley(2) (str: cmpt: led over 3f: sn wknd) 9	**4**	10/1
		(SP 110.6%) **4 Rn**

67.96 secs (9.56) CSF £3.35 TOTE £1.40 (£1.90) OWNER Mr C. J. Wates (NEWMARKET) BRED Lowquest Ltd

Blue Movie	94
I'm Still Here	92
Wagga Moon	65
C-Harry	38

C-Harry has looked very moderate on his first and third outings, but has run to ratings of 38 and 36. This would appear to give us a line to a second Doncaster race, via:-

HAYDOCK (L-H) (Good)
Saturday April 6th
WEATHER: fine WIND: slt half bhd

568   BNFL BRASS AND MALE VOICE MAIDEN AUCTION STKS (2-Y.O) (Class E)
4-00 (4-02) **5f** £2,932.50 (£885.00: £430.00: £202.50) Stalls: High GOING minus 0.04 sec per fur (G)

			SP
	Aztec Traveller (JBerry) 2-8-5 JCarroll(8) (lt-f: mde all: drew clr fnl f) .... —	**1**	5/1 [3]
452³	**Spondulicks (IRE)** (RHannon) 2-8-3 RHills(3) (sn bhd & drvn along: swtchd lft over 1f out: fin wl) 2	**2**	9/4 [1]
476⁴	**C-Harry (IRE)** (RHollinshead) 2-7-12(5) FLynch(4) (a.p: jnd wnr ½-wy: rdn & wknd appr fnl f) 3	**3**	25/1
	Absolutely Abstone (PDEvans) 2-7-12 NAdams(1) (lt-f: unf: prom centre: rdn & one pce appr fnl f) ....s.h	**4**	8/1
452⁵	**Classic Partygoer** (MWEasterby) 2-8-4ᵒʷ¹ MBirch(5) (hdwy 2f out: nt rch ldrs) ....nk	**5**	100/30 [2]
	Senate Swings (WRMuir) 2-8-7 KDarley(6) (small: cmpt: bkwd: dwlt: hdwy 2f out: nvr nr to chal) 3	**6**	6/1
	Weet A Bit (IRE) (RHollinshead) 2-8-7 LDettori(9) (leggy: bit bkwd: s.i.s: a bhd & outpcd) ....s.h	**7**	6/1
452⁹	**Lucybod** (NTinkler) 2-8-2 LCharnock(2) (bkwd: a outpcd) ....½	**8**	33/1
	Champagne On Ice (PDEvans) 2-8-0 CRutter(7) (lt-f: unf: bit bkwd: gd spd over 3f) ....nk	**9**	14/1
			(SP 123.6%) **9 Rn**

62.92 secs (3.72) CSF £17.16 TOTE £7.40: £2.10 £1.30 £3.70 (£8.60) Trio £47.40 OWNER Mr J. K. Brown (COCKERHAM) BRED J. R. Thompson

Aztec Traveller	61
Spondulicks	53
C-Harry	38
Absolutely Abstone	33
Classic Partygoer	38
Senate Swings	32
Lucybod	25
Champagne On Ice	22
Weet A Bit	23

N.B. Later results would show this line to be a little wide of the mark. This is why you always need to be watching for form that is turning out better or worse than you anticipate.

As three of these ran in the same race at Doncaster, we can now take a look at this.

0446-DONCASTER (L-H) (Soft)
Saturday March 23rd
WEATHER: overcast WIND: almost nil

452 GREY FRIARS MAIDEN AUCTION STKS (2-Y.O) (Class D)
2-00 (2-02) 5f £3,526.75 (£1,054.00: £504.50: £229.75) Stalls: High GOING: 0.82 sec per fur (S)

		SP
Kingsinger (IRE) (MRChannon) 2-8-6 TQuinn(12) (neat: trckd ldrs: carried lft over 1f out: led ins fnl f: r.o)	— 1	9/2 [2]
Magical Times (RBoss) 2-8-4 AClark(11) (cmpt: sn trckng ldrs: led over 2f out: hung bdly lft: hdd & no ex ins fnl f)	1¼ 2	7/1
Spondulicks (IRE) (RHannon) 2-8-0(5)ow1 DaneO'Neill(2) (leggy: scope: cl up tl outpcd appr fnl f)	2½ 3	6/1
Fan of Vent-Axia (CNAllen) 2-8-5 CHodgson(7) (cmpt: unf: sn pushed along: hdwy 2f out: styd on wl towards fin)	hd 4	20/1
Classic Partygoer (MWEasterby) 2-8-4 MBirch(10) (str: cmpt: led tl hdd over 2f out: styd on one pce)	s.h 5	20/1
Nervous Rex (WRMuir) 2-8-9 JReid(1) (w'like: scope: cl up tl appr fnl f)	5 6	4/1 [1]
Highland Pass (IRE) (MMcCormack) 2-8-6ow1 RCochrane(3) (cmpt: gd spd 3f: wknd)	½ 7	5/1 [3]
Majaro (JBerry) 2-8-4 LeTolboll(6) (lt-f: unf: spd to ½-wy: sn wknd)	5 8	10/1
Lucybod (NTinkler) 2-8-2 GCarter(8) (cmpt: bkwd: dwlt: a outpcd & bhd)	8 9	12/1
Magic Blue (IRE) (RHollinshead) 2-8-8 KDarley(9) (lengthy: dwlt: a bhd)	3½ 10	11/1
Seamus (AGNewcombe) 2-8-3 JQuinn(4) (cmpt: bit bkwd: s.i.s: sn trckng ldrs: wknd over 2f out)	3 11	33/1
Risky Flight (ASmith) 2-8-5ow2 DHarrison(5) (lt-f: unf: sn outpcd & bhd)	1¾ 12	20/1
		(SP 124.0%) 12

65.94 secs (7.54) CSF £35.16 TOTE £5.20: £2.10 £2.70 £1.80 (£19.60) Trio £40.20 OWNER Maygain Ltd (UPPER LAMBOURN) BRED Bernard Eivers

Spondulicks, rated 53, suffered a 13lb beating, suggesting a winner's rating of 66. Classic Partygoer and Lucybod suggest 53 and 98 respectively. As the former employed totally different tactics in the two races and the latter was beaten a very long way at Doncaster, Spondulicks looks the safest option.

Kingsinger	66
Magical Times	60
Spondulicks	53
Fan of Vent-Axia	52
Classic Partygoer	51
Nervous Rex	41
Highland Pass	36
Majaro	19
Lucybod	NR
Magic Blue	NR
Seamus	NR
Risky Flight	NR

Kingsinger met another winner, Iechyd-Da, at Lingfield.

0498-LINGFIELD (L-H) (Turf Good to soft, Soft patches, AWT Standard)
Thursday April 4th
WEATHER: sunny WIND: almost nil

552 BAKERS LANE CONDITIONS STKS (2-Y.O) (Class D)
2-30 (2-30) 5f £3,297.50 (£910.00: £432.50) Stalls: High GOING: 0.29 sec per fur (G)

			SP
490*	**Iechyd-Da (IRE)** (MBell) 2-8-11 MFenton(2) (hld up: rdn over 2f out: str run to ld wl ins fnl f: r.o wl)	— 1	5/2 [2]
452*	**Kingsinger (IRE)** (MRChannon) 2-9-2 JWeaver(3) (led: edgd lft wl over 1f out: sn hdd: ev ch wl ins fnl f: unable qckn)	2½ 2	11/10 [1]
	Salty Behaviour (IRE) (RHannon) 2-8-6(5) DaneO'Neill(1) (leggy: chsd ldr: led over 1f out: hung lft ins fnl f: sn hdd: one pce)	¾ 3	5/2 [2]
			(SP 104.8%) 3 Rn

62.93 secs (5.93) CSF £5.00 TOTE £3.30 (£2.90) OWNER Mr & Mrs K Mercer, Mr & Mrs H Ceredig (NEWMARKET) BRED W. Powell-Harris

Iechyd-Da	69
Kingsinger	66
Salty Behaviour	59

This uses Kingsinger as the yardstick and implies that Iechyd-Da did not need to reproduce his debut effort to score.

Five of our twenty five-races are still without ratings and, ironically, one is the Brocklesby. As I explained at the beginning, this is going to be a difficult race to rate accurately and we need all the help we can get. To continue, we take a really tentative line at face value, namely Silver Raj who was last to Sweet Emmaline at Musselburgh. He had previously run at Catterick.

481 TOYTOP CONDITIONS STKS (2-Y.O) (Class D)
4-00 (4-02) **5f** £3,125.50 (£934.00: £447.00: £203.50) Stalls: Low GOING: 0.73 sec per fur (S)

		SP
441³ **Muchea** (MRChannon) 2-8-11 RHughes(5) (lw: led after 1½f: qcknd clr over 1f out: easily) ....—	**1**	4/9¹
Red Garter (IRE) (KMcAuliffe) 2-8-6 KDarley(3) (neat: unf: chsd ldrs: rdn ½-wy: styd on: no ch w wnr) 10	**2**	3/1²
Perfect Bliss (PDEvans) 2-8-6 SSanders(2) (lt-f: unf: led 1½f: outpcd fr ½-wy) 1	**3**	7/1³
Silver Raj (WTKemp) 2-8-11 KFallon(4) (lt-f: unf: s.s: a wl bhd)...10	**4**	33/1
Chilled Wine (NBycroft) 2-8-6 LCharnock(1) (neat: bkwd: prom to ½-wy: wknd qckly)......................5	**5**	66/1
		(SP 111.2%) **5 Rn**

64.7 secs (7.20) CSF £2.22 TOTE £1.50: £1.10 £1.50 (£1.70) OWNER Albion Investments (UPPER LAMBOURN) BRED Lady Richard Wellesley

Muchea	89
Red Garter	54
Perfect Bliss	51
Silver Raj	26
Chilled Wine	6

First impressions of this line are not too bad. This was Chilled Wine's debut and her four performance ratings in race order would be 6, 27, 47, 49 - a reasonable progression. As all else has failed, we use Muchea to rate the Brocklesby giving us ratings of:-

Indian Spark	112
Joint Venture	100
Muchea	89
Fredrik The Fierce	74
Mr Fortywinks	74
Mujova	72
M T Vessel	42

As for the race won by Weet Ees Girl at Nottingham, well your guess is as good as mine.

523 E.B.F. CINDERHILL MAIDEN STKS (2-Y.O) (Class D)
2-30 (2-35) **5f 13y** £3,175.75 (£946.00: £450.50: £202.75) Stalls: High GOING: 0.32 sec per fur (G)

		SP
Weet Ees Girl (IRE) (PDEvans) 2-8-9 LDettori(3) (chsd ldrs: rdn 2f out: chal fnl f: styd on to ld wl ins fnl f) ....—	**1**	14/1³
452⁶ **Nervous Rex** (WRMuir) 2-9-0 JReid(5) (led: rdn over 1f out: chal fnl f: edgd lft & hdd wl ins fnl: no ex)..........½	**2**	4/1²
441⁶ **Mujova (IRE)** (RHollinshead) 2-9-0 KDarley(4) (w ldr: rdn 2f out: no ex ins fnl f) 3½	**3**	16/1
441² **Joint Venture (IRE)** (BJMeehan) 2-9-0 BDoyle(1) (swvd bdly lft s: sn pushed along: hdwy ½-wy: prom 2f out: btn over 1f out: eased)...10	**4**	4/11¹
Bold Welcome (JWharton) 2-9-0 JQuinn(2) (s.i.s & wnt lft s: hdwy & in tch ½-wy: sn outpcd: wknd qckly appr fnl f) 12	**5**	14/1³
		(SP 112.5%) **5 Rn**

66.1 secs (7.50) CSF £59.53 TOTE £10.50: £3.50 £1.50 (£21.00) OWNER Ed Weetman (Haulage & Storage) Ltd (WELSHPOOL) BRED Mrs Catherine Flanagan

Our ratings on the three to have run before are Nervous Rex 41, Mujova 72 and Joint Venture 100. These have been turned upside down. What I can say in such a situation is that Nervous Rex was clearly expected to win on his debut, as he started favourite, and his good run at Nottingham was anticipated by the market. It seems reasonable to assume that he has made significant improvement from that first run. Those who know Nottingham will tell you that high numbers often have a very big advantage when the stalls are against the stands' rail. This is not normally so in five-runner races, but on this occasion, Joint Venture swerved badly towards the centre of the course at the start, probably racing on the slowest ground throughout as a result. Mujova seems the least bad yardstick.

Weet Ees Girl	80
Nervous Rex	83
Mujova	72
Joint Venture	42
Bold Welcome	6

This is as far as we can go with this method, as the other two races in our sample contain horses which ran only once.

We said at the start of the chapter that there were rough average values for the winners of certain types of race. We now have ratings on twenty-three race winners, so how do these assessments compare with our expectations?

Sellers (expected figure 60)

Hit Or Miss	78
Lawful Find	75
Folly Foot Fred	60
Contravene	60

Maiden Auction (expected figure 70)

Kingsinger	66
Jennelle	87
Iechyd-Da	86
Enchanting Eve	79
Northern Sal	69
Sweet Emmaline	92
Aztec Traveller	61
Connemara	103
Express Girl	92
Masterstroke	74
Superior Premium	95

Maiden (expected figure 85)

Blue Movie	94
Weet Ees Girl	80
Bilko	88
Herecomestheknight	82
Bettynouche	74

Conditions (expected figure 95)

Indian Spark	112
Muchea	89
Iechyd-Da	69

By comparing the ratings of the twenty-three winners with the expected norms, we find that the winner's rating exceeds what was expected by a total of 145lb (just above 6lb per race). At this point, it would be advisable to reduce all the ratings we have calculated by 6lb.

That is the basic way to get a handicap up and running, those couple of races we are missing will soon be ready for inclusion. Look at this result from just six days after the end of our sample.

THIRSK (L-H) (Good to firm)
Friday April 19th
WEATHER: cloudy WIND: mod half bhd

715 CLIFTON CONDITIONS STKS (2-Y.O F) (Class C)
3-20 (3-20) 5f £4,691.80 (£1,736.20: £833.10: £340.50: £135.25: £53.15) Stalls: High GOING minus 0.23 sec per fur (GF)

			SP
465* **Jennelle** (CADwyer) 2-8-5(3) JStack(2) (mde virtually all: shkn up over 1f out: r.o wl) ......—	**1**		13/8 [1]
608[2] **Double Park (FR)** (MJohnston) 2-8-8 JWeaver(5) (w ldrs: rdn ½-wy: hung lft & wandered: nt qckn ins fnl f).1½	**2**		4/1 [3]
446* **Hit Or Miss** (MRChannon) 2-8-8 DHarrison(3) (a chsng ldrs: kpt on same pce fnl 2f) 2½	**3**		7/1
538* **Northern Sal** (JBerry) 2-8-10 GCarter(1) (unruly s: s.s: sn chsng ldrs: rdn & hung bdly lft 2f out: kpt on fnl f) 2½	**4**		15/2
630[3] **Nightingale Song** (MartynMeade) 2-8-3(5) RHavlin(6) (chsd ldrs: outpcd ½-wy: grad wknd) 5	**5**		14/1
506* **Enchanting Eve** (CNAllen) 2-8-3(5) MHenry(4) (chsd ldrs to ½-wy: sn lost pl & bhd: eased)...................12	**6**		11/4 [2]

(SP 115.7%) **6 Rn**
59.8 secs (1.80) CSF £8.46 TOTE £3.00: £1.40 £1.80 (£5.10) OWNER Mrs J. A. Cornwell (NEWMARKET) BRED Mrs A. J. Owen

This represents a solid line of form back to one of the races, via the runner-up Double Park.

RIPON (R-H) (Good)
Wednesday April 10th
WEATHER: raining WIND: almost nil

608 E.B.F. SPA WELTER MAIDEN STKS (2-Y.O) (Class D)
2-10 (2-10) 5f £3,452.50 (£1,045.00: £510.00: £242.50) Stalls: Low GOING minus 0.28 sec per fur (GF)

			SP
Proud Native (IRE) (APJarvis) 2-9-0 JTate(1) (cmpt: cl up: led over 1f out: styd on wl) ....—	**1**		8/1
Double Park (FR) (MJohnston) 2-8-9 JWeaver(4) (leggy: scope: led tl hdd over 1f out: no ex)...................1½	**2**		3/1 [2]
The Gay Fox (BAMcMahon) 2-9-0 GCarter(6) (w'like: unf: chsd ldrs: m green appr fnl f: nt qckn) 1¾	**3**		10/1
Danehill Princess (IRE) (RHollinshead) 2-8-9 WRyan(2) (neat: chsd ldrs: n.m.r over 1f out: kpt on) 2	**4**		7/1
Bold African (PDEvans) 2-9-0v[1] KFallon(5) (cmpt: chsd ldrs: hmpd over 1f out: styd on one pce) ....hd	**5**		9/2 [3]
The Bee Man (MWEasterby) 2-9-0 DaleGibson(8) (leggy: spd to ½-wy) 6	**6**		16/1
Foolish Flutter (IRE) (GROldroyd) 2-8-5(7)ow3 AColgan(7) (neat: unf: dwlt: a bhd) ....¾	**7**		66/1
Prince of Parkes (JBerry) 2-9-0 JCarroll(3) (cmpt: scope: s.s: a bhd) 1	**8**		13/8 [1]

(SP 121.4%) **8 Rn**
61.0 secs (2.60) CSF £32.32 TOTE £16.90: £4.00 £1.50 £1.90 (£32.30) OWNER Mr L. Fust (ASTON UPTHORPE) BRED Mrs B. A. Headon

Despite the fact that we have managed to tie most of the early form together, you may well have the uneasy feeling that our handicap is built as much on quicksand as on concrete. I would agree. It is never easy getting a handicap started, but there is more information at our disposal than we think. Read on.

CHAPTER 5

EASIER WAYS TO GET YOUR HANDICAP STARTED

The previous chapter describes a perfectly sensible way to get a handicap started. It is based purely on the form the horses have shown against each other in the opening weeks of the season. Now, with a little work, we can uncover so much more.

The chances are that the race has been run in previous years. We can use this information to answer some of the following questions: What were the winners worth on those occasions? How does the time that year compare with the time this year? Was the going similar? What about speed figures?

By studying the Brocklesby a bit more closely we can use various methods to rate it. Here are my eventual assessments of the previous few Brocklesbys, also shown are weight carried, the race time and the official going.

			My Rating	Time	Going
1995	World Premier	8-11	87	63.49	Good
1994	Mind Games	8-11	78	62.28	Good to firm
1993	Bandon Castle	8-11	90	60.53	Good to firm
1992	Touch Silver	8-11	84	63.38	Good
1991	Sylvan Sabre	8-11	80	63.88	Soft
1990	Itsagame	8-11	77	62.14	Good to firm
1996	Indian Spark	8-11	??	62.03	Good

The first point to make is that ratings gained early in a two-year-old career are not necessarily the be all and end all. Of recent Brocklesby winners, Mind Games must surely be the best, yet he received one of the poorest winning ratings. The ratings do not take into account the style of victory, but merely the horse's performance, based on the opposition and the winning distances.

Nevertheless, we have learnt some quite interesting facts. The previous six Brocklesby winners have been rated between 77 and 90. This doesn't sound like a stunning piece of information, but it's how you use it that counts. If your early calculations put a figure of 65 or 100 on the Brocklesby winner, you are entitled to smell a rat. The average is 83, which has never been more than 7lb away from the final figure. In the previous chapter, the 1996 Brocklesby winner Indian Spark was given a figure well above 100, so we appear to have a problem.

The race times, when viewed in conjunction with the official going, do suggest that Indian Spark is a very useful horse. He has completed the course in over a second less than World Premier and Touch Silver on the same ground. Both of these were rated in the 80s. Given that a second over five furlongs is worth roughly 18lb, that rating of 100 begins to look reasonable again.

The chances are that you have access to a much better guide to race times, a set of speed figures. Speed figures vary considerably, but those in *Raceform* publications do not include any weight-for-age and are on a scale of 0-100. The figures for the twenty-five races looked at in the previous chapter are:-

Race 441	Indian Spark	44
Race 446	Hit Or Miss	12
Race 452	Kingsinger	32
Race 465	Jennelle	0
Race 476	Blue Movie	18
Race 481	Muchea	33
Race 490	Iechyd-Da	0
Race 506	Enchanting Eve	12
Race 523	Weet Ees Girl	0
Race 533	Lawful Find	5
Race 538	Northern Sal	0
Race 551	Bilko	8
Race 552	Iechyd-Da	18
Race 557	Sweet Emmaline	22
Race 568	Aztec Traveller	24
Race 569	Herecomestheknight	11
Race 585	Marathon Maid	9
Race 590	Folly Foot Fred	0
Race 596	Connemara	30
Race 608	Proud Native	30
Race 618	Express Girl	0
Race 624	Contravene	12
Race 630	Masterstroke	24
Race 639	Superior Premium	27
Race 643	Bettynouche	0

Using the above speed figures, we can generate reasonably accurate ratings for the races, by adding 18 plus to the weight-for-age, from our table. What follows is a justification of this. Those of you who are not interested in the whys and wherefores, may wish to skip the paragraphs preceding 'Another way of using race times'.

By giving those with speed figures the weight-for-age, we would get:-

Race 441	Indian Spark	44 + 18 + 47	=	109
Race 446	Hit Or Miss	12 + 18 + 47	=	77
Race 452	Kingsinger	32 + 18 + 47	=	97
Race 465	Jennelle	0		
Race 476	Blue Movie	18 + 18 + 47	=	83
Race 481	Muchea	33 + 18 + 47	=	98
Race 490	Iechyd-Da	0		
Race 506	Enchanting Eve	12 + 18 + 47	=	77
Race 523	Weet Ees Girl	0		

N.B. weight-for-age changes between late March and early April from 47 to 44lb.

| Race 533 | Lawful Find | 5 + 18 + 44 | = | 67 |

Race 538	Northern Sal	0		
Race 551	Bilko	8 + 18 + 44	=	70
Race 552	Iechyd-Da	18 + 18 + 44	=	80
Race 557	Sweet Emmaline	22 + 18 + 44	=	84
Race 568	Aztec Traveller	24 + 18 + 44	=	86
Race 569	Herecomestheknight	11 + 18 + 44	=	73
Race 585	Marathon Maid	9 + 18 + 44	=	71
Race 590	Folly Foot Fred	0		
Race 596	Connemara	30 + 18 + 44	=	92
Race 608	Proud Native	30 + 18 + 44	=	92
Race 618	Express Girl	0		
Race 624	Contravene	12 + 18 + 44	=	74
Race 630	Masterstroke	24 + 18 + 44	=	86
Race 639	Superior Premium	27 + 18 + 44	=	89
Race 643	Bettynouche	0		

Justification

As these ratings are on a 0-100 rather than a 0-140 scale and do not include weight-for-age, they need some adjustment to make them usable on the latter scale. However, the figure required for addition is not 40. After all, Dancing Brave was the last horse most people had rated at 140, but these speed figures give figures of 100 or just above quite a few times a season. *Raceform*'s speed figure calculation will give any truly-run handicap winner a speed figure of 18lb less than the horse's performance rating, assuming maturity.

So, by adding 18 to the speed figure, you will get a weight-for-age-free rating for the two-year-olds shown. The only thing left to do is to add the relevant weight-for-age to all the ratings from our weight-for-age table. A good theory, but beware, in practice you will soon start believing that you have found a superstar or two adopting this method. The reason for this is that the weight-for-age table shows the amount in pounds that the AVERAGE horse is away from full maturity at any particular time.

The two-year-olds that race early in the season are often considerably more mature than the average. The highest early season two-year-old rating in recent years is this one:-

0508-NEWMARKET (R-H) (Good to soft becoming Soft)
Thursday April 14th

521 THETFORD STKS 2-Y.O) (Class C)
5-20 (5-21) 5f **(Rowley)** £4,368.00 (£1,508.00: £721.50: £292.50) Stalls: High GOING: 0.00 sec per fur (G)

		SP	RR
414* **Statom** (MRChannon) 2-9-2 TQuinn(1) (lw: racd alone centre: mde all: clr appr fnl f: unchal) .... — 1		8/11 1	87+
365* **Rupert's Princess (IRE)** (MJHeaton-Ellis) 2-8-4(3) StephenDavies(3) (chsd wnr: rdn appr fnl f: no imp)........10 2		4/1 3	48
369* **Sound the Trumpet (IRE)** (JBerry) 2-9-2 JCarroll(4) (unruly in stalls: s.i.s: sn wnt prom: outpcd wl over 1f out) 3 3		5/2 2	48
Powder River Grey (IRE) (GAPritchard-Gordon) 2-8-9 DHarrison(2) (cmpt: leggy: sn pushed along: a outpcd)6 4		20/1	23
		(SP 111.2%)	

63.42 secs (4.72) TOTE£1.80 (£2.10) OWNER Mrs N. K. Crook (UPPER LAMBOURN) BRED P. and Mrs Venner

If allowed the full weight-for-age, Statom would appear to be Group One material.

	65	
+	18	
+	44	(the official weight-for-age at the time)
	==	
	127	would be Statom's rating

You only need to look at the International Classifications for the year to expose the inaccuracy. Rather than rating 127, Statom is awarded 106, no less than 24lb behind the top two-year-old of the year, Celtic Swing. According to the weight-for-age table, Statom should have improved 27lb between the Newmarket race and the end of the season. The implication of the International Classification is that he improved just 6lb.

My collateral rating for Statom ends up, coincidentally, as 106, and the fact that time is not always the ultimate guide to ability is illustrated on that very same day.

0508-NEWMARKET (R-H) (Good to soft becoming Soft)
Thursday April 14th

520   E.B.F. STUNTNEY STKS   Mdn 2-Y.O.C & G) (Class D
4-45 (4-46) **5f (Rowley)** £4,425.00 (£1,320.00: £630.00: £285.00) Stalls: High   GOING: 0.00 sec per fur (G)

		SP	RR	SF
Silca Blanka (IRE) (MRChannon) 2-9-0 TQuinn(3) (cmpt: scope: prom: led 2f out: qcknd clr: r.o) ....— 1		9/4 2	69	28
330³ Hinton Rock (IRE) (MBell) 2-9-0 MHills(4) (lw: hld up: hdwy 2f out: rdn & unable qckn fnl f) 1¾ 2		4/6 1	64	25
Bernard Seven (IRE) (SPCWoods) 2-9-0 WWoods(6) (neat: unf: prom tl outpcd over 1f out: rallied nr fin)...1¼ 3		12/1	60	21
330¹⁵ Risky Romeo (GCBravery) 2-8-11(3) CHodgson(1) (s.s: swtchd rt: sn chsng ldrs: rdn appr fnl f: one pce).....hd 4		20/1	59	21
Petoskin (RHannon) 2-9-0 PatEddery(5) (w'like: scope: slt ld 3f: shkn up over 1f out: one pce) ....hd 5		8/1 3	58	20
Tumbleweed Cottage (IRE) (BJMeehan) 2-9-0 BRaymond(2) (w'like: leggy: spd 3f) 3½ 6		33/1	47	9

(SP 117.3%) **6 Rn**

65.54 secs (6.84) TOTE£3.70: £2.00 £1.10 (£2.20) OWNER Aldridge Racing Ltd (UPPER LAMBOURN) BRED Luzi S P A in Ireland

Silca Blanka, over two seconds slower and carrying less weight, is rated 109 in the International Classifications.

To establish the link between the two-year-old ratings calculated from the speed figures and the official handicap ratings, I have ignored the race winners, as they could well have won their races with plenty in hand. Instead, I have taken the second and third in each of our twenty-five races and compared the rating they receive via the speed figures with the first rating they were given by the BHB Handicappers, when they were entered for nurseries. Those who never received a handicap mark are ignored.

March 1996

Race mark	Horse	Speed Figure	First handicap
441	Joint Venture	97	80
	Muchea	86	117
446	Hello Dolly	75	67
	Rahona	60	52
452	Magical Times	91	98
	Spondulicks	84	62
476	I'm Still Here	81	60
	Wagga Moon	54	76
481	Red Garter	63	68
	Perfect Bliss	60	56

| 506 | Full Traceability | 69 | 60 |

Race Mark	Horse	Speed Figure	First	Handicap
533	Contravene	58	58	
	Abstone Queen	43	56	
551	Irish Fiction	66	74	
	Molly Music	46	65	
552	Salty Behaviour	70	85	
557	Swino	76	83	
	Tribal Mischief	69	58	
568	Spondulicks	78	62	
	C-Harry	63	71	
569	Rude Awakening	71	89	
	Masterstroke	65	74	
585	Top of The Wind	67	71	
596	Wait for Rosie	74	91	
	Hello Dolly	65	67	
608	Double Park	82	88	
	The Gay Fox	82	93	
624	Abstone Queen	65	56	
630	Royal Emblem	75	62	
	Nightingale Song	75	71	
639	Castle House	74	75	

As can be seen from the ratings above, two-year-olds can appear to improve and deteriorate alarmingly in the early months. However, the overall level of our ratings is not too bad. In the sample above, the average speed figure generated rating is 70.45, less than 2lb below the first official handicap mark. And half of the discrepancy is down to one horse, Muchea, who improved on his maiden defeat in March to go mighty close to winning a Group One.

Another way of using race times

In the early weeks of the Flat season, I try to pick out cards which feature both a two-year-old race and a five-furlong handicap featuring older horses. Any two-year-old race will do, because all early season two-year-old races are over the minimum trip. My method for rating the five-furlong handicap is to assume that the runner-up has run to it's official handicap mark. I then raise the winner's rating accordingly, using 3lb for each length the race was won by. This done, remove any weight-for-age from the winner's mark. This will only apply to three-year-olds, as four-year-olds are already regarded by the weight-for-age table to be fully mature at this distance.

Now consider the relative times of the two races. The two-year-old race will almost certainly be slower. As explained later in the chapter on time handicapping, this difference can be turned into pounds. The formula used in this book suggests that each second on the race time is worth 18lb at five furlongs.

By now you should have a rating for the handicap winner and a time difference expressed in pounds between that race and the two-year-old race. If we then take the pounds difference from the rating of the handicap winner, it gives us a figure for the two-year-old winner. However, this figure disregards two facts. Not only is it almost certain that the two-year-old carried a different weight to the handicap winner, but also no weight-for-age is included in the figure. To solve this, adjust the rating to allow for the relative weights (e.g. if the two-year-old winner carried 9st and the handicap winner 8st, add 14 to the two-year-olds figure to allow for the extra weight carried) and add on the weight-for-age for two-year-olds as we discussed earlier.

To make this method clear to anyone who is still in any doubt, I have included a worked example.

443 MITSUBISHI DIAMOND VISION H'CAP (0-90) (3-Y.O) (Class C)
3-40 (3-42) **5f** £6,108.00 (£1,824.00: £872.00: £396.00) Stalls: High GOING: 0.13 sec per fur (G)

			SP	RR	SF
	Little Noggins (IRE) (72) (CADwyer) 3-8-5(3) JStack(3) (chsd ldrs: r.o u.p to ld ins fnl f) ....—	1	16/1	83	46
	Lady Caroline Lamb (IRE) (60) (MRChannon) 3-7-10 AGorman(8) (chsd ldrs: led ½-wy tl ins fnl f) ......½	2	20/1	69	32
	Passion For Life (85) (GLewis) 3-9-7 PatEddery(17) (lw: w ldrs stands' side: edgd lft 2f out: r.o wl ins fnl f) ....nk	3	4/1¹	93	56
	Secret Voucher (67) (BAMcMahon) 3-7-12(5)ow¹ LNewton(5) (hmpd & swtchd lft after 1f: hdwy & nt clr run over 1f out: swtchd rt: styd on wl towards fin) 1	4	16/1	72	34
	Amy Leigh (IRE) (66) (CaptJWilson) 3-8-2 GCarter(4) (chsd ldrs: edgd lft over 1f out: no ex) 1¾	5	12/1	66	29
293*	Krystal Max (IRE) (80) (TDBarron) 3-8-9(7) KimberleyHart(14) (sn outpcd & bhd: styd on fnl f: nt rch ldrs) 1½	6	9/1³	75	38
	Polly Golightly (82) (MBlanshard) 3-8-9-4b KDarley(10) (led to ½-wy: wknd over 1f out) ......nk	7	16/1	76	39
335*	Princely Sound (70) (MBell) 3-8-6 MFenton(16) (chsd ldrs tl wknd 2f out) 1½	8	5/1²	59	22
	Ed's Folly (IRE) (67) (SDow) 3-7-12(5) ADaly(6) (sme hdwy 2f out: nvr nr ldrs) ......nk	9	25/1	55	18
	Welsh Mountain (76) (MJHeaton-Ellis) 3-8-9(3) SDrowne(13) (a in rr) 2	10	20/1	58	21
	U-No-Harry (IRE) (70) (RHollinshead) 3-8-1(5) FLynch(9) (lw: in tch: outpcd fr ½-wy) ......nk	11	33/1	51	14
	Opening Chorus (60) (MrsMReveley) 3-7-10 LCharnock(7) (sn rdn: nvr wnt pce) 1	12	10/1	38	1
	Ramsey Hope (78) (CWFairhurst) 3-9-0 NKennedy(15) (a bhd) ......¾	13	33/1	53	16
	Marjorie Rose (IRE) (75) (ABailey) 3-8-8(3) DWright(12) (s.i.s: a bhd) ......¾	14	25/1	48	11
	Miss Bigwig (78) (JBerry) 3-8-9(5) PRoberts(18) (in tch tl lost pl ½-wy) ......½	15	12/1	49	12
407⁹	Johayro (75) (WGMTurner) 3-8-6b(3) CAdamson(2) (in tch: wknd 2f out) ......nk	16	25/1	45	8
160*	Chemcast (67) (DNicholls) 3-8-3 JQuinn(11) (in tch: lost pl 2f out) 5	17	10/1	21	—
	Imp Express (IRE) (77) (GMMoore) 3-8-13 JWeaver(1) (unruly & swvd lft s: wl bhd fr ½-wy) 20	18	20/1	—	—

(SP 129.6%) **18 Rn**

61.78 secs (3.38) CSF £278.01 CT £1,443.57 TOTE £18.00: £2.70 £4.30 £1.50 £3.90 (£148.60) Trio £636.10 OWNER Mr M. E. Hall (NEWMARKET) BRED A. M. F. Persse

Little Noggins' handicap mark is 72, which includes 12lb weight-for-age, or to put it another way, a fully mature horse rated 60 would, in theory, equal Little Noggins' performance. He won the race by half a length, or 2lb, and is therefore worth a figure of 62 (60+2).

His time is 0.25 of a second faster than the two-year-old Indian Spark in the Brocklesby. With time being worth 18lb a second at five furlongs, this difference is worth 5lb (18 x 0.25). However, Indian Spark carried 3lb more than Little Noggins, (8st 11lb as opposed to 8st 8lb) and so Indian Spark's figure for the Brocklesby is 62 - 5 + 3 = 60. I advise you to hold two figures for each two-year-old, a weight-for-age free figure (in this case 60) and one with weight-for-age included (in this case 107 which is 60 + the weight-for-age figure of 47 from the table). Holding both figures does allow the early gauging of whether an animal is making natural improvement or not.

This has dealt fully with two-year-olds and similar methods can be applied to starting a juvenile hurdle handicap. Virtually all cards that feature a juvenile hurdle will also have other hurdle races over the same distance. The method is to compare times between the two races and adjust for weight carried and weight-for-age, as in the Flat example.

To demonstrate, I have taken the following two races:-

49

BANGOR-ON-DEE (L-H) (Good, Good to firm patches)
Saturday September 14th
WEATHER: fine

638
DICK FRANCIS H'CAP HURDLE (0-130) (4-Y.O+) (Class C)
3-10 (3-12) **2m 1f (9 hdls)** £3,371.25 (£1,020.00: £497.50: £236.25) GOING minus 0.30 sec per fur (GF)

			SP	R
341[3]	Star Market (119) (JLSpearing) 6-12-0b APMcCoy (mde all: clr fr ½-wy: unchal)................—	1	7/1	102
538*	Sarmatian (USA) (100) (MDHammond) 5-10-9 RGarritty (lw: hld up in rr: stdy hdwy 5th: nt rch wnr)................8	2	9/4[1]	76
582*	Red Valerian (119) (GMMoore) 5-12-0v MAFitzgerald (hld up & bhd: effrt appr 3 out: nt rch ldrs)................6	3	5/2[2]	89
416[6]	Robert's Toy (IRE) (118) (MCPipe) 5-11-13b AMaguire (chsd wnr fr 4th tl wknd appr 2 out)................17	4	9/2[3]	72
	Don du Cadran (FR) (106) (CaptTAForster) 7-11-1 AThornton (bit bkwd: prom tl wknd appr 5th: t.o)................15	5	14/1	46
453*	Have a Nightcap (100) (NPLittmoden) 7-10-9b MRichards (trckd ldrs to 5th: sn wknd: t.o)................9	6	10/1	31
591[U]	Windward Ariom (108) (PMitchell) 10-11-3 ALarnach (pushed along fr 3rd: no ch whn fell 3 out)................	F	20/1	—

(SP 110.5%)

3m 52.1 (-2.90) CSF £21.56 TOTE £9.00: £4.10 1.80 (£9.00) OWNER Mrs P. Joynes (ALCESTER) BRED M. H. D. Madden and Partners

640
GORDON MYTTON HOMES HURDLE (3-Y.O) (Class D)
4-10 (4-13) **2m 1f (9 hdls)** £2,827.00 (£856.00: £418.00: £199.00) GOING minus 0.30 sec per fur (GF)

			SP	RR
	Silverdale Knight (KWHogg) 3-10-10 MFoster (trckd ldng pair: led appr 2 out: sn clr: easily)................—	1	8/1	77+
	Flying Green (FR) (NJHWalker) 3-10-7[3] GuyLewis (chsd ldr: led after 6th: hdd & mstke 2 out: sn btn)................14	2	5/2[2]	64
501[4]	Bath Knight (DJSffrenchDavis) 3-10-10b[1] SMcNeill (plld hrd: led & sn clr: wknd & hdd after 6th).,................24	3	25/1	41
589[2]	Song For Jess (IRE) (FJordan) 3-10-5 SWynne (lw: in tch: no hdwy fr 6th)................7	4	12/1	30
	Welcome Royale (IRE) (MHTompkins) 3-10-10 AMaguire (lw: hld up & bhd: sme hdwy fr 3 out: nvr nrr)................2½	5	5/1[3]	32
458[4]	Balmoral Princess (JHPeacock) 3-10-12b RBellamy (a in rr)................1¼	6	16/1	33
501*	Sheath Kefaah (JRJenkins) 3-11-3 GBradley (lw: trckd ldrs tl wknd 5th: t.o)................9	7	2/1[1]	30
	Flood's Fancy (LJBarratt) 3-10-5 CLlewellyn (a bhd: t.o)................dist	8	33/1	—
	Krasnik (IRE) (MrsDHaine) 3-10-10 JFTitley (bkwd: a bhd: t.o)................hd	9	14/1	—
	Tallulah Belle (NPLittmoden) 3-10-5 MRichards (hld up: sme hdwy whn fell 5th)................	F	33/1	—
	Peyton Jones (ADSmith) 3-10-10 FJousset (bkwd: mid div: rdn 4th: t.o whn p.u bef 6th)................	P	50/1	—

(SP 121.6%) 1

3m 57.9 (2.90) CSF £27.81 TOTE £9.80: £2.20 1.70 £5.10 (£27.70) Trio £111.80 OWNER Auldyn Stud Ltd (ISLE OF MAN) BRED Auldyn

Star Market, officially rated 119 and carrying 12st, has completed Bangor's two mile one furlong course 5.8 seconds faster than Silverdale Knight has taken in the juvenile race.

To assess the method by the same means we used for Flat racing, estimate the new handicap rating that Star Market will receive for the Bangor win. My estimate was 125, although he was in fact actually rated 126. Star Market is a fully mature horse and subject to no weight-for-age. Therefore, this rating does not need any element of weight-for-age adding back in.

At 10st 10lb, Silverdale Knight has carried 18lb less than Star Market. Were Silverdale Knight a fully mature horse who had completed the course in the same time as Star Market, his rating would be:-

$$
\begin{array}{r}
125 \\
-\quad 18 \\
\hline
107
\end{array}
$$

However, this does not allow for Silverdale Knight's slower time. At two miles, one second is worth between 5 and 6lb. Multiplying the amount slower by 5.5, we get:-

$$
\begin{array}{r}
5.8 \\
\times\quad 5.5 \\
\hline
31.9 \text{ or } 32lb
\end{array}
$$

Therefore, had Silverdale Knight been fully mature, the performance would rate:-

107

                  -        32
                         ===
                           75

But three-year-old hurdlers in September get 18lb weight-for-age and the final rating for Silverdale Knight is:-

                           75
              +   18
                         ==
                           93

We have now considered the options available for starting both two-year-old and juvenile hurdle handicaps. You will be pleased to hear that most others are easier to start. Let us begin with a three-year-old handicap.

What we have at our disposal, quite apart from a lot of ratings in newspapers and *the Form Book*, are the official handicap ratings. My advice would be to use these whenever possible, as your handicap ought to then dovetail nicely with the official one. Let us look at a few early-season three-year-old races to see just how easy it is to get started.

NEWMARKET (R-H) (Good to firm)
Tuesday April 16th
WEATHER: overcast WIND: fresh half against

671 CONSTANT SECURITY MAIDEN STKS (3-Y.O) (Class D)
2-00 (2-02) 1m 4f **(Rowley)** £4,269.00 (£1,272.00: £606.00: £273.00) Stalls: High GOING minus 0.26 sec per fur (GF)

	SP	RR	SF
Sherpas (IRE) (HRACecil) 3-9-0 PatEddery(11) (gd sort: wl grwn: led after 2f: shkn up over 2f out: r.o gamely)..— 1	7/2 [1]	94+	61
Sasuru (106) (GWragg) 3-9-0 PaulEddery(3) (b: lw: trckd ldrs: stdy hdwy to disp ld 1f out: r.o)......................hd 2	9/2 [2]	94	61
Valedictory (HRACecil) 3-9-0 WRyan(2) (gd sort: bit bkwd: hld up: stdy hdwy to chal 2½f out: outpcd appr fnl f: kpt on wl towards fin)...1 3	9/1 [3]	93+	60
Wilawander (99) (BWHills) 3-9-0 MHills(1) (hld up: smooth hdwy to chal 2f out: sn rdn & nt qckn).................½ 4	9/2 [2]	92	59
Highland Legend (IRE) (RCharlton) 3-8-9 RHughes(9) (w'like: leggy: s.i.s: sn trckng ldrs: rdn 3f out: kpt on same pce) 1¾ 5	10/1	85	52
Zaforum (95) (LMontagueHall) 3-9-0 LDettori(4) (in tch: drvn along over 3f out: r.o one pce) ....s.h 6	33/1	90	57
Qasida (IRE) (CEBrittain) 3-9-0 MJKinane(5) (w'like: leggy: trckd ldrs tl wknd fnl 2½f)................................1½ 7	25/1	88	55
Lakeline Legend (IRE) (MAJarvis) 3-9-0 EmmaO'Gorman(7) (hld up: effrt over 3f out: no imp)................1¼ 8	14/1	86	53
Chief Contender (IRE) (PWChapple-Hyam) 3-9-0 JReid(10) (gd sort: str: led 2f: w wnr tl rdn & wknd 2f out)...nk 9	9/2 [2]	85	52
Glowing Reeds (CNAllen) 3-8-2[7] CWebb(6) (outpcd & hung lft 5f out: sn bhd)..26 10	100/1	52	19
Petrolio (IRE) (LMCumani) 3-9-0 JWeaver(8) (Withdrawn not under Starter's orders: lame at s) .... W	25/1	—	—

(SP 114.1%) **10 Rn**

2m 32.88 (2.38) CSF £17.42 TOTE £3.30: £1.50 £1.50 £3.20 (£6.80) Trio £8.70 OWNER Mr K. Abdulla (NEWMARKET) BRED Juddmonte

This is a good-quality maiden, but all the runners are making their seasonal debut. The official marks give the budding Handicapper something to play with. Using our one and a half mile conversion table, the official marks of Sasuru, Wilawander and Zaforum suggest the following ratings for the winner, Sherpas:-

Sasuru	106
Wilawander	101
Zaforum	99

It takes a good maiden winner to get a figure above 100. Anything around 110 is normally at least listed race class. There are few maiden races where more than the odd one goes on to Group races, rather than handicaps. From the three horses with official ratings, a figure of somewhere around 100 for Sherpas would seem entirely acceptable. If you were trying to be flexible with your ratings, you could give the winner 107 on the basis that he has beaten a 106 horse at level weights, and then rate the rest of the field through the other two horses. This sort of idea would leave you with ratings of:-

Sherpas	107
Sasuru	106
Valedictory	100
Wilawander	99
Highland Gift	90
Zaforum	95

This assumes that each horse was worth its handicap mark and no more. Therefore, beating them will determine your rating. Sherpas gets his rating by beating Sasuru, Valedictory by beating Wilawander, and Highland Gift by beating Zaforum. If you go down this avenue, you will compile ratings rather different to those seen in print. Certainly, *Raceform*'s are tied to looking strictly at the order in which horses pass the post and the distances beaten. There is no allowance for making any judgements on individual horses. You may have seen this race live and decided that Valedictory would come on 5lb for the outing, so why not rate him 105?

Once you run your own handicap, you become your own boss, so frankly you can do what you like! Just remember you will make mistakes, but that's fine as long as you learn from them.

Good horses are dealt with later on, but this was the main race on that day of the Craven meeting:-

NEWMARKET (R-H) (Good to firm)
Tuesday April 16th
WEATHER: overcast WIND: fresh half against

674 SHADWELL STUD NELL GWYN STKS (Gp 3) (3-Y.O F) (Class A)
3-40 (3-40) **7f (Rowley)** £19,362.00 (£7,158.00: £3,429.00: £1,395.00: £547.50: £208.50) Stalls: Centre GOING minus 0.26 se
fur (GF)

	SP	RR
Thrilling Day (104) (NAGraham) 3-8-9 DHarrison(9) (hld up & bhd: hdwy u.p 2f out: r.o wl fnl f to ld cl home) ....— 1	20/1	108
Bint Salsabil (USA) (113) (JLDunlop) 3-8-12 WCarson(6) (lw: led: qcknd over 2f out: hdd cl home: rallied) ..s.h 2	7/2 [1]	111
Honest Guest (IRE) (108) (MHTompkins) 3-8-9 PRobinson(1) (bhd: rdn & hdwy over 2f out: styd on wl fnl f)2½ 3	16/1	102
My Melody Parkes (108) (JBerry) 3-8-9 GCarter(4) (a chsng ldrs: hdwy u.p 4f out: ev ch 1f out: nt qckn) ......hd 4	12/1	102
Maid For The Hills (DRLoder) 3-8-9 RHughes(3) (trckd ldr: outpcd over 2f out: hdwy over 1f out: no ex ins fnl f)..1¼ 5	7/2 [1]	99
Darling Flame (USA) (109) (JHMGosden) 3-8-9 LDettori(7) (lw: in tch: effrt over 2f out: r.o one pce) ....½ 6	15/2	98
Mezzogiorno (112) (GWragg) 3-8-9 MHills(2) (lw: hld up & bhd: effrt over 2f out: btn & eased appr fnl f).......½ 7	9/2 [2]	73
Wild Rumour (IRE) (PWChapple-Hyam) 3-8-9 JReid(11) (prom tl outpcd fnl 2f)....................................2 8	7/1 [3]	68
572[6] **Cyrillic (92)** (PAKelleway) 3-8-9 JFEgan(10) (lw: outpcd ½-wy: n.d after) ....½ 9	50/1	67
548[2] **Marl (90)** (RAkehurst) 3-8-9 SSanders(5) (chsd ldr tl wknd wl over 1f out)................................hd 10	16/1	67
572[8] **Coachella (85)** (MJRyan) 3-8-9 MJKinane(8) (in tch tl rdn & wknd 3f out) 4 11	50/1	58
	(SP 115.0%) 1

1m 25.31 (0.81) CSF £81.73 TOTE £26.50: £5.20 £1.70 £3.40 (£44.50) Trio £228.30 OWNER Bloomsbury Stud (NEWMARKET) BRED
Bloomsbury Stud

Most of these either have handicap marks or are featured in the International Classifications, which is essentially the same thing. Adjusting these marks according to the conversion table and allowing for weights carried, the following ratings are suggested for the winner, Thrilling Day, who was currently rated 104 by the official Handicapper:-

Bint Salsabil	110	(was giving the winner 3lb)
Honest Guest	113	

My Melody Parkes	114
Maid For The Hills	NR
Darling Flame	119

Mezzogiorno	146
Wild Rumour	NR
Cyrillic	131
Marl	130
Coachella	134

All of those below the line were the wrong side of an eleven length gap in a seven furlong race. It does seem reasonable to suppose that none of these were at their best so early in the season.

The winner has clearly improved on what she had done previously and you may well decide to average those horses which appear to have run a race.

	104
+	110
+	113
+	114
+	119
	===
	560

which would rate Thrilling Day at 112

If allowing yourself flexibility, you may approach the race with the view that My Melody Parkes did not stay seven furlongs. Therefore, she can not have run to her best, so she should end up with a rating below her official mark.

There was a seven-furlong, three-year-old handicap on this day:-

NEWMARKET (R-H) (Good to firm)
Tuesday April 16th
WEATHER: overcast WIND: fresh half against

676 EQUITY FINANCIAL COLLECTIONS H'CAP (0-95) (3-Y.O) (Class C)
4-45 (4-45) 7f **(Rowley)** £6,212.00 (£1,856.00: £888.00: £404.00) Stalls: Centre GOING minus 0.26 sec per fur (GF)

			SP	RR	SF
	Sky Dome (IRE) (75) (MHTompkins) 3-8-4 PRobinson(9) (hdwy over 2f out: swtchd & r.o u.p to ld cl home).— 1		14/1	86	28
	Welville (89) (PJMakin) 3-9-4 JWeaver(10) (lw: led after 2f: clr over 1f out: sn rdn: jst ct)................hd 2		11/2 2	100	42
493 3	**White Plains (IRE) (67)** (MBell) 3-7-3(7) RMullen(5) (hdwy 3f out: chsng wnr over 1f out: nt qckn ins fnl f)........2 3		7/1 3	73	15
484*	**Waypoint (73)** (RCharlton) 3-8-2 TSprake(11) (a chsng ldrs: rdn 2f out: kpt on fnl f)......................s.h 4		9/2 1	79	21
	Jerry Cutrona (IRE) (69) (NACallaghan) 3-7-12 JFEgan(2) (hld up & bhd: hdwy 2f out: r.o: nvr plcd to chal)1½ 5		14/1	72	14
453 11	**Rebel County (IRE) (68)** (DJSCosgrove) 3-7-11 NAdams(7) (hld up: hdwy over 2f out: shkn up over 1f out:				
	eased whn btn)..hd 6		25/1	70	12
453 8	**Beas River (IRE) (72)** (WRMuir) 3-7-12(3)ow2 DRMcCabe(14) (effrt 3f out: nvr trbld ldrs)...............3½ 7		16/1	66	6
453*	**Sualtach (IRE) (81)** (RHollinshead) 3-8-10 LDettori(4) (w ldrs tl wknd wl over 1f out)..................1¾ 8		9/2 1	71	13
	Consordino (87) (LMCumani) 3-9-2 MJKinane(13) (lw: hld up: stdy hdwy over 2f out: nvr rchd ldrs) ....s.h 9		10/1	77	19
	Lyzia (IRE) (80) (CEBrittain) 3-8-9 BDoyle(1) (bhd: rdn ½-wy: no imp) ....s.h 10		16/1	70	12
	Ocean Grove (IRE) (92) (PWChapple-Hyam) 3-9-7 JReid(12) (unf: led 2f: cl up tl wknd 2f out) 1½ 11		14/1	79	21
	Red Rusty (USA) (67) (DMorris) 3-7-10 LCharnock(8) (lw: prom 5f)..................................1½ 12		16/1	50	—
571 10	**Missile Toe (IRE) (72)** (JEBanks) 3-7-10b1(5) FLynch(3) (gd spd 5f).................................½ 13		16/1	54	—

(SP 120.7%) **13 Rn**
1m 27.8 (3.30) CSF £83.57 CT £546.68 TOTE £16.40: £3.00 £2.20 £2.50 (£88.10) Trio £208.70 OWNER Miss D. J. Merson (NEWMARKET)

How do we deal with handicaps? After all, the horses have run off their official marks unless they are out of the handicap - that is carrying more weight than they were allotted by the Handicapper because that weight was below the minimum for the race. Consequently, these ratings are predicting a multiple dead-heat.

As the idea of this handicap is to run alongside the official one, the obvious move is to try and estimate the new mark that will be given to the winner. I have looked at a busy week during the summer of 1996 to give you a few guidelines. Of the fifty-eight handicaps that were won by horses without penalties, the most common rise was 5lb, which happened to sixteen of the winners.

The total handicap mark rise of all the winners was 316lb, an average of 5.45lb. The smallest rise was 1lb and the biggest fourteen. In general, the more clear cut the winner, the more the official handicap mark rises.

If you judge this run by Sky Dome to have been an average one, then you would rate Sky Dome at 80 and the rest of the field accordingly.

Such a method would work for starting an all-age handicap but, when different age groups start meeting, you need to remember that weight-for-age is deducted from the weights carried by immature horses, as per the official weight-for-age table. Here is an example:-

1625-NEWMARKET (R-H) (Good to firm)
Saturday June 8th
WEATHER: fine WIND: almost nil

1807 BAILEYS IRISH CREAM LIQUEUR H'CAP (0-90) (3-Y.O+) (Class C)
8-35 (8-35) 1m (July) £8,155.00 (£2,440.00: £1,170.00: £535.00) Stalls: Low GOING minus 0.29 sec per fur (GF)

		SP	RR	S
1126[5] Mawingo (IRE) (69) (GWragg) 3-8-1 JQuinn(1) (lw: hld up & plld hrd: hdwy & squeezed thro over 1f out: sn led: rdn out)	— 1	3/1 [2]	80	29
876[2] Master Charter (76) (MrsJRRamsden) 4-9-5 KFallon(7) (lw: trckd ldrs: edgd lft & led over 1f out: sn hdd & no ex) 1½ 2		11/4 [1]	84	44
Insatiable (IRE) (85) (MRStoute) 3-9-3 JReid(10) (lw: hld up: hdwy 3f out: r.o fnl f) 1½ 3		4/1 [3]	90+	39
1625* Saifan (78) (DMorris) 7-9-7b CHodgson(4) (s.i.s: rdn 4f out: styng on whn edgd lft fnl f) ......½ 4		7/1	82	42
1469[3] Classic Leader (78) (RHarris) 3-8-10b[1] AMackay(9) (hld up: hdwy 2f out: no ex ins fnl f) 1¾ 5		25/1	79	28
1528[5] Mountgate (74) (MPBielby) 4-9-3 DRMcCabe(6) (hld up & plld hrd: effrt 2f out: no imp) 1¼ 6		20/1	72	32
1412[11] Wild Palm (69) (WAO'Gorman) 4-8-12b EmmaO'Gorman(2) (lw: dwlt: sn prom: wknd over 1f out) 3 7		25/1	61	21
1506[5] Cim Bom Bom (IRE) (70) (MBell) 4-8-13 PatEddery(8) (led over 5f out tl over 1f out: sn wknd) ......nk 8		12/1	61	21
1321[3] Toujours Riviera (84) (JPearce) 6-9-13 GBardwell(5) (plld hrd: prom: wkng whn hmpd over 1f out) 4 9		16/1	67	27
1088[7] Bentico (65) (MrsNMacauley) 7-8-8 PBloomfield(3) (led over 2f: wknd 2f out) 2½ 10		25/1	43	3
1449[23] Risky Romeo (64) (GCBravery) 4-8-7 MHills(11) (rel to race: a t.o) 20 11		14/1	2	

(SP 120.7%) 11 Rn

1m 40.39 (3.19) CSF £11.51 CT £29.36 TOTE £4.10: £1.90 £1.70 £2.00 (£5.50) Trio £9.20 OWNER Mrs Claude Lilley (NEWMARKET) BRED Miss Geraldine Browne
WEIGHT FOR AGE 3yo-11lb

The two horses to look at here are Insatiable and Mountgate. Both were ridden by non-claiming Jockeys and both carried 9st 3lb. There was a difference in their official handicap marks. As you can see from the race result, Insatiable ran off 85 but Mountgate off only 74. This is because the three-year-old Insatiable receives 11lb weight-for-age in a mile race at this time of year. The message is to take great care when handicapping horses of more than one age.

Remember, this is only a method to get a handicap started. Continue in this mode permanently and your handicap may prove virtually identical to the official one. My feeling is that, after three or four weeks, your ratings will be ready to stand on their own.

We have studied methods of starting your handicap, discussing both master and performance ratings. What now needs to be resolved is how we store our ratings, how we use them to assess a forthcoming race, and how we adjust them after that race is run.

CHAPTER 6

THE DAY TO DAY RUNNING OF A HANDICAP

What we have dealt with so far is how to calculate performance ratings. Now we need a way of storing our ratings in a consistent form. This will allow us to analyse races before they are run for the purposes of making selections. Once the race is over, this same data should be used to reassess the race, store new performance ratings and amend master ratings where necessary.

It has been mentioned already that Flat ratings are kept on a scale of 0-140 and jump ratings on a scale of 0-175. This is because 10st, or 140lb, tends to be the maximum weight carried in Flat races, whilst the weights over jumps go up to 12st 7lb, or 175lb.

To allow us to compare the horses in each type of race within a category, we need to adjust our ratings to take into account the weight being carried. Our highest-rated horse will often be carrying topweight, but it may be conceding 20lb to a horse rated only 10lb inferior. What we need is a way of comparing each horse in relation to its competitors. Until then, we can not begin to make judgements. Take the following race as an example:-

2.15 Yarmouth 25th June, 1996
TOTE DUAL FORECAST H'CAP, for three-year-olds only

Alwarqa	9-7
Soldier Mak	9-5
Ship's Dancer	8-10
Influence Pedler	8-9
Pearl Anniversary	8-8
Glowing Reeds	8-2

Going into the race, our master ratings were:-

Soldier Mak	69
Alwarqa	68
Influence Pedler	60
Ship's Dancer	58
Glowing Reeds	52
Pearl Anniversary	47

Soldier Mak and Alwarqa are rated some way above the other four, but are carrying the biggest weights. What we need is a method which allows us to compare our previous assessments with today's weights.

As previously stated, the method generally used for Flat racing is to adjust the ratings to 10st (140lb). That is to say, for every pound carried below 10st, one point is added, and for every pound carried above 10st, one point is deducted. Under jump racing rules, the adjustments are normally made to 12st 7lb (175lb). If you find it quicker at first to refer to tables rather than rely on your mental arithmetic, here they are:-

Flat Table

9st 13lb	plus 1		8st 11lb	plus 17
9st 12lb	plus 2		8st 10lb	plus 18
9st 11lb	plus 3		8st 9lb	plus 19
9st 10lb	plus 4		8st 8lb	plus 20
9st 9lb	plus 5		8st 7lb	plus 21
9st 8lb	plus 6		8st 6lb	plus 22
9st 7lb	plus 7		8st 5lb	plus 23
9st 6lb	plus 8		8st 4lb	plus 24
9st 5lb	plus 9		8st 3lb	plus 25
9st 4lb	plus 10		8st 2lb	plus 26
9st 3lb	plus 11		8st 1lb	plus 27
9st 2lb	plus 12		8st	plus 28
9st 1lb	plus 13		7st 13lb	plus 29
9st	plus 14		7st 12lb	plus 30
8st 13lb	plus 15		7st 11lb	plus 31
8st 12lb	plus 16		7st 10lb	plus 32

Jumps Table

12st 6lb	plus 1		11st 2lb	plus 19
12st 5lb	plus 2		11st 1lb	plus 20
12st 4lb	plus 3		11st	plus 21
12st 3lb	plus 4		10st 13lb	plus 22
12st 2lb	plus 5		10st 12lb	plus 23
12st 1lb	plus 6		10st 11lb	plus 24
12st	plus 7		10st 10lb	plus 25
11st 13lb	plus 8		10st 9lb	plus 26
11st 12lb	plus 9		10st 8lb	plus 27
11st 11lb	plus 10		10st 7lb	plus 28
11st 10lb	plus 11		10st 6lb	plus 29
11st 9lb	plus 12		10st 5lb	plus 30
11st 8lb	plus 13		10st 4lb	plus 31
11st 7lb	plus 14		10st 3lb	plus 32
11st 6lb	plus 15		10st 2lb	plus 33
11st 5lb	plus 16		10st 1lb	plus 34
11st 4lb	plus 17		10st	plus 35
11st 3lb	plus 18			

Making the adjustments from the Flat table for this particular race, we would get adjusted master ratings as follows:-

Rating			Master Rating		Adjustment for Weight Carried		Adjusted Master
Alwarqa	9-7		68	+	7	=	75
Soldier Mak	9-5		69	+	9	=	78
Ship's Dancer	8-10		58	+	18	=	76
Influence Pedler	8-9		60	+	19	=	79
Pearl Anniversary	8-8		47	+	20	=	67
Glowing Reeds	8-2		52	+	26	=	78

Although Soldier Mak and Alwarqa have our best master ratings, once the ratings are adjusted for today's weights, the picture changes. Now, Influence Pedler looks the pick in an open race. I call this race open as five of the six are rated within just 4lb of each other.

To get a more in-depth view of the race, each of the competitors' last three performance ratings is adjusted to allow for today's weights and we end up with:-

YARMOUTH- Tuesday 25 June

0215 **TOTE DUAL FORECAST H'CAP (0-70) (3-Y.O) (CLASS E) 1m 6f 17y**

RHR	HORSE,AGE,WEIGHT	LAST THREE OUTINGS		
79	Influence Pedler (3-8-9)	79	67	75
78	Glowing Reeds (3-8-2)	67	46	78
78	Soldier Mak (3-9-5)	73	78	69
76	Ship's Dancer (3-8-10)	76	74	76
75	Alwarqa (3-9-7)	75	75	70
67	Pearl Anniversary (IRE) (3-8-8)	85A	89A	76A

What is shown here are the master ratings once adjusted to today's weights, followed by the horse name and weight. Also shown are the last three performance ratings adjusted to today's weights, with the most recent on the left. These performance ratings should help you form a view on whether the horse is improving, consistent, or on the downgrade. What it will also enable you to do is refer quickly to *the Form Book* or a racing paper to view the key performances, based upon which your selection may depend. This is the way in which you will find the pre-race ratings displayed throughout the rest of this book.

The ratings shown with an 'A' are the All-Weather performance ratings gained by Pearl Anniversary on his latest three starts. As I have said earlier, I keep a separate set of master ratings for Turf and All-Weather racing. In this case, the separation of the two sets of ratings served us well, as Influence Pedler, our top-rated on Turf, actually won the race.

1903-**YARMOUTH** (L-H) (Firm)
Tuesday June 25th
WEATHER: warm WIND: almost nil

2204 TOTE DUAL FORECAST H'CAP (0-70) (3-Y.O) (Class E)
2-15 (2-15) **1m 6f 17y** £3,179.40 (£949.20: £453.60: £205.80) Stalls: Low GOING minus 0.66 sec per fur (HD)

			SP	RR	SF
1679² **Influence Pedler (52)** (CEBrittain) 3-8-9 BDoyle(3) (hld up gng wl: hdwy to ld 4f out: rdn clr over 2f out: eased ins fnl f) ....—	1	11/4¹	65+	36	
1814⁴ **Glowing Reeds (45)** (CNAllen) 3-8-2v¹ JQuinn(5) (s.i.s: bhd 10f: drvn & nt keen after: mod late hdwy to take 2nd nr fin) 7	2	25/1	50	21	
1984³ **Soldier Mak (62)** (AHide) 3-9-2⁽³⁾ MHenry(2) (hld up: wnt 2nd 4f out: drvn & no ch w wnr fnl 2f) ....nk	3	6/1	67	38	
1877* **Alwarqa (64)** (RWArmstrong) 3-9-7 WCarson(4) (chsd ldrs: pushed along ½-wy: rdn & v.onepcd fnl 3f)........2½	4	3/1²	66	37	
1814² **Pearl Anniversary (IRE) (51)** (MJohnston) 3-8-8 DHarrison(6) (sn pushed along: prom tl hrd rdn & no rspnse 4f out) 3	5	5/1	50	21	
1877³ **Ship's Dancer (53)** (JLDunlop) 3-8-10b PatEddery(1) (led 10f: sn btn: t.o 2f out: sn eased) ....dist	6	7/2³	—	—	
		(SP 108.7%)	**6 Rn**		

3m 0.5 (1.10) CSF £40.85 TOTE £3.10: £1.80 £5.90 (£27.60) OWNER Mr C. E. Brittain (NEWMARKET) BRED Stetchworth Park Stud Ltd

We have dealt with weight, but what about weight-for-age? In a race like the one at Yarmouth which concerns horses of just one age group, it is easiest to ignore it. However, once horses of different ages meet in races that you are trying to assess, you need to employ the weight-for-age table. If doing your ratings by hand, you will need to have the table printed on a sturdy piece of card that will stand up to plenty of use (the one printed on the front card of *Raceform, the Form Book* is ideal). Here is another race from June 1996.

Ayr 22nd June, 1996
ALLOWAY H'CAP, 1m 2f for three-year-olds and upwards

Far Ahead	9-12
Dr Edgar	9-0
Efizia	8-13
Shabanaz	8-13
Keep Battling	8-1
Lucky Bea	8-1
Stormless	7-10

These horses had the following master ratings going in to the race:-

Far Ahead	82
Lucky Bea	71
Efizia	67
Stormless	66?
Shabanaz	65
Dr Edgar	65
Keep Battling	53

Adjusting these as before we get:-

Rating		Master Rating		Adjustment for Weight Carried		Adjusted Master Rating
Far Ahead	9-12	82	+	2	=	84
Dr Edgar	9-0	65	+	14	=	79
Efizia	8-13	67	+	15	=	82
Shabanaz	8-13	65	+	15	=	80
Keep Battling	8-1	53	+	27	=	80
Lucky Bea	8-1	71	+	27	=	98
Stormless	7-10	66?	+	32	=	98?

This appears to suggest that the two bottom weights, Lucky Bea and Stormless, have been very leniently treated by the official Handicapper. This is often referred to as being well in. However, Lucky Bea is a three-year-old.

When we stored our ratings, weight-for-age was added in. Remember, the stored rating is a best-guess assessment of the horse's ability when it is fully mature. However, this horse is only three, and so is not fully mature. Therefore, we should remove the weight-for-age allowance to allow us to do a fair comparison. Reference to the official weight-for-age table will tell us that, in a mile and a quarter race, in the second half of June, three-year-olds are still 12lb short of full maturity. So, now we need to remove 12lb from the rating of Lucky Bea. This gives an adjusted master rating of 86.

Although Stormless now has an adjusted rating of 98, the question mark indicates some doubt in the rating. If the figure could be relied upon, it would give him an outstanding chance.

AYR- Saturday 22 June

0345 ALLOWAY H'CAP (0-80) (3-Y.O+) (CLASS D) 1m 2f

RHR	HORSE,AGE,WEIGHT	LAST THREE OUTINGS		
98?	Stormless (5-7-10)	84	98	43
86	Lucky Bea (3-8-1)	86	61	74
84	Far Ahead (4-9-12)	71	63	75
82	Efizia (6-8-13)	82	76	72
80	Keep Battling (6-8-1)	80	77	77
80	Shabanaz (11-8-13)	72	72	68
79	Dr Edgar (4-9-0)	79	62	79

Calculating your new assessments after the race is run

This is the acid test of your rating ability. Look at the result and adjust your pre-race ratings, using the performance of each horse to generate a new figure for the winner. How to calculate a conversion table for beaten distances was discussed earlier. What follows is a conversion table for each furlong up to a mile; and each two furlongs up to fourteen furlongs (1m 6f). This should be enough to get you started.

Flat Conversion Table

Distance (lengths)	5 furlongs	6 furlongs	7 furlongs	1 mile	1¼ miles	1½ miles	1¾ miles
s.h	0	0	0	0	0	0	0
hd	1	1	1	0	0	0	0
nk	1	1	1	1	1	1	0
½	2	1	1	1	1	1	1
¾	2	2	2	1	1	1	1
1	3	3	2	2	2	1	1
1¼	4	3	3	2	2	2	1
1½	5	4	3	3	2	2	2
1¾	5	4	4	3	3	2	2
2	6	5	4	4	3	3	2
2¼	7	6	5	4	3	3	2
2½	8	6	5	5	4	3	3
2¾	8	7	6	5	4	3	3
3	9	8	6	6	5	4	3
3½	11	9	7	7	5	4	4
4	12	10	9	8	6	5	4
4½	14	11	10	8	7	6	5
5	15	13	11	9	8	6	5
6	18	15	13	11	9	8	6
7	21	18	15	13	11	9	8
8	24	20	17	15	12	10	9
9	27	23	19	17	14	11	10
10	30	25	21	19	15	13	11

11	33	28	24	21	17	14	12
12	36	30	26	23	18	15	13
13	39	33	28	24	20	16	14
14	42	35	30	26	21	18	15
15	45	38	32	28	23	19	16
16	48	40	34	30	24	20	17
17	51	43	36	32	26	21	18
18	54	45	39	34	27	23	19
19	57	48	41	36	29	24	20
20	60	50	43	38	30	25	21

Jumps Conversion Table

Distance	2 miles	2½ miles	3 miles
s.h	0	0	0
hd	0	0	0
nk	0	0	0
½	0	0	0
¾	1	1	0
1	1	1	1
1¼	1	1	1
1½	1	1	1
1¾	2	1	1
2	2	2	1
2¼	2	2	1
2½	2	2	2
2¾	3	2	2
3	3	2	2
3½	3	3	2
4	4	3	3
4½	4	3	3
5	5	4	3
6	6	5	4
7	7	5	4
8	8	6	5
9	8	7	6
10	9	8	6
11	10	8	7
12	11	9	8
13	12	10	8
14	13	11	9
15	14	11	9
16	15	12	10
17	16	13	11
18	17	14	11
19	18	14	12
20	19	15	13
21	20	16	13
22	21	17	14
23	22	17	14

24	23	18	15
25	23	19	16
26	24	20	16
27	25	20	17
28	26	21	18
29	27	22	18
30	28	23	19

The best way to demonstrate how the procedure works is by way of an example. Here are the pre-race ratings of one of the races we worked on earlier:-

AYR- Saturday 22 June

0345 ALLOWAY H'CAP (0-80) (3-Y.O+) (CLASS D) 1m 2f

RHR	HORSE,AGE,WEIGHT	LAST THREE OUTINGS		
98?	Stormless *(5-7-10)*	84	98	43
86	Lucky Bea *(3-8-1)*	86	61	74
84	Far Ahead *(4-9-12)*	71	63	75
82	Efizia *(6-8-13)*	82	76	72
80	Keep Battling *(6-8-1)*	80	77	77
80	Shabanaz *(11-8-13)*	72	72	68
79	Dr Edgar *(4-9-0)*	79	62	79

And this was the result of the race:-

2118-**AYR (L-H) (Good to firm)**
Saturday June 22nd
5th race was hand timed
WEATHER: fine WIND: mod against

2152 ALLOWAY H'CAP (0-80) (3-Y.O+) (Class D)
3-45 (3-46) **1m 2f** £3,615.00 (£1,095.00: £535.00: £255.00) Stalls: Low GOING minus 0.14 sec per fur (G) **SP**

1585²	**Stormless (43)** (PMonteith) 5-7-7(3) DarrenMoffatt(4) (lw: hld up & bhd: hdwy to join ldrs ent st: led over 1f out: all out)..—	1	9/2²
2020*	**Keep Battling (48)** (JSGoldie) 6-8-1 5x TWilliams(5) (hld up & bhd: hdwy on bit 3f out: swtchd outside over 1f out: ev ch ins fnl f: kpt on)...hd	2	9/4¹
1861⁶	**Far Ahead (73)** (JLEyre) 4-9-12 RLappin(3) (chsd ldrs: hdwy & ev ch ins fnl f: nt qckn) 1¼	3	14/1
2077³	**Dr Edgar (61)** (MDods) 4-9-0 JCarroll(6) (led tl hdd over 1f out: wknd ins fnl f) 2½	4	11/2³
1698³	**Efizia (60)** (GMMoore) 6-8-13 JFortune(7) (chsd ldrs tl outpcd fnl 2f) 3½	5	6/1
1772²	**Shabanaz (60)** (WRMuir) 11-8-13 WJO'Connor(2) (cl up tl wknd over 2f out) ....s.h	6	11/2³
2123³	**Lucky Bea (60)** (MWEasterby) 3-8-1 JFanning(1) (lw: prld hrd: trckd ldrs: outpcd over 2f out: sn btn)............2½	7	8/1

(SP 111.8%) **7 Rn**

2m 8.9 (4.30) CSF £14.21 TOTE £7.10: £3.00 £1.60 (£6.90) OWNER Mr D. St Clair (ROSEWELL) BRED D. V. St Clair
WEIGHT FOR AGE 3yo-12lb

Taking the pre-race ratings, add the pounds value of the beaten distances to each horse's figure in turn. This gives us what I refer to as the 'suggested winner's rating'. In this case this would be:-

Stormless	98?	
Keep Battling	80	as a head is not worth even 1lb on the 1m 2f conversion table
Far Ahead	86	84 + 2, the 2lb coming for the 1¼ length margin between the second and third
Dr Edgar	85	79 + 2 + 4, 4lb for the 2½ lengths from the conversion table
Efizia	93	82 + 2 + 4 + 5
Shabanaz	91	80 + 2 + 4 + 5 + 0
Lucky Bea	101	86 + 2 + 4 + 5 + 0 + 4

How you rate the race from this point on is a matter of personal style. This is probably a good time to mention the level of your ratings, as it will be the decision you make now that will determine whether the overall level of your ratings rises, falls, or ideally stays the same.

If your standard decision in a case like this would be to take most notice of Keep Battling's figure and opt for a figure in the very low 80s, then your ratings will probably end up falling through the year. You need to remember that the case shown is based on my use of master ratings, which gives us the best performance rating in the last few runs. An average of all the runners here would give a figure of about 93, and if this is the figure used, your ratings will undoubtedly climb throughout the course of a season. This is not altogether a bad thing, as it gives recent form a slight edge and may allow your percentage of winners top-rated to climb slightly. However, it renders your ratings invalid when trying to make comparisons between different seasons if you wish to run your handicap over a long period.

The answer for maintaining the level of the ratings lies somewhere in the middle, and at the time I settled on 85, being unable to justify raising the master rating of the joint third-favourite Dr Edgar, who had finished fourth in the race.

However, this is not where the mathematics end. The rating for the winner of 85 assumes a fully mature horse but it also assumes a weight carried of 10st. (N.B. for the purposes of handicapping, I always include the jockey's claim in the weight carried and thus consider Stormless to have carried 7st 10lb).

Defeat in the race is worth the following value in pounds from the conversion table:-

Stormless	0	obviously, as the winner
Keep Battling	0	
Far Ahead	2	
Dr Edgar	6	
Efizia	11	
Shabanaz	11	
Lucky Bea	15	

The Performance Ratings generated are as follows:-

Stormless	53	The suggested winner's rating of 85 minus the 32lb the horse carried less than 10st.
Keep Battling	58	85 - 27
Far Ahead	81	85 - 2 - 2 The suggested winner's rating of 85 minus the 2lb carried below 10st, minus the 2lb beaten from the table above.
Dr Edgar	65	85 - 14 - 6
Efizia	59	85 - 15 - 11
Shabanaz	59	85 - 15 - 11

Lucky Bea	55	85 - 27 - 15 + 12 The calculation is as before but weight-for-age is now added back in. To not do so would rate Lucky Bea as a fully mature horse when, as a three-year-old, we know from the weight-for-age table that he is 12lb short of it.

Chester 9th May, 1996
ORMONDE STAKES, 1m 5f 89y

The pre-race ratings were:-

CHESTER- Thursday 9 May

0340 ORMONDE STKS (GP 3) (4-Y.O+) (CLASS A) 1m 5f 89y

RHR	HORSE,AGE,WEIGHT	LAST THREE OUTINGS		
139	Shambo *(9-8-11)*	135	139	135
139	Oscar Schindler (IRE) *(4-8-11)*	139	138	129
136	Minds Music (USA) *(4-8-11)*	130	136	124
134	Dance A Dream *(4-8-8)*	133	124	134
134	Further Flight *(10-9-0)*	130	97	134
133	Poppy Carew (IRE) *(4-8-8)*	125	119	131
109	Election Day (IRE) *(4-8-11)*	109	66	

And the result,

1002-CHESTER (L-H) (Good)
Thursday May 9th
WEATHER: cloudy WIND: str half bhd

1017 ORMONDE STKS (Gp 3) (4-Y.O+) (Class A)
3-40 (3-40) **1m 5f 89y** £29,520.00 (£11,038.50: £5,294.25: £2,297.25) Stalls: Low GOING minus 0.10 sec per fur (G)

		SP	RR	SF
	Oscar Schindler (IRE) (KPrendergast,Ireland) **4-8-11** MJKinane(2) (gd sort: lw: hld up gng wl: qcknd to ld ins fnl f: readily) ....— **1**	11/4[2]	121	55
687*	**Election Day (IRE)** (MRStoute) **4-8-11** WCarson(1) (lw: trckd ldrs: n.m.r 7f out: hdwy on ins over 1f out: fin wl) 1½ **2**	10/1	119	53
	Minds Music (USA) (114) (HRACecil) **4-8-11** PatEddery(3) (lw: chsd ldr: led 7f out tl ins fnl f: r.o)..............s.h **3**	2/11[1]	119	53
831[7]	**Poppy Carew (IRE) (104)** (PWHarris) **4-8-8** GHind(4) (hld up & bhd: hdwy ent st: kpt on u.p fnl f) 2½ **4**	20/1	113	47
	Dance a Dream (116) (MRStoute) **4-8-8** LDettori(8) (lw: led over 6f: prom tl rdn & one pce appr fnl f)...........nk **5**	9/23[3]	113	47
751*	**Further Flight (110)** (BWHills) **10-9-0** MHills(6) (hld up: effrt & rdn 2f out: nt pce to chal) ....¾ **6**	9/1	118	52
	Shambo (111) (CEBrittain) **9-8-11** BDoyle(7) (bkwd: hld up: hdwy 6f out: pushed along 3f out: one pce appr fnl f) 1 **7**	8/1	114	48

(SP 113.1%) **7 Rn**

2m 55.39 (5.39) CSF £25.82 TOTE £3.10: £1.70 £3.40 (£16.00) OWNER Mr Oliver Lehane BRED Oliver Lehane

Using the conversion table for 1m 6f gives values to the beaten distances. If you wish, you could work out a table for the exact thirteen furlong distance by the method shown earlier in the book. This, added to the horse's pre-race ratings, gives us the following suggested winning ratings:-

Oscar Schindler	139	
Election Day	111	(109 + 2)
Minds Music	138	(136 + 2)
Poppy Carew	138	(133 + 5)
Dance A Dream	139	(134 + 5)
Further Flight	140	(134 + 6)

Given that Shambo received the paddock comment of backward, it seems safe to assume that he ran below his best as a result. Ignoring the winner is always a good policy if at all possible, as even an apparently flat-out winner can be idling in front. Looking at the others, the only question requiring an answer is, can Election Day really have shown all this improvement? As a horse who had won just a small maiden on the second of his two starts, a second in Group Three company was clearly a step up, and 138 was a confident assessment of the race.

The assumption about Election Day was confirmed nine days later when, on better terms, Election Day gave Minds Music a much more emphatic beating.

In races where the runners have carried similar weights, you may prefer to work out each new performance rating by referring to the horse that finished in front of it, as in the example below:-

1   Oscar Schindler (8-11) gets a performance rating of 121, that is 138 minus one point for every pound he shouldered under than 10st
2   1½   Election Day (8-11), carrying the same weight, but taking a 2lb beating, gets a rating of 121 - 2 = 119
3   s.h   Minds Music (8-11) also gets 119
4   2½   Poppy Carew (8-8) 119 - 3 - 3 = 113
5   nk   Dance A Dream (8-8), also gets 113 as a neck is not worth a point at 1m 5f
6   ¾   Further Flight (9-0) 113 + 6 -1 = 118, carrying 6lb more than the fifth horse, Dance A Dream.
7   1   Shambo (8-11) 118 - 3 - 1 = 114

Looking up your assessments
You will need to look through the racing every day to establish which races are covered by your handicap.

To produce ratings for races, you need to store your assessments of previous races in some way, before looking up each runner in the race being studied.

Keeping Your Ratings
When I first started with *Raceform*, I built up huge trays of 5 x 3 inch index cards, one for each horse. Every one had all its performances logged, so that its career efforts could be glanced through by removing the card from the deck. Apart from the obvious problem of being unable to carry your cards around, you always run the risk of knocking them on the floor. Sorting them out is no fun. I can assure you of that from personal experience! The system works quite well but is very time consuming and fixing ratings in the light of subsequent events is very laborious. My advice with cards is stick to poker!

I have also used notebooks (or address books) for a similar purpose, lettering up each page of the book and entering horses as they come to hand. The problem with this method is that the spread of horses through the alphabet seems to vary from one year to the next. There always seem to be some pages with just half a dozen entries and others that are crammed and that eventually fall out of strict alphabetic order. This can make looking up horses a bit of a nightmare. As with the cards, changing previous ratings can be a nightmare. However, a book of this type is more easily transported.

If your mental arithmetic is particularly swift, you could try putting a rating for the winner against the race returns in one of the weekly papers such as *Raceform Update*. Use the index from the paper to find each horse's previous effort and work out its rating from the winner's figure. However, the weekly results pull-outs become dog-eared after a time, and are not as easy to carry around.

Whichever method you use, if you only have access to fresh results on a weekly basis, make sure you keep them safe, otherwise you will end up duplicating a lot of work. Believe me, if you leave papers lying around, someone will tidy them up - normally into the bin!

I find all the above methods both time-consuming and frustrating. If you can possibly afford it, I would recommend investing in one of the computer formbook packages. This 'bells and whistles' approach may seem over the top, but the time you save by having the information at your fingertips makes it well worth it. As you can guess, there are many computer formbooks on the market, so make sure you choose one which allows you to store and retrieve your own ratings. Even though I compile handicap ratings for a living, I still dabble in my own ratings for hurdlers and two-year-olds, as my colleague Walter Glynn compiles these for *Raceform*. You will not be surprised to hear that I use *Computer Raceform*, but then I would, wouldn't I!

Picking an area for specialisation
I can not emphasise enough the need to specialise, whether you're limited by time or just starting from scratch. Let us consider some possible areas in which it is possible to specialise, and then look at the pros and cons.

Handicapping two-year-olds
This area has already been dealt with in detail. The one real downside of the two-year-old handicap is that, just as you feel the form is dropping into place, the six-furlong races start and the whole game changes, as stamina comes into play.

Sprint handicaps
Now that access to the official handicap ratings is so easy, I would advise that these are used as the basis of any handicap that deals with handicap races. The big plus with sprinters is that the horses run frequently, and meet each other regularly. The big minus is that far too many of the races are unduly influenced by the effects of the draw, and *the Form Book* is often the last place to look to find the winner. Also, the big fields will mean that your winning percentage is quite low and you may lose heart as well as some of your bank balance!

Group and listed races
This is a good one to try as most of the races you rate will be televised, and you are likely to be familiar with most of the horses. The down side is that Group races resemble London buses; none for weeks and then ten come along at the same time.

Other problems include getting started, as the official ratings are printed only up to a ceiling of 120 during the season, and the fact that many Group and listed winners will be graduating from top handicap company.

Juvenile hurdlers
As with two-year-old racing on the Flat, all Handicappers start from scratch with these, and this is the area to which the habitual two-year-old Handicapper seems drawn in the winter.

Two mile handicap hurdlers and chasers
Both are fascinating fields. You run the danger of horses with varying trips coming in and out of your races during the season, and both spheres are invaded by hordes of novices in the later stages of the season.

Hunter chasers
This can be a real moneyspinner, although probably not as much now as in the past, given the better coverage in the sporting press. If you include point-to-points as well, you are liable to spend seven months of the year twiddling your thumbs, and three or four of the remaining five worked off your feet.

CHAPTER 7

WORKED EXAMPLES

I think the best way to learn about handicapping is to see how someone else has done it. By following through their thought processes, it should give you an idea of why we make certain decisions, and how they are reflected in our ratings. The ratings used in the examples I am about to give you are real. As you will see, no handicap will ever be perfect, but it's how we correct our assessments that counts.

The Cheltenham Festival 1996

We will all adopt a slightly different way of handicapping a race after it has happened. Some of you will concentrate on the most recent form, whilst others will look at the best performances of the competitors. The trick is to try to and find a system which will not make the overall level of your ratings fall or, far more likely, rise. In this chapter, I aim to give you an insight into the way a Handicapper's mind works.

I only hope that the way I approach this task will point you in the right direction.

0405 RITZ CLUB NATIONAL HUNT H'CAP CHASE (5-Y.O+) (CLASS B) 3m 1f

RHR	HORSE,AGE,WEIGHT	LAST THREE OUTINGS		
188d	Chatam (USA) (12-10-2)	—	—	188
187	Flyer's Nap (10-10-0)	172	187	180
181	Unguided Missile (IRE) (8-10-10)	181	180	174
179	Flashing Steel (11-12-0)	—	179	179
178	Amtrak Express (9-10-9)	—	178	—
177	Percy Smollett (8-10-10)	177	177	176
170	Maamur (USA) (8-9-4)	170	167	162
165	James Pigg (9-9-1)	150	165	165
156	Kilfinny Cross (IRE) (8-8-0)	122	145	156
154+	Billygroat Gruff (7-9-1)	141	154	150

As you can see, the two best handicapped horses were Chatam on 188 and Flyer's Nap on 187. On his previous start in the Mandarin, Chatam had run poorly. Flyer's Nap was also beaten in the Mandarin, but he was running over a half-mile shorter trip than looked ideal. Normally, a vital factor for a handicap win at the Festival is to identify horses still on the upgrade. Unguided Missile appeared the best weighted of these, as both Maamur and the novice Billygoat Gruff were some way out of the handicap.

2745 RITZ CLUB NATIONAL HUNT H'CAP CHASE (5-Y.O+) (Class B)
4-05 (4-13) 3m 1f (Old) (19 fncs) £33,712.00 (£10,096.00: £4,848.00: £2,224.00) GOING: 0.59 sec per fur (S)

			SP	RR
2541*	**Maamur (USA)** (138) (CaptTAForster) 8-10-0 3x AThornton (a.p: disp ld fr 4 out: shkn up to ld flat: styd on strly)	— 1	13/2 3	150
2160*	**Unguided Missile (IRE)** (148) (GRichards) 8-10-10 RDunwoody (trckd ldrs: lft in ld 4 out: hrd rdn, hdd & no ex flat)	7 2	11/4 1	156
2251P	**Chatam (USA)** (140) (MCPipe) 12-10-2 DBridgwater (hld up: hdwy & mstke 12th: hmpd 4 out: n.d after)	13 3	28/1	139
2251⁴	**Flyer's Nap** (138) (RHAlner) 10-9-9(5) PHenley (bhd: mstke 8th: rdn 10th: effrt appr 4 out: sn wknd: t.o)	dist 4	7/1	—
2482U	**Amtrak Express** (147) (NJHenderson) 9-10-9 MAFitzgerald (prom to 14th: sn wknd: t.o)	30 5	7/1	—
2331*	**Billygoat Gruff** (138) (DNicholson) 7-9-11(3) RJohnson (hld up: hdwy 10th: rdn 4 out: no ch whn fell 2 out)	F	7/1	—
2450⁵	**Kilfinny Cross (IRE)** (138) (JPearce) 8-10-0 JMcLaughlin (led tl fell 4 out: dead)	F	66/1	—
2359a⁷	**Flashing Steel** (166) (JEMulhern,Ireland) 11-12-0 JOsborne (lw: lost pl 8th: t.o whn p.u bef 4 out)	P	8/1	—
728³	**James Pigg** (138) (MCPipe) 9-10-0 CMaude (a bhd: t.o whn p.u bef 14th)	P	25/1	—
2482²	**Percy Smollett** (148) (DNicholson) 8-10-10 BPowell (nt j.w: a bhd: t.o whn p.u bef 4 out)	P	4/1 2	—

(SP 117.4%)

6m 22.9 (13.90) CSF £23.65 CT £432.99 TOTE £7.30: £2.00 £1.50 £4.70 (£9.20) Trio £90.60 OWNER Mrs A. L. Wood (LUDLOW) BRED Maverick Productions Ltd in USA

LONG HANDICAP Maamur (USA) 9-1 Kilfinny Cross (IRE) 8-0 James Pigg 9-1 Billygoat Gruff 9-1

Maamur continued his climb up the ladder and Unguided Missile ran well, being the only one to give him a race. Although Chatam is best when fresh and on a flatter track, he ran his best race in a while to be a slightly unlucky third. Flyer's Nap flopped.

Using our three mile conversion table, the suggested ratings for the winner are:-

Maamur	170
Unguided Missile	185
Chatam	200d
Flyer's Nap	218

A difficult race to find a line and the only option was to take Unguided Missile's run at face value, giving Maamur a Performance Rating of 150 (185 - 35).

0250 QUEEN MOTHER CHAMPION CHASE (GD 1) (5-Y.O+) (CLASS A) 2m

RHR	HORSE,AGE,WEIGHT	LAST THREE OUTINGS		
180	Viking Flagship (9-12-0)	168	179	165
176	Strong Platinum (IRE) (8-12-0)	—	179	176
176+	Sound Man (IRE) (8-12-0)	170	176	173
176	Coulton (9-12-0)	—	158	—
173	Travado (10-12-0)	173	171	167
165	Klairon Davis (FR) (7-12-0)	165	—	—
154	Dancing Paddy (8-12-0)	154	150	154

The rating of championship races is often one of the easiest parts of a Handicapper's task. After all, so much is known about most of the competitors, and comparing them should be easy. Sound Man, beaten by Klairon Davis in the previous year's Arkle, was considered the contender on the up. However, Viking Flagship was sure not to give up his crown without a fight.

2761 QUEEN MOTHER CHAMPION CHASE (Gd 1) (5-Y.O+) (Class A)
2-50 (2-55) 2m (Old) (12 fncs) £82,085.00 (£30,515.00: £14,757.50: £6,162.50: £2,581.25: £1,148.75) GOING: 0.56 sec per fur

			SP	RR
2207a²	**Klairon Davis (FR)** (ALTMoore,Ireland) 7-12-0 FWoods (lw: hld up: hdwy 7th: mstkes 4 out & 3 out: led last: drvn clr)	— 1	9/1	177
2479*	**Viking Flagship** (170) (DNicholson) 9-12-0 CFSwan (a.p: jnd ldr & mstke 3 out: hit next: ev ch last: no ex flat)	5 2	9/4 2	172
2297*	**Sound Man (IRE)** (169) (EJO'Grady,Ireland) 8-12-0 RDunwoody (lw: led & hdd & mstke 3rd: led 6th: mstkes 3 out & 2 out: hdd last: one pce)	1¼ 3	11/8 1	171
2252²	**Travado** (164) (NJHenderson) 10-12-0 MAFitzgerald (lw: trckd ldrs: outpcd appr 3 out: btn whn mstke 2 out)	5 4	16/1	166
2574a²	**Strong Platinum (IRE)** (171) (PBurke,Ireland) 8-12-0 CO'Dwyer (lw: hld up: j.slowly 7th: wknd after 4 out)	3½ 5	5/1 3	162
2297F	**Coulton** (168) (OSherwood) 9-12-0 JOsborne (hld up & bhd: hdwy 8th: mstkes 4 out & 3 out: sn bhd)	1¼ 6	20/1	161
2479²	**Dancing Paddy** (144) (KOCunningham-Brown) 8-12-0 WMarston (led 3rd to 6th: hit 8th: mstke 4 out: sn btn)	3 7	50/1	158?

(SP 112.1%)

4m 0.4 (7.40) CSF £27.94 TOTE £8.70: £2.70 £1.60 (£10.50) OWNER Mr C. Jones (NAAS) BRED M. C. Quellier in France

A bit of a surprise to most of us, as Klairon Davis confirms his liking for Cheltenham, pouncing at the last to win fair and square.

The result suggests winner's ratings of:-

Klairon Davis	165
Viking Flagship	185
Sound Man	182+
Travado	184
Strong Platinum	193
Coulton	191
Dancing Paddy	172

Viking Flagship and Travado have reproduced their Newbury form of the previous month, virtually to the inch. Therefore, rating this race was comparatively easy. According to our figures, Viking Flagship ran 1lb below his very best that day. Therefore, Travado is taken as having run to his very best, giving Klairon Davis a rating of 177 (184 - 7).

0405 SUN ALLIANCE CHASE (GD 1) (5-Y.O+) (CLASS A) 3m 1f

RHR	HORSE, AGE, WEIGHT	LAST THREE OUTINGS		
166+	Mr Mulligan (IRE) (8-11-4)	166	153	129
157	Johnny Setaside (IRE) (7-11-4)	157	157	117
154	Minella Lad (10-11-4)	150	154	165
152	Major Rumpus (8-11-4)	152	—	133
149	Nahthen Lad (IRE) (7-11-4)	149	140	138
144d	Linden's Lotto (IRE) (7-11-4)	121	128	144
141	Dark Honey (11-11-4)	140	—	135
140+	Betty's Boy (IRE) (7-11-4)	137	140	—
135	River Lossie (7-11-4)	135	135	114
134	Punters Overhead (IRE) (8-11-4)	—	134	—
132	Do Rightly (IRE) (7-11-4)	132	—	129
110	Tothewoods (8-11-4)	109	102	—

Mr Mulligan was so impressive in the Reynoldstown at Ascot that he looked something of a banker. Add to that the fact that the opposition have shown no more than ordinary form, and he looks a possible bet, even at such a short price.

2742-CHELTENHAM (L-H) (Good to soft, Good patches)
Wednesday March 13th
WEATHER: overcast, dry & very cold WIND: str half bhd

2763 SUN ALLIANCE NOVICES' CHASE (Gd 1) (5-Y.O+) (Class A)
4-05 (4-10) **3m 1f** (Old) (19 fncs) £54,672.50 (£20,427.50: £9,963.75: £4,256.25: £1,878.13: £926.87) GOING: Not Established

			SP	RR	SF
2298²	Nahthen Lad (IRE) (131) (MrsJPitman) 7-11-4 WMarston (lw: hld up: hdwy 9th: rdn 3 out: led last: drvn out)	—	1	7/1³	146+	68
2298*	Mr Mulligan (IRE) (153) (NoelChance) 8-11-4 RJohnson (blnd 1st: hdwy 6th: mstke 11th: led 13th: j.slowly 4 out: hdd last: sn btn)	8	2	11/8¹	141++	63
2514²	Do Rightly (IRE) (100) (MBradstock) 7-11-4 PHolley (lw: led: pckd 1st: blnd & hdd 12th: wkng whn mstke 4 out: lft poor 3rd last)	28	3	40/1	123	45
1494²	Betty's Boy (IRE) (127) (KCBailey) 7-11-4 MAFitzgerald (prom to 14th: sn wknd: t.o)	16	4	8/1	113	35
2447a*	Johnny Setaside (IRE) (NMeade,Ireland) 7-11-4 GBradley (a bhd: t.o fr 9th)	27	5	5/1²	95	17
2298⁶	Tothewoods (NATwiston-Davies) 8-11-4 CLlewellyn (prom to 9th: sn wknd: t.o)	½	6	66/1	95	17
2254*	River Lossie (122) (CREgerton) 7-11-4 JOsborne (lw: prom tl lost pl 7th: t.o whn fell 12th)		F	16/1	—	—
1939a²	Minella Lad (APO'Brien,Ireland) 10-11-4 CFSwan (mstke 3rd: blnd 5th: t.o whn fell 3 out)		F	11/1	—	—
2358a*	Major Rumpus (ALTMoore,Ireland) 8-11-4 FWoods (lw: w ldrs: lft in ld 12th: hdd next: 3rd & btn whn fell last: dead)		F	8/1	—	—
2344³	Dark Honey (120) (SDow) 11-11-4 DBridgwater (bhd: blnd 2nd: p.u bef next)		P	66/1	—	—
1430⁵	Linden's Lotto (IRE) (120) (JWhite) 7-11-4 JFTitley (lw: a bhd: t.o whn p.u bef 3 out)		P	50/1	—	—
2480ᶠ	Punters Overhead (IRE) (8-11-4) (PFNicholls) 8-11-4 APMcCoy (lw: hld up & bhd: lost tch 14th: blnd & uns rdr 4 out)		U	25/1	—	—

(SP 118.9%) **12 Rn**

6m 22.3 (13.30) CSF £16.21 TOTE £8.60: £1.90 £1.70 £7.90 (£6.20) Trio £103.80 OWNER Mr J. Shaw (UPPER LAMBOURN) BRED Mrs M. Brennan

Those who lumped on the favourite heavily suspected their fate early when he failed to lead from the off and was all but down at the first. Nahthen Lad, second at Ascot, reversed form with the favourite, even on 7lb worse terms.

69

Suggested ratings for winner:-

Nahthen Lad	149
Mr Mulligan	171+
Do Rightly	155
Betty's Boy	173+
Johnny Setaside	207
Tothewoods	160

Nahthen Lad must have improved and it seems unfair to use Mr Mulligan as a yardstick, given his antics. Johnny Setaside's jockey reported that his mount disliked the ground, and the least bad option seems to be to average the remaining three.

$$
\begin{array}{r}
155 \\
+ \quad 173 \\
+ \quad 160 \\
\hline
488
\end{array}
$$
which, divided by three, gives us roughly 163

This generates a rating of 146 (163 - 17) for Nahthen Lad. The ill-fated Major Rumpus looked to be confirming our assessment when falling fatally at the last.

RHR	HORSE,AGE,WEIGHT	LAST THREE OUTINGS		
193	One Man (IRE) *(8-12-0)*	193	175	168
187	Imperial Call (IRE) *(7-12-0)*	187	168	—
184	Monsieur Le Cure *(10-12-0)*	182	184	172
177	Young Hustler *(9-12-0)*	—	177	177
176	Dublin Flyer *(10-12-0)*	176	176	170
173	Barton Bank *(10-12-0)*	173	—	171
168	Couldnt Be Better *(9-12-0)*	—	168	158
164	Rough Quest *(10-12-0)*	164	—	162
162	Lord Relic (NZ) *(10-12-0)*	—	—	161
156	King Of The Gales *(9-12-0)*	—	156	155

One Man was most people's banker to overcome his poor record at Cheltenham, but the Irish had found a serious danger in Imperial Call.

2785 TOTE CHELTENHAM GOLD CUP CHASE (Gd 1) (5-Y.O+) (Class A)
3-30 (3-39) **3m 2f 110y (New) (21 fncs)** £131,156.00 (£49,004.00: £23,902.00: £10,210.00: £4,505.00: £2,223.00) GOING: 0.59 s per fur (S)

		SP	RR	
2359a* Imperial Call (IRE) (174) (FSutherland,Ireland) 7-12-0 CO'Dwyer (hld up: led after 16th to 17th: led 4 out: r.o wl fr 2 out)	—	1	9/2 2	182	9
2482* Rough Quest (149) (TCasey) 10-12-0 MAFitzgerald (hld up & bhd: stdy hdwy 18th: chsd wnr fr 2 out: one pce)	...4	2	12/1	180	9
1433F Couldnt Be Better (157) (CPEBrooks) 9-12-0 GBradley (lw: a.p: led 14th to 16th: led 17th to 4 out: rdn & wknd 3 out)	...19	3	11/1	168	7
2482 4 Barton Bank (168) (DNicholson) 10-12-0 APMcCoy (prom: blnd 7th: wknd 4 out)	...3	4	16/1	166	7
2482P Young Hustler (163) (NATwiston-Davies) 9-12-0 CMaude (chsd ldr: led briefly 16th: wknd 18th)	...nk	5	25/1	166	7
1802* One Man (IRE) (179) (GRichards) 8-12-0 RDunwoody (lw: hld up: hdwy 16th: hit 17th: ev ch 3 out: wknd qckly appr last: fin tired)	...8	6	11/8 1	161	7
2682a 2 King of the Gales (JEKiely,Ireland) 9-12-0 CFSwan (hld up: mstke 12th: sn bhd: t.o)	...17	7	50/1	151	6
2359a 3 Monsieur le Cure (167) (JACEdwards) 10-12-0 JFTitley (lw: prom: 5th whn fell 6th: dead)		F	14/1	—	—
1849* Dublin Flyer (168) (CaptTAForster) 10-12-0 BPowell (led to 14th: wknd 16th: t.o whn p.u bef 2 out)		P	5/1 3	—	—
2373P Lord Relic (NZ) (147) (MCPipe) 10-12-0 DBridgwater (lw: bhd: j.slowly 5th: t.o whn p.u bef 15th)		P	100/1	—	—

(SP 112.3%) 10

6m 42.5 (7.50) CSF £48.90 TOTE £4.90: £1.90 £3.00 £2.30 (£47.90) Trio £84.60 OWNER Lisselan Farms Ltd (KILLINARDRISH)

With the tragic loss of Monsieur le Cure early on, this looked a two-horse race come the third last. Then, on the home turn, One Man went from cruising to unconscious in a few strides. In my opinion, he stays no better than his pedigree suggests. Couldnt Be Better, who looked a danger to all at the top of the hill, and Rough Quest, who finished to great effect, both ran the races of their lives.

The performances suggest:-

Imperial Call	187
Rough Quest	167
Couldnt Be Better	183
Barton Bank	190
Young Hustler	194
One Man	215
King of The Gales	189

If we ignore Rough Quest and One Man and then average the others, we get a rating of 189, which fits the facts well. Couldnt Be Better has excelled and his rating goes up. Barton Bank made one bad mistake, but ran on strongly and is only 1lb below his best. Young Hustler was unable to lead, but he too is only slightly below his rating. This converts to a winner's rating for Imperial Call of 182 (189 - 7).

0405 CHRISTIES FOXHUNTER CHALLENGE CUP AMATEUR CHASE (5-Y.O+) (CLASS B) 3m 2f 110y

RHR	HORSE,AGE,WEIGHT	LAST THREE OUTINGS		
147	Elegant Lord (IRE) *(8-12-0)*	141	141	135
140	Holland House *(10-12-0)*	130	134	140
140+	Cool Dawn (IRE) *(8-12-0)*	140	—	117
138?	Kerry Orchid *(8-12-0)*	—	122	—
136	Proud Sun *(8-12-0)*	—	136	89
133+	What AHand *(8-12-0)*	133	104	—
128d	Hermes Harvest *(8-12-0)*	111	128	—
122	Mr Golightly *(9-12-0)*	—	122	117
119	Clare Man (IRE) *(8-12-0)*	116	—	113
115	Colonial Kelly *(8-12-0)*	115	102	—
115	Cape Cottage *(12-12-0)*	115	—	109
110	Country Tarrogen *(7-12-0)*	—	110	108
107	Royal Stream *(9-12-0)*	107	—	—
88	Lewesdon Hill *(9-12-0)*	—	86	—
	The Bird O'Donnell *(10-12-0)*	—		
	Goolds Gold *(10-12-0)*	—		
	Earlydue *(9-12-0)*			

Thought likely to be much better suited by the ground than when third in the race twelve months earlier, Elegant Lord was 7lb clear and had the look of a banker.

2786 CHRISTIES FOXHUNTER CHALLENGE CUP CHASE (5-Y.O+) (Class B)

4-05 (4-19) **3m 2f 110y (New) (22 fncs)** £19,363.75 (£5,785.00: £2,767.50: £1,258.75) GOING: 0.59 sec per fur (S)

				SP	RR	SF
2360a*	**Elegant Lord (IRE)** (EBolger,Ireland) **8-12-0** MrEBolger (lw: hld up gng wl: hdwy 10th: led 3 out: r.o wl)	1	3/1 [1]	140+	69
2458*	**Cool Dawn (IRE)** (RHAlner) **8-12-0** MissDHarding (led to 8th: led 12th to 3 out: one pce) 6	2	9/2 [2]	136	65
2578a*	**Kerry Orchid** (EJO'Grady,Ireland) **8-12-0**v¹ MrPFenton (hdwy 11th: blnd 16th: rdn 18th: 3rd & btn whn j.rt & mstke last) 7	3	12/1	132	61
2458F	**Proud Sun (122)** (SPike) **8-12-0** MrsSMulcaire (w.r.s: hmpd 3rd: mstke 9th: hmpd 12th: hdwy 13th: lost pl & mstke 17th: styd on fr 2 out) ....s.h	4	13/2 [3]	132	61
2306*	**Holland House (124)** (PRChamings) **10-12-0** MrCVigors (lw: bhd tl styd on fr 3 out: nvr nrr) 3½	5	14/1	130	59
	Goolds Gold (DavidBrace) **10-12-0** MissPJones (mstke 8th: nvr nr to chal) 2½	6	66/1	129	58
2454*	**Clare Man (IRE) (110)** (NATwiston-Davies) **8-12-0** MrMRimell (prom: led 8th: j.rt 10th: hdd 12th: mstke 13th: sn wknd) 4	7	16/1	126	55
	The Bird O'Donnell (RBarber) **10-12-0** MrTJBarry (bhd: mstke 5th: hmpd 12th: hdwy 13th: mstke 3 out: sn wknd) 2	8	25/1	125	54
	Lewesdon Hill (RBarber) **9-12-0** MrTMitchell (mstkes: a bhd) 15	9	33/1	116	45
	Earlydue (PMJDoyle,Ireland) **9-12-0** MrDCostello (bhd whn mstke 13th: t.o) 15	10	50/1	107	36
2454U	**Country Tarrogen (110)** (TDWalford) **7-12-0** MrNWilson (lw: prom: hmpd 3rd: mstke 12th: sn wknd: t.o) .....dist	11	20/1	—	—
2619*	**What A Hand** (RBarber) **8-12-0** MissPCurling (lw: fell 1st)	F	13/2 [3]	—	—
2564*	**Colonial Kelly** (MrsDMGrissell) **8-12-0** MrPHacking (lw: prom: 3rd when fell 3rd)	F	16/1	—	—
2624³	**Hermes Harvest (128)** (DLWilliams) **8-12-0**v MrABalding (prom: 4th whn fell 12th)	F	12/1	—	—
2543²	**Cape Cottage** (DJCaro) **12-12-0** MrAPhillips (hmpd 3rd: t.o 11th: p.u bef 2 out)	P	100/1	—	—
	Royal Stream (MrsDBJohnstone) **9-12-0** MrAParker (nt j.w: hmpd 12th: bhd whn blnd 15th: t.o whn p.u bef 18th)	P	20/1	—	—
2306R	**Mr Golightly** (MrsSCobden) **9-12-0** MrsJReed (prom: hit 9th: rdn 18th: 6th & wkng whn blnd & uns rdr 4 out)	U	14/1	—	—

(SP 131.1%) **17 Rn**

6m 51.0 (16.00) CSF £17.22 TOTE £3.20: £1.70 £2.10 £2.50 (£6.20) Trio £28.40 OWNER Mr J. P. McManus (BRUREE) BRED Joseph Smiddy

A good result for the Handicapper, with Elegant Lord a fluent winner and the top five filling the first five places.

Suggested winner's rating:-

Elegant Lord	147
Cool Dawn	144+
Kerry Orchid	146?
Proud Sun	144
Holland House	150
Goolds Gold	---
Clare Man	134
The Bird O'Donnell	---
Lewesdon Hill	113
Earlydue	---

Run in a time only eight and a half seconds slower than the Gold Cup itself, it seems reasonable to assume that the first five home have run somewhere near their best. This is certainly what I assumed at the time, taking the winner Elegant Lord, to have run to 140, his best figure. However, there is a sting in the tail. The clue is in the ratings of Clare Man and Lewesdon Hill. Subsequent efforts by Goolds Gold, Clare Man and The Bird O'Donnell suggested the race had been wildly over-rated. It rather looks as if it was Clare Man who ran to form.

I have included this race to show that even when you are right, you are often wrong! Hunter chases are notorious for moderate horses finishing much closer to good ones than they should. Always be very wary of using a rating that an animal gained in defeat in a hunter chase when it is entered for a handicap.

Royal Ascot 1996

0230   QUEEN ANNE STKS (GP 2) (3-Y.O+) (CLASS A) 1m

RHR	HORSE,AGE,WEIGHT	LAST THREE OUTINGS		
139	Charnwood Forest (IRE) (4-9-2)	139	109	130
137	Young Ern (6-9-2)	129	136	126
135	Soviet Line (IRE) (6-9-7)	135	134	123
134	Timarida (IRE) (4-9-2)	134	132	130
134d	Prince Of India (4-9-2)	97	120	116
132	Mistle Cat (USA) (6-9-2)	135	132	125
131	Restruture (IRE) (4-9-2)	131	125	128
130	Gabr (6-9-5)	112	130	126
120	Mr Martini (IRE) (6-9-2)	120	92	112

The first race of the meeting, and our ratings suggest that Charnwood Forest is presented with an obvious chance to win his first Group race. This represented a theoretical drop in class for the horse, who had been beaten in a photo in the Group One Lockinge Stakes on his previous outing and was now 5lb better of with his conqueror, Soviet Line.

0874-**ASCOT** (R-H) (Good to firm)
Tuesday June 18th
WEATHER: sunny periods WIND: almost nil

2037   QUEEN ANNE STKS (Gp 2) (3-Y.O+) (Class A)
2-30 (2-31) **1m** (straight) £59,890.00 (£22,418.25: £10,771.63: £4,695.12) Stalls: Centre GOING minus 0.40 sec per fur (F)

			SP	RR	SF
1177²	**Charnwood Forest (IRE) (119)** (SbinSuroor) 4-9-2 MJKinane(6) (lw: hld up: hdwy to ld over 1f out: edgd rt: sn clr)	1	10/11¹	128	95
1824*	Restructure (IRE) (106) (MrsJCecil) 4-9-2 PaulEddery(8) (swtg: a.p: rdn over 2f out: unable qckn fnl f) 4	2	11/1	120	87
1582a*	Mistle Cat (USA) (117) (SPCWoods) 6-9-2 WWoods(1) (led tl over 1f out: one pce) ....hd	3	20/1	120	87
1582a³	**Young Ern (119)** (SDow) 6-9-2 CAsmussen(4) (hld up & bhd: hdwy 2f out: kpt on ins fnl f) 1¼	4	20/1	117	84
1177*	Soviet Line (IRE) (120) (MRStoute) 6-9-7 JReid(2) (b.off hind: s.i.s: sn chsng ldrs: hrd rdn 2f out: no imp) 1½	5	13/2³	119	86
1768³	Mr Martini (IRE) (113) (CEBrittain) 6-9-2 BDoyle(5) (hld up: effrt & rdn over 2f out: nvr nr to chal) 4	6	40/1	106	73
	Prince of India (107) (LordHuntingdon) 4-9-2 JWeaver(9) (lw: hld up & bhd: effrt over 2f out: no imp).........½	7	50/1	105	72
1575a²	Timarida (IRE) (JOxx,Ireland) 4-9-2 JPMurtagh(7) (lw: prom tl wknd over 3f out: t.o.) 15	8	6/1²	75	57
1177⁵	Gabr (113) (RWArmstrong) 6-9-5 WCarson(3) (plld hrd: prom tl wknd over 2f out. t.o) ....hd	9	12/1	78	45

(SP 109.9%) **9 Rn**

1m 38.71 (-2.49) CSF £10.32 TOTE £2.00: £1.10 £2.20 £2.60 (£9.60) Trio £51.60 OWNER Godolphin (NEWMARKET)

72

A good start to the meeting for form students, but our well-rated Young Ern was slightly disappointing.
Suggested winner's ratings:-

Charnwood Forest	139	
Restructure	139	
Mistle Cat	140	
Young Ern	147	
Soviet Line	148	has a tendency to hang and could not race by a rail
Mr Martini	141	
Prince of India	156d	but best of 142 recently
Timarida	184	broke blood-vessel
Gabr	180	eased

I rated this race on the basis that Mr Martini had not improved. Because I have used our conversion tables for these examples, this gives Charnwood Forest a rating of 129 (141 - 12), 1lb lower than used at the time. As was said earlier, there can be slight discrepancies between using exact calculations and conversion tables.

0305 PRINCE OF WALES'S STKS (GP 2) (3-Y.O+) (CLASS A) 1m 2f

RHR	HORSE,AGE,WEIGHT	LAST THREE OUTINGS		
133	Pilsudski (IRE) *(4-9-3)*	133	124	119
133+	Cap Juluca (IRE) *(4-9-3)*	133	124	119
133	Montjoy (USA) *(4-9-6)*	128	129	131
132	Lucky Di (USA) *(4-9-3)*	132	129	108
132	First Island (IRE) *(4-9-3)*	132	126	129
131	Fahal (USA) *(4-9-3)*	122	124	131
131	Cezanne *(7-9-3)*	126	110	123
130	Tamayaz (CAN) *(4-9-3)*	124	129	130
130	Desert Shot *(6-9-3)*	126	78	130
130	Needle Gun (IRE) *(6-9-6)*	—	130	114
114	Dankeston (USA) *(3-8-5)*	114	113	100
107	Clever Cliche *(3-8-5)*	107	101	

An extraordinarily open race, with ten of the twelve runners rated within 3lb of each other.

0874-ASCOT (R-H) (Good to firm)
Tuesday June 18th
WEATHER: sunny periods WIND: almost nil

2038   PRINCE OF WALES'S STKS (Gp 2) (3-Y.O+) (Class A)
3-05 (3-06) 1m 2f £63,325.00 (£23,735.00: £11,430.00: £5,010.00) Stalls: High GOING minus 0.40 sec per fur (F)

			SP	RR	SF
1112* First Island (IRE) (114) (GWragg) 4-9-3 MHills(3) (hld up: hdwy over 2f out: led ent fnl f: drvn out)	...—	1	9/1	125	103
1749a⁴ Montjoy (USA) (119) (PFICole) 4-9-6 RHills(13) (plld hrd: a.p: led wl over 1f out: sn hdd: no ex nr fin)	...1¼	2	16/1	126	104
1509⁴ Tamayaz (CAN) (SbinSuroor) 4-9-3 OPeslier(11) (mid div: hdwy over 2f out: r.o ins fnl f)	...1¼	3	12/1	121	99
1754a³ Dankeston (USA) (101) (MBell) 3-8-5 MRoberts(12) (lw: trckd ldrs: outpcd ent st: styd on again appr fnl f)...3½		4	50/1	115	81
1135a⁶ Cezanne (SbinSuroor) 7-9-3 JPMurtagh(1) (lw: hld up & bhd: hdwy over 2f out: nrst fin)	...nk	5	25/1	115	93
1355⁴ Fahal (USA) (117) (DMorley) 4-9-3 WCarson(5) (lw: hld up mid div: nvr nr to chal)	...s.h	6	7/1	115	93
680⁶ Desert Shot (115) (MRStoute) 6-9-3 CAsmussen(4) (hld up in rr: hdwy over 2f out: nt rch ldrs)	...1¼	7	20/1	113	91
1509* Pilsudski (IRE) (105) (MRStoute) 4-9-3 PatEddery(9) (b.nr hind: lw: chsd ldr: disp ld fr 3f out tl wknd over 1f out)	...1¼	8	4/11	111	89
1509² Lucky Di (USA) (113) (LMCumani) 4-9-3 JWeaver(10) (b.nr fore: mid div: rdn over 4f out: bhd fnl 3f)...2½		9	9/2²	107	85
918⁴ Clever Cliche (HRACecil) 3-8-6ᵒʷ1 JReid(7) (lw: chsd ldrs: rdn 3f out: wkng when hmpd 2f out)	...½	10	16/1	107	72
Cap Juluca (IRE) (112) (RCharlton) 4-9-3 RHughes(8) (lw: led tl over 2f out: eased whn btn appr fnl f)...nk		11	5/13	106	84
1938a* Needle Gun (IRE) (118) (CEBrittain) 6-9-6 MJKinane(6) (prom: hrd rdn ent st: sn wknd: t.o)	...9	12	16/1	94	72
			(SP 114.0%)	**12 Rn**	

2m 2.76 (0.55 under best) (-4.04) CSF £121.20 TOTE £11.20: £2.70 £4.60 £5.90 (£73.90) Trio £412.60 OWNER Mollers Racing (NEWMAR-KET) BRED Citadel Stud
WEIGHT FOR AGE 3yo-12lb

A very fast-run race in which the twenty-year-old course-record was broken. So no doubt about the value of the form, but the two who set the race up, Cap Juluca and Pilsudski, effectively put paid to each other's chances.

73

First Island	132	
Montjoy	135	(but 133 his best in last three outings, which is used in calculations)
Tamayaz	134	
Dankeston	123	(three-year-old stepping up in trip)
Cezanne	141	(but 136 his best in last three outings, used in calculations)
Fahal	141	
Desert Shot	142	
Pilsudski	147	(went too fast)
Lucky Di	150	(below form and eased, ground too fast)
Clever Cliche	125	(unexposed)
Cap Juluca	153+	(blew up, first time out)
Needle Gun	164	(had an off-day)

By Elmaamul, it seems that Dankeston has left his previous form behind for the step up beyond a mile. Of the others in the first seven, it seems hard to decide which horses have run to form. Therefore they are averaged:-

	132
+	133
+	134
+	136
+	141
+	142
	===
	818

which gives an average of 136

As a result, First Island receives a Performance rating of 125.

0345 ST JAMES PALACE STKS (GP 1) (3-Y.O C & F) (CLASS A) 1m

RHR	HORSE,AGE,WEIGHT	LAST THREE OUTINGS		
138	Mark Of Esteem (IRE) (3-9-0)	138	98	103
138	Bijou d'Indel (3-9-0)	128	138	111
136	Beauchamp King (3-9-0)	134	122	136
132+	Ashkalani (IRE) (3-9-0)	132	126	—
131+	Spinning World (USA) (3-9-0)	131	118	—
128	Cayman Kai (IRE) (3-9-0)	128	126	121
124+	Sorbie Tower (IRE) (3-9-0)	124	121	118
120	World Premier (3-9-0)	113	115	120
114+	Wall Street (USA) (3-9-0)	92	114	

A chance to compare the 2000 Guineas winners from England, Ireland and France.

2039 ST JAMES'S PALACE STKS (Gp 1) (3-Y.O C & F) (Class A)
3-45 (3-47) 1m (round) £135,720.00 (£50,546.00: £24,073.00: £10,261.00) Stalls: High GOING minus 0.40 sec per fur (F)

			SP	RR	SF
1574a⁴	Bijou d'Inde (120) (MJohnston) 3-9-0 JWeaver(7) (led after 2f tl over 1f out: rallied gamely to ld last stride) ......—	1	9/1	126	78
1141a*	Ashkalani (IRE) (AdeRoyerDupre,France) 3-9-0 MJKinane(9) (w'like: scope: lw: hld up: a.p: led over 1f out: hrd rdn: ct post) .....hd	2	13/8¹	126	78
1441²	Sorbie Tower (IRE) (108) (MissGayKelleway) 3-9-0 RHughes(6) (hr.bhind: lw: hld up: hdwy on outside over 2f out: drifted rt fnl f: styd on) 1	3	33/1	124	76
1574a³	Beauchamp King (115) (JLDunlop) 3-9-0 JReid(8) (trckd ldrs: hrd drvn wl over 1f out: nt pce to chal) 1¼	4	14/1	121	73
1141a⁴	Cayman Kai (IRE) (117) (RHannon) 3-9-0 PatEddery(3) (lw: bhd: drvn along ent st: styd on wl appr fnl f) 1¼	5	12/1	119	71
1574a*	Spinning World (USA) (JEPease,France) 3-9-0 CAsmussen(5) (leggy: scope: hld up in tch: outpcd 2f out: sn btn) 1¾	6	100/30²	115	67
1627*	Wall Street (USA) (SbinSuroor) 3-9-0 BThomson(2) (swtg: prom tl wknd over 2f out) 5	7	16/1	105	57
926¹	Mark of Esteem (IRE) (120) (SbinSuroor) 3-9-0 OPeslier(1) (mid div tl rdn & outpcd 2f out) 1½	8	11/2³	102	54
1151³	World Premier (111) (CEBrittain) 3-9-0 BDoyle(4) (led 2f: wknd fnl 2f) .....½	9	100/1	101	53

(SP 110.7%) 9 Rn
1m 39.7 (-1.10) CSF £22.09 TOTE £9.70: £2.10 £1.30 £4.70 (£12.80) Trio £111.30 OWNER Mr J. S. Morrison (MIDDLEHAM) BRED Whitsbury Manor Stud

All three Classic winners are upstaged by Bijou d'Inde, who rallies to snatch a race Ashkalani seems to have won at the furlong pole. My feeling at the time was that this might have been a 'box race', that is one unduly influenced by the draw. This conclusion is offered by the very poor run of Mark of Esteem from stall one and the fact that the first four home occupied the four stalls nearest the inside rail. Mark of Esteem's connections later said that the horse should not have run so soon after his injury scare, before the Derby. However, in the light of subsequent events, Mark of Esteem going on to be the top-rated European miler, our 'box race' interpretation still holds water.

Suggested ratings for winner:-

Bijou d'Inde	138
Ashkalani	132+
Sorbie Tower	126+
Beauchamp King	140
Cayman Kai	134
Spinning World	140+
Wall Street	132+
Mark of Esteem	159
World Premier	142

The moral of this tale is that you should allow your judgement to influence your figures. I was simply unwilling to allow Beauchamp King any improvement for finishing what I interpreted as last in a four-horse race. Therefore, Bijou d'Inde could rate no more than 126. You will not always be right, but follow your instincts. After all, they are YOUR ratings!

0345 CORONATION STKS (GP 1) (3-Y.O F) (CLASS A) 1m

RHR	HORSE,AGE,WEIGHT	LAST THREE OUTINGS		
135+	Shake The Yoke *(3-9-0)*	121	135	122
125	Dance Design (IRE) *(3-9-0)*	125	119	112
122	Thrilling Day *(3-9-0)*	97	122	113
122	Ta Rib (USA) *(3-9-0)*	122	104	104
118	Priory Belle (IRE) *(3-9-0)*	118	113	115
115	Miss Universal (IRE) *(3-9-0)*	112	113	103
94+	Last Second (IRE) *(3-9-0)*	—	94	

A rematch between the surprise French 1000 Guineas winner Ta Rib and the second, Shake the Yoke, considered unlucky in running that day.

2052 CORONATION STKS (Gp 1) (3-Y.O F) (Class A)
3-45 (3-46) **1m (round)** £120,726.00 (£44,890.80: £21,320.40: £9,022.80) Stalls: High GOING minus 0.25 sec per fur (GF)

		SP	RR	SF
1140a²	**Shake the Yoke** (ELellouche,France) 3-9-0 OPeslier(4) (unf: hld up: shkn up 3f out: led ins fnl f: comf)........—	1 Evens¹	121	76
	Last Second (IRE) (SirMarkPrescott) 3-9-0 GDuffield(7) (swtchd lft over 2f out: hdwy over 1f out: str run fnl f: fin wl) ....nk	2 12/1	120	75
1567a²	**Dance Design (IRE)** (DKWeld,Ireland) 3-9-0 MJKinane(1) (leggy: lw: led: rdn 2f out: hdd ins fnl f: unable qckn) ....½	3 9/2³	119	74
1140a*	**Ta Rib (USA) (113)** (EALDunlop) 3-9-0 WCarson(2) (swtg: chsd ldr 6f out to 1f out: sn wknd) 2½	4 100/30²	114	69
1639²	**Miss Universal (IRE) (99)** (CEBrittain) 3-9-0 BDoyle(5) (lw: chsd ldr 2f: rdn over 2f out: r.o one pce fnl f) ....¾	5 50/1	113	68
1129¹¹	**Thrilling Day (110)** (NAGraham) 3-9-0 DHarrison(3) (a bhd) 4	6 16/1	105	60
1567a⁵	**Priory Belle (IRE)** (JSBolger,Ireland) 3-9-0 KJManning(6) (lengthy: scope: bhd fnl 2f) 2	7 16/1	101	56

(SP 112.7%) **7 Rn**

1m 40.45 (-0.35) CSF £12.21 TOTE £2.30: £1.60 £3.10 (£12.50) OWNER Mr S. Brunswick BRED Sussex Stud & Calogo Bloodstock

Shake the Yoke comfortably reverses the form with Ta Rib, but has to withstand a stern challenge from the unexposed Last Second. The last two home ran some way below their best. The form is devalued by the proximity of Miss Universal, who was beaten almost ten lengths further in the Newmarket 1000 Guineas than she was here.

Suggested winner's ratings:-

Shake the Yoke	135+	
Last Second	97+	
Dance Design	127	
Ta Rib	129	
Miss Universal	123	(121 best in last three outings)
Thrilling Day	138	(had already looked best at 7 furlongs)
Priory Belle	138	

Looking at the above figures, using Shake The Yoke would raise the next four home considerably, as would using either of the last two. Last Second has clearly improved and is not a reliable yardstick.

In the end, the least poor option seems to be to average Dance Design, Ta Rib and Miss Universal, giving the winner a rating of 112 (126 - 14).

ROYAL ASCOT- Thursday 20 June

0530 KING GEORGE V H'CAP (0-105) (3-Y.O) (CLASS B) 1m 4f

RHR	HORSE,AGE,WEIGHT	LAST THREE OUTINGS		
113	Warning Reef (3-8-7)	105	113	105
113	Nador (3-9-0)	113	104	75
112	Arctic Fancy (USA) (3-8-4)	112	108	102
112	Samraan (USA) (3-9-3)	112	103	102
111	Illuminate (3-8-2)	103	111	101
111	Orinoco River (USA) (3-8-9)	111	88	105
111	Pleasant Surprise (3-9-5)	111	103	104
110+	Harbour Dues (3-8-12)	110	96	81
108	Montecristo (3-7-12)	108	101	105
108	Traceability (3-8-3)	108	93	106
108	Warbrook (3-8-13)	98	108	99
108	Migwar (3-9-7)	108	98	73
107	Private Song (USA) (3-8-10)	107	103	85
107	Gold Disc (USA) (3-8-13)	107	85	96
106+	A Chef Too Far (3-7-12)	106	97	88
106	Shenango (IRE) (3-8-3)	106	65	94
105	Count Basie (3-8-11)	105	92	101
104	Serendipity (FR) (3-8-7)	104	102	76
103	Male-Ana-Mou (IRE) (3-8-10)	103	103	94
97	Get Away With It (IRE) (3-8-3)	97	93	79

A typically open Ascot handicap, further complicated by the apparent number of horses in the line-up that are still improving.

2074 KING GEORGE V H'CAP (0-105) (3-Y.O) (Class B)
5-30 (5-31) **1m 4f** £26,215.00 (£7,945.00: £3,885.00: £1,855.00) Stalls: Low GOING minus 0.25 sec per fur (GF)

		SP	RR	SF
1175*	**Samraan (USA) (94)** (JLDunlop) 3-9-3 TQuinn(17) (lw: hld up in tch: hdwy to chal 1f out: kpt on u.p to ld nr fin)..— 1	14/1	105	74
1305*	**Private Song (USA) (87)** (RCharlton) 3-8-10 PatEddery(19) (led: rdn 2f out: ct wl ins fnl f)............................½ 2	8/1 [2]	97	66
1712*	**Harbour Dues (89)** (LadyHerries) 3-8-12 PaulEddery(2) (hld up & bhd: hdwy over 2f out: styd on strly towards fin)..2 3	6/1 [1]	97	66
1798*	**Pleasant Surprise (96)** (MJohnston) 3-9-5 JWeaver(14) (lw: chsd ldr: rdn over 2f out: one pce appr fnl f)....2½ 4	20/1	100	69
1175[2]	**Nador (91)** (DRLoder) 3-9-0 RHughes(4) (trckd ldrs: outpcd 4f out: styd on again fnl 2f)............................½ 5	16/1	95	64
1002[D]	**Montecristo (75)** (RGuest) 3-7-12 JQuinn(8) (hld up & bhd: hdwy on ins fnl 2f: nvr nrr)........................hd 6	12/1	79	48
1771[9]	**Warning Reef (84)** (MRChannon) 3-8-2[5] PPMurphy(15) (hld up: hdwy & sltly hmpd 3f out: kpt on appr fnl f)..1 7	33/1	86	55
1666[4]	**Serendipity (FR) (84)** (JLDunlop) 3-8-7 MJKinane(9) (prom tl rdn & wknd over 1f out)..................................1 8	14/1	85	54
1711*	**Male-Ana-Mou (IRE) (87)** (DRCElsworth) 3-8-10 MRoberts(20) (hld up: hdwy over 4f out: 7th & styng on whn hmpd 3f out)..½ 9	16/1	87	56
1195*	**A Chef Too Far (75)** (RRowe) 3-7-7[5] (lw: hdwy: rdn over 3f out: wknd 2f out)..3 10	25/1	71	40
1666*	**Gold Disc (USA) (90)** (BWHills) 3-8-4 GHind(13) (dwlt: hdwy 5f out: wkng whn hmpd 3f out: t.o)............16 11	14/1	65	34
1711[5]	**Illuminate (79)** (JARToller) 3-8-2 SSanders(18) (lw: hld up: effrt 4f out: wknd over 2f out: t.o).................5 12	12/1	47	16
1175[6]	**Warbrook (90)** (IABalding) 3-8-13 KDarley(10) (lw: trckd ldrs: 8th whn hmpd & lost pl 3f out: t.o)............1½ 13	33/1	56	25
1090[2]	**Get Away With It (IRE) (80)** (MRStoute) 3-8-3v[1] WCarson(6) (lw: hld up: hdwy 5f out: rdn over 3f out: sn wknd: t.o)..1¼ 14	8/1 [2]	45	14
1669*	**Orinoco River (USA) (86)** (PWChapple-Hyam) 3-8-9v JReid(1) (trckd ldrs: rdn 5f out: carried wd ent st: sn bhd: t.o)..4 15	16/1	45	14
1782*	**Arctic Fancy (81)** (PWHarris) 3-8-4 GHind(5) (lw: hld up: hdwy 5f out: wkng whn hmpd 3f out: t.o)..........21 16	16/1	12	—
1656[3]	**Shenango (IRE) (80)** (GWragg) 3-8-3 MHills(7) (hld up: a in rr: t.o)..3½ 17	20/1	7	—
1656*	**Count Basie (88)** (HRACecil) 3-8-11 WRyan(12) (trckd ldrs: 6th & drvn along whn slipped & almost fell 3f out: t.o)..¾ 18	14/1	14	—
1476*	**Migwar (98)** (LMCumani) 3-9-7 KFallon(16) (lw: effrt whn bdly hmpd 3f out: eased: t.o)...........................17 19	10/1 [3]	1	—
1687*	**Traceability (80)** (SCWilliams) 3-8-0[3] MHenry(11) (mid div tl lost pl ½-wy: t.o)..................................dist 20	33/1	—	—
		(SP 133.4%) **20 Rn**		

2m 31.11 (1.11) CSF £118.61 CT £698.77 TOTE £17.70: £3.90 £2.50 £2.00 £3.90 (£92.80) Trio £175.00 OWNER Mr K. M. Al-Mudhaf (ARUNDEL) BRED Mrs Afaf A. Al Essa

A race with numerous hard luck stories, including the favourite Harbour Dues, who made a lot of ground in the home straight. Half of the field have finished tailed off and are ignored for assessment purposes.

Suggested winner's ratings:-

Samraan	112	
Private Song	108	
Harbour Dues	114+	(very unlucky in running)
Pleasant Surprise	118	
Nador	121	
Montecristo	116	
Warning Reef	122	(hampered)
Serendipity	114	(unexposed)
Male-Ana-Mou (IRE)	114	(unexposed)
A Chef Too Far	121+	(first time beyond seven furlongs)

With so many problems in the race, this is a tricky one to rate accurately. I took the option of averaging Samraan, Pleasant Surprise, Nador and Montecristo, all of whom have proven handicap form over the trip. I could have given the winner a performance rating of 106, but settled for 105 (116 - 11).

0305 HARDWICKE STKS (GP 2) (4-Y.O+) (CLASS A) 1m 4f

RHR	HORSE,AGE,WEIGHT	LAST THREE OUTINGS		
141	Oscar Schindler (IRE) (4-8-9)	140	120	141
141	Annus Mirablis (FR) (4-8-9)	137	106	114
139	Election Day (IRE) (4-8-9)	139	138	111
136	Dance A Dream (4-8-6)	135	135	126
136	Punishment (5-8-9)	136	136	131
134	Phantom Gold (4-8-9)	117	134	120
133	Lear White (USA) (5-8-9)	133	133	129
128	Posidonas (4-9-0)	127	125	128

This looks something of a three-horse race and the Bookmakers end up going 8/1 bar three.

2113 HARDWICKE STKS (Gp 2) (4-Y.O+) (Class A)
3-05 (3-06) **1m 4f** £70,970.00 (£26,588.50: £12,794.25: £5,597.25) Stalls: High GOING minus 0.19 sec per fur (GF)

						SP	RR
1017*	Oscar Schindler (IRE) (KPrendergast,Ireland) 4-8-9 MJKinane(8) (hdwy over 2f out: led 1f out: hrd rdn: r.o wl)	—	1	7/4 [1]	122	9
1575a[3]	Annus Mirabilis (FR) (119) (SbinSuroor) 4-8-9 JCarroll(2) (lw: chsd ldr: led 3f out to 1f out: r.o)	½	2	5/1 [3]	121	9
1176[3]	Posidonas (116) (PFICole) 4-9-0 TQuinn(7) (b.off hind: lw: a.p: hrd rdn & edgd lft over 2f out: unable qckn)	3½	3	16/1	122	9
1355[3]	Lear White (USA) (106) (PAKelleway) 5-8-9 JWeaver(5) (lw: led 9f: rdn: one pce)	s.h	4	33/1	117	8
1509[9]	Phantom Gold (112) (LordHuntingdon) 4-8-9 MHills(1) (hld up: rdn & n.m.r over 2f out: one pce)	1¼	5	10/1	115	8
1017[5]	Dance a Dream (116) (MRStoute) 4-8-6 PatEddery(6) (rdn over 4f out: a bhd)	1	6	8/1	111	8
1794[4]	Punishment (CEBrittain) 5-8-9 BDoyle(3) (lw: bhd fnl 2f)	hd	7	16/1	114	8
1176*	Election Day (IRE) (115) (MRStoute) 4-8-9 WCarson(4) (lw: nvr gng wl: rdn thrght: a bhd: t.o fnl 5f)	dist	8	100/30 [2]	—	—

(SP 111.0%) **8**

2m 27.84 (-2.16) CSF £10.06 TOTE £2.20: £1.20 £1.50 £3.30 (£3.90) OWNER Mr Oliver Lehane BRED Oliver Lehane

With Election Day completely lost on the fast ground, our joint-top rated duo fight out the finish.

Suggested winner's ratings:-

Oscar Schindler	141
Annus Mirabilis	142
Posidonas	133
Lear White	138
Phantom Gold	141
Dance A Dream	144
Punishment	144
Election Day	(clearly did not run his race)

The only decision that needs making here is, have Posidonas and Lear White improved? Posidonas had won an Italian Group One race the previous autumn. Therefore, it was not difficult to see that 114 was rather a low master rating for such a horse going into the race. Lear White was stepping up to one and a half miles and certainly seemed to stay on well enough, suggesting that he could have easily improved at the longer trip. I rate the race through Oscar Schindler, as Annus Mirabilis seems to have surrendered a winning chance rather tamely, giving the winner a performance rating of 122 (141 - 19).

My assumptions prove well founded, as within three outings Lear White steps up to two miles and is narrowly beaten in the Goodwood Cup. As for Posidonas, he reverses form with Annus Mirabilis next time and gets a performance rating of 129.

0420 KING'S STAND STKS (GP 2) (3-Y.O+) (CLASS A) 5f

RHR	HORSE, AGE, WEIGHT	LAST THREE OUTINGS		
139	Mind Games (4-9-2)	139	123	102
138	Lucky Lionel (USA) (3-8-10)	137	138	110
138d	Hever Golf Rose (5-9-2)	125	113	110
133	Royale Figurine (IRE) (5-8-13)	133	118	122
133	Struggler (4-9-2)	133	123	131
132	Eveningperformance (5-8-13)	123	132	126
130	Royal Applause (3-8-13)	101	130	117
128d	Ya Malak (5-9-2)	106	116	128
124	Lidanna (3-8-7)	124	116	
123	Titus Livius (FR) (3-8-10)	124	—	123
123	Almaty (IRE) (3-8-10)	114	89	123
123	Loch Patrick (6-9-2)	115	118	123
121	Double Quick (IRE) (4-8-13)	113	111	121
120	Mubhij (IRE) (3-8-10)	92	120	118
118	Aileacht (USA) (4-8-13)	113	118	117
114	Wavian (4-9-2)	94	107	113
107+	Pivotal (3-8-10)	107	106	81

Beaten at odds-on in the race the previous season, Mind Games seems to have found a slightly easier renewal this time, with Hever Golf Rose struggling to find her form.

2115 KING'S STAND STKS (Gp 2) (3-Y.O+) (Class A)

4-20 (4-24) **5f** £65,390.00 (£24,449.50: £11,724.75: £5,085.75) Stalls: Centre GOING minus 0.19 sec per fur (GF)

		SP	RR	SF
	Pivotal (104) (SirMarkPrescott) 3-8-10 GDuffield(7) (h.d.w: a.p: rdn over 1f out: led last strides)........— 1	13/2 [3]	128	88
1483*	Mind Games (117) (JBerry) 4-9-2 JCarroll(14) (lw: racd far side: led: clr over 1f out: hrd rdn: hdd last stride) ....½ 2	3/1 [1]	126	92
1911a[4]	Almaty (IRE) (CCollins,Ireland) 3-8-10 KDarley(10) (lw: racd far side: a.p: rdn over 2f out: one pce) 3½ 3	20/1	115	75
1945a[2]	Hever Golf Rose (119) (TJNaughton) 5-9-2 PatEddery(11) (lw: racd far side: a.p: rdn over 2f out: one pce) .1¾ 4	11/1	110	76
1129[3]	Royale Figurine (IRE) (107) (MJFetherston-Godley) 5-8-13 JReid(16) (racd far side: rdn over 2f out: hdwy fnl f: nvr nrr) ....hd 5	25/1	106	72
926[10]	Royal Applause (120) (BWHills) 3-8-13 MHills(6) (hld up: rdn over 2f out: one pce) ....nk 6	11/2 [2]	111	71
1621[5]	Loch Patrick (105) (MMadgwick) 6-9-2 AMcGlone(18) (lw: racd far side: nvr nr to chal) ....hd 7	50/1	108	74
1566a*	Lidanna (DHanley,Ireland) 3-8-7 MJKinane(15) (lt-f: racd far side: a.p: rdn over 2f out: wknd fnl f) ....nk 8	9/1	104	64
1581a[4]	Titus Livius (FR) (JEPease,France) 3-8-10 CAsmussen(12) (unf: racd far side: nvr nrr) ....hd 9	20/1	107	67
927[6]	Eveningperformance (112) (HCandy) 5-8-13 WNewnes(5) (lw: spd over 3f) ....½ 10	14/1	102	68
1129[12]	Mubhij (IRE) (111) (BWHills) 3-8-10 WCarson(4) (a.p: rdn over 2f out: wknd fnl f) ....nk 11	25/1	104	64
1129[4]	Lucky Lionel (USA) (115) (RHannon) 3-8-10 TQuinn(13) (lw: racd far side: a.p: rdn over 2f out: a bhd) ....½ 12	14/1	103	63
1818[11]	Wavian (97) (RHannon) 4-9-2 WJO'Connor(9) (lw: bhd fnl 3f) ....nk 13	100/1	102	68
1911a[2]	Ailleacht (USA) (JSBolger,Ireland) 4-8-13 KJManning(3) (lw: bhd fnl 3f) ....nk 14	33/1	98	64
2003*	Double Quick (IRE) (102) (MJohnston) 4-8-13 JWeaver(1) (lw: a bhd) 1¼ 15	25/1	94	60
1483[2]	Struggler (110) (DRLoder) 4-9-2v[1] RHughes(1) (stumbled s: a bhd) 2½ 16	15/2	89	55
2003[5]	Ya Malak (110) (JWPayne) 5-9-2b[1] BThomson(8) (spd 3f) 11 17	50/1	53	19

(SP 126.1%) **17 Rn**

Pivotal has won just a Newcastle maiden and a Folkestone conditions race, but has always been a bit of a talking horse. Turning the talk dramatically into action, he pounces inside the final furlong. With the pair split by the width of the course, Pivotal just pipped Mind Games to the post.

Pivotal	107+	
Mind Games	141	
Almaty	136	
Hever Golf Rose	156d	(best of 143 in last three outings)
Royale Figurine	152	
Royal Applause	150	
Loch Patrick	144	
Lidanna	146	
Titus Livius	146	
Eveningperformance	157	
Mubhij	146	
Lucky Lionel	166	
Wavian	143	
Ailleacht	148	
Double Quick	155	(best of 147 last three outings)
Struggler	175	
Ya Malak	203d	

During the meeting, the general feeling was that horses racing on the far side were at a disadvantage. However, my study of the Wokingham result earlier in the afternoon suggests that there was little or no advantage whichever side you raced on. The one thing you could not do during the meeting was to race down the centre of the track. I took the view that Mind Games had run right to his best and rated Pivotal as having beaten him by 1lb (our conversion table gives the distance value as two, but this seemed a mighty close race from the Stands). Therefore, Pivotal gets a performance rating of 128 (140 - 18 + 6 weight-for-age).

RHR	HORSE,AGE,WEIGHT	LAST THREE OUTINGS		
144	Shantou (USA) (3-8-8)	144	123	106
134	Prize Giving (3-8-8)	134	127	124
126	Desert Boy (IRE) (3-8-8)	126	114	73
124	Legal Right (USA) (3-8-8)	124	108	105
116d	Amfortas (IRE) (3-8-8)	56	116	106
115	Germano (3-8-8)	115	112	94
98+	Don Vito (3-8-8)	98		

History suggests that Shantou is taking a chance in reappearing just thirteen days after finishing third in the Derby. Epsom is the equivalent of the Cup Final for thoroughbreds and horses generally need time to recover after the race. The temptation is there for all to see, as Shantou looks to have an easy task.

2116 KING EDWARD VII STKS (Gp 2) (3-Y.O C & G) (Class A)

4-55 (4-55) 1m 4f £70,204.00 (£26,371.95: £12,748.48: £5,640.57) Stalls: High GOING minus 0.19 sec per fur (GF)

					SP	RR	S
1180¹⁰	Amfortas (IRE) (86) (CEBrittain) 3-8-8 BDoyle(6) (mde virtually all: drvn out)	—	1	66/1	118	79
1015²	Desert Boy (IRE) (106) (PWChapple-Hyam) 3-8-8 JReid(5) (hld up: chsd wnr fnl 2f: hrd rdn: r.o)	½	2	13/2³	117	78
1791³	Shantou (USA) (JHMGosden) 3-8-8 MJKinane(1) (lw: n.m.r over 2f out: rdn & hdwy over 1f out: r.o)	nk	3	9/4¹	117	78
1427⁵	Germano (95) (GWragg) 3-8-8 PaulEddery(7) (lw: rdn & hdwy on ins 3f out: wknd over 1f out)	7	4	16/1	108	69
1329²	Prize Giving (112) (GWragg) 3-8-8 MHills(2) (lw: stdy hdwy 9f out: wknd 2f out)	1½	5	9/4¹	106	67
691*	Don Vito (RCharlton) 3-8-8 PatEddery(4) (lw: plld hrd: bhd fnl 3f)	3	6	7/2²	102	63
1329⁴	Legal Right (USA) (102) (PWChapple-Hyam) 3-8-10ᵒʷ² RHughes(3) (lw: chsd wnr 10f: sn wknd)	1	7	11/1	102	61

(SP 112.8%) 7 Rn

2m 29.85 (-0.15) CSF £377.45 TOTE £50.00: £9.50 £2.80 (£144.60) OWNER Mr B. H. Voak (NEWMARKET)

This race is included just to show the sort of things that a Handicapper has to make sense of. Amfortas was seventh in the Wood Ditton behind, among others, Shantou. He has been well beaten in the Sandown Derby Trial and beaten almost half a furlong in a soft-ground maiden on his last two starts. Presumably appreciating the faster ground, Amfortas makes all for an extraordinary win.

Amfortas	116d	
Desert Boy	127	
Shantou	146	
Germano	126	
Prize Giving	147	
Don Vito	115+	(unexposed)
Legal Right	142	

This is the sort of result that can have you tearing out your hair - well that's my excuse for a receding hairline, and I'm sticking to it! What in the race has run to form? Amfortas has clearly improved. Shantou is surely well below his Derby form. If Shantou doesn't make the race a 146, then Prize Giving's 147 ought to be ignored as well. Don Vito's win in a Pontefract maiden told us nothing about him. Legal Right has flopped and probably ran below form, but Germano and Desert Boy have run much better than their position in the market. Any figure between 127 and 142 would probably have been justifiable, but I settle on 138, giving Amfortas a performance rating of 118.

I do hope this last example hasn't put you off. Nearly always there are good lines of form if you look hard enough. Although sometimes it feels like you're trying to find a needle in a haystack, there will normally be something you can use. Handicapping really can change the way you watch a race. A mistake in a chase often registers in the brain as, "that's going to be a couple of pounds below its best".

Having taken you through a large portion of a couple of big meetings, you may think you have grasped the hardest part. Unfortunately, not so. In general, the worse the race, the harder it is to rate accurately. Don't be put off, handicapping can be very satisfying. Just don't blame me if your closest friends think you should be locked up, and there will be days when you think that they are right!

CHAPTER 8

HOW TRAINERS HANDICAP THEIR HORSES

Some horses do seem to get a raw deal in handicap races. If you are not given a fair chance to win in such races, your options become limited to claiming and selling contests.

The system looks fair on paper and is impartially run by the BHB's team of professional Handicappers, but if all races were really weighted to be multiple dead-heats, where do all these hot favourites come from in this type of contest? The most vital handicap mark of any horse's career is its first one. This will determine if confidence can be boosted by a few wins off a lenient mark or if it is going to be some time before the horse can get competitive. Each horse has a different handicap mark for each code it runs under. Turf Flat form is taken into account when a horse is given an All-Weather mark and vice versa, but neither mark affects a horse's mark over hurdles and fences.

One loophole made use of to good effect by jump trainers is the running of horses in handicap chases that have only previously run over hurdles. Trainers have exploited the fact that these horses tend to get into handicap chases on a mark a few pounds lower than they would in handicap hurdles. The logic of the official Handicapper in this area is perfectly reasonable. A horse who has never run over fences is going to be at a disadvantage, running in a handicap against what are probably seasoned chasers. In most cases their logic is correct, but what about a horse who has run only over hurdles that has always looked ideally made for fences, and has schooled well at home? Then, off something normally like a 7lb lower mark over fences than over hurdles, the trainer has something to go to war with.

The first trainer I noticed shrewdly using this ploy was David Nicholson, very successfully during the early careers of Waterloo Boy and Long Engagement. Even now, he takes advantage when the opportunity arises. After six runs over hurdles in the '95/'96 season, Ballyea Boy finished his campaign with this run in a handicap hurdle:-

3117-NEWTON ABBOT (L-H) (Soft)
Saturday April 13th
WEATHER: sunny

3200 EIRE CONDITIONAL H'CAP HURDLE (0-125) (4-Y.O+) (Class E)
2-00 (2-00) 2m 6f (10 hdls) £2,664.70 (£749.20: £366.10) GOING: 1.26 sec per fur (HY)

		SP	RR	SF
3051* **Jovial Man (IRE) (108)** (RJO'Sullivan) 7-10-12 SCurran (lw: hld up med div: hdwy 5th: led appr last: drvn out) .... — 1		7/2 1	88	37
2940* **Spring Grass (99)** (BJMRyall) 8-10-3 TDascombe (racd wd: a.p: led 7th tl appr last: styd on flat)...............½ 2		14/1	79	28
3122³ **Lansdowne (119)** (PFNicholls) 8-11-6(3) MGriffiths (lw: hdwy 5th: rdn next: one pce appr last)...............1½ 3		6/1 2	98	47
2551⁷ **Ballyea Boy (IRE) (109)** (DNicholson) 6-10-13 RJohnson (chsd ldrs: wknd 8th: nrst fin)...................8 4		12/1	82	31
2886⁴ **Marine Society (96)** (AGNewcombe) 8-10-0 BFenton (hld up & bhd: gd hdwy 8th: nt rch ldrs)............1¾ 5		14/1	68	17
3062⁴ **Touch Silver (96)** (HJManners) 6-10-0 SophieMitchell (bhd tl hdwy 7th: nt rch ldrs)...............2½ 6		12/1	66	15
3060³ **Jadidh (109)** (CPWildman) 8-10-13 DSalter (nvr trbld ldrs).................................¾ 7		12/1	78	27
2928⁶ **Fly by North (USA) (98)** (DNicholson) 8-9-9(7) XAizpuru (in tch tl lost pl 5th: r.o appr 7th: wknd next) 2 8		20/1	66	15
2553ᴾ **Sticky Money (97)** (MCPipe) 8-10-1 OBurrows (a bhd) 12 9		20/1	56	5
2348⁵ **Robero (96)** (MrsJPitman) 5-10-0v ABates (led 2nd to 4th: wknd after next) 3 10		20/1	53	2
2886* **Selatan (IRE) (111)** (DRGandolfo) 4-10-8 DFortt (racd wd: led to 2nd: wknd 7th) 2½ 11		15/2	66	8
2818* **Sheriffmuir (103)** (MrsLWadham) 7-10-7 GHogan (lw: chsd ldrs: ev ch 8th: wkng & mstke 2 out: nt rcvr) 1 12		7/2 1	58	7
2762¹⁶ **Pondering (121)** (MCPipe) 6-11-4v(7) BMoore (chsd ldrs 3rd: led next: hdd 7th: wknd qckly).................¾ 13		33/1	75	24
3063⁶ **Mu-Tadil (103)** (RJBaker) 4-10-0b RMassey (a bhd: t.o 7th)...................................dist 14		66/1	—	—
2966³ **Country Store (101)** (APJones) 7-10-5 LAspell (a bhd: t.o whn p.u after 6th) .... P		7/1 3	—	—

5m 40.4 (28.40) CSF £54.73 CT £284.91 TOTE £5.60: £2.40 £4.60 £2.60 (£76.40) Trio £245.62; £34.63 to Musselburgh 15/4/96 OWNER Mrs Barbara Marchant (WHITCOMBE) BRED John B. Hughes
(SP 138.1%) **15 Rn**
LONG HANDICAP Robero 9-8 Touch Silver 9-12 Mu-Tadil 7-10 Marine Society 9-7
WEIGHT FOR AGE 4yo-7lb

81

As you can see, this lightly-raced gelding ran a perfectly respectable race of an official mark of 109. After failing to win over hurdles, Ballyea Boy was able to make a good start over the larger obstacles having been dropped that vital few pounds.

0819-TOWCESTER (R-H) (Good)
Thursday November 14th
WEATHER: fine

1338 TIFFIELD H'CAP CHASE (0-125) (5-Y.O+) (Class D)
1-50 (1-50) **3m 1f** (**18 fncs**) £3,738.00 (£1,119.00: £537.00: £246.00) GOING minus 0.05 sec per fur (G)

		SP	RR
Ballyea Boy (IRE) (101) (DNicholson) 6-11-6 AMaguire (j.w: led 10th: rdn & wandered appr last: sn hdd: led again nr fin) .... — 1		3/1 2	107
1122⁴ **Ardcroney Chief (90)** (DRGandolfo) 10-10-9 RDunwoody (w ldrs: rdn & led last: ct nr fin) .... nk 2		5/1	96
1142² **Celtic Silver (93)** (MrsSJSmith) 8-10-12 RichardGuest (hld up: hit 8th: hdwy 11th: rdn appr 2 out: nt clr run & swtchd appr last: one pce) 4 3		7/4 1	96
1194* **Drumcullen (IRE) (102)** (KCBailey) 7-11-0⁽⁷⁾ ⁶ˣ MrRWakley (led: hit 6th: hdd 10th: mstke 12th: sn no ch) ....dist 4		4/1 3	—
Nicklup (105) (CaptTAForster) 9-11-10 AThornton (lw: fell 2nd) .... F		9/2	—
		(SP 116.2%) 5	

6m 23.7 (8.70) CSF £16.46 TOTE £3.50: £1.80 £3.00 (£12.60) OWNER Mr Denis Barry (TEMPLE GUITING) BRED Ted O'Rourke

1171-EXETER (R-H) (Good)
Friday December 6th
WEATHER: misty

1765 BONUSPRINT H'CAP CHASE (0-120) (5-Y.O+) (Class D)
2-20 (2-21) **2m 7f 110y** (**17 fncs**) £4,192.20 (£1,254.60: £601.80: £275.40) GOING: 0.29 sec per fur (GS)

		SP	RR
1338* **Ballyea Boy (IRE) (106)** (DNicholson) 6-11-3 AMaguire (lw: a.p: led 14th: hld on u.p flat) .... — 1		5/2 1	117
1428⁴ **Rocky Park (92)** (GBBalding) 10-10-3 BFenton (a.p: lost pl 15th: mstke last: rallied flat) .... ¾ 2		14/1	103
Red Parade (NZ) (95) (NJHawke) 8-10-6 RGreene (bit bkwd: hld up: hdwy 11th: ev ch 15th: one pce) 3 3		9/1	103
1426* **Orswell Lad (105)** (PJHobbs) 7-10-13⁽³⁾ GTormey (hdwy & mstke 14th: one pce) 4 4		13/2	111
1540⁴ **Spuffington (114)** (JTGifford) 8-11-11 PHide (lw: led to 14th: ev ch 2 out: wknd qckly appr last) 1½ 5		10/1	119
1473* **Andre Laval (IRE) (113)** (KCBailey) 7-11-3⁽⁷⁾ MrRWakley (bhd: hdwy 12th: nvr nrr) .... ¾ 6		5/1 2	117
1119⁶ **Garrylough (IRE) (113)** (DRGandolfo) 7-11-10 RDunwoody (bhd: hdwy 12th: nvr nrr) .... ½ 7		6/1 3	117
1057* **Special Account (97)** (CRBarwell) 10-10-8 APMcCoy (lw: chsd ldrs tl wknd 13th) .... nk 8		8/1	101
Ghia Gneuiagh (113) (NATwiston-Davies) 10-11-10 CLlewellyn (bit bkwd: a bhd: t.o) .... dist 9		20/1	—
Mr Invader (102) (NAGaselee) 9-10-13 WMarston (bit bkwd: a bhd: t.o) 2½ 10		16/1	—
1379⁴ **Kindle's Delight (101)** (MissHCKnight) 8-10-12 JOsborne (prom to 13th: grad wknd: t.o whn p.u bef last) ..... P		20/1	—
		(SP 125.1%) 11	

6m 8.7 (21.70) CSF £36.32 CT £257.41 TOTE £3.90: £1.90 £5.50 £1.80 (£114.30) Trio £105.60 OWNER Mr Denis Barry (TEMPLE GUITING) BRED Ted O'Rourke

What options are open to trainers if their horse's first handicap mark is based on form under the same code? It is placement of the horse that is all-important. One run in the wrong place and your handicap mark can suffer permanent damage. I have to say at this stage that the examples I use to demonstrate when a horse has got itself a harsh handicap mark should not really be judged against the trainer. I am writing with the benefit of hindsight and do not know what went on behind the scenes. What if the owners were local to a certain track and insisted that their horse ran there? What if there were no other suitable races for the horse at the time?

I will start with an example of when things really do go right. This is the career of a fairly modest horse called Frog. A rangy but backward two-year-old, Frog didn't race until October. Within just twenty days, she had qualified for a handicap mark by finishing nearer last than first in three six furlong maiden races. She was given a handicap mark of 61, before running down the field in a nursery on Equitrack on her final start at two. Dropped to 55 after that effort, she then disappeared until the middle of her three-year-old season.

What do you do with a filly rated 55 who has a middle-distance pedigree? Run her in a mile and a quarter 0-55 Limited Stakes where she gets a sex allowance from the colts and geldings who can be rated no higher.

NOTTINGHAM (L-H) (Firm, Good to firm st)
Saturday July 6th
WEATHER: fine WIND: mod across

2542 'FUN FOR ALL THE FAMILY' LIMITED STKS (0-55) (3-Y.O) (Class F)
9-20 (9-22) 1m 1f 213y £1,932.00 (£532.00: £252.00) Stalls: Low GOING minus 0.64 sec per fur (F)

			SP	RR	SF
Frog (55) (SirMarkPrescott) 3-8-11 WWoods(8) (in tch: hdwy to ld over 1f out: sn pushed clr)............	—	1	9/4 [1]	64	11
2191[2] Two Socks (57) (MMcCormack) 3-9-0 RHughes(4) (hdwy 5f out: led over 1f out: sn hdd & one pce)........3½		2	11/2 [3]	61	8
595[4] Fiona Shann (USA) (53) (JLDunlop) 3-8-11 WCarson(2) (prom: rdn over 3f out: swtchd & r.o fnl f)........¾		3	7/2 [2]	57	4
1821* Spa Lane (54) (PJMakin) 3-8-9[5] RHavlin(11) (chsd ldrs: rdn & ev ch over 1f out: one pce appr fnl f)........s.h		4	6/1	60	7
1908[5] Sylvella (53) (MAJarvis) 3-8-11 PRobinson(3) (bhd: hdwy 4f out: one pce fnl 2f)........................3		5	6/1	52	—
2014[5] Miss Pravda (53) (PTWalwyn) 3-8-6[5] MartinDwyer(7) (led 3f out tl over 1f out: wknd fnl f)........1¼		6	16/1	50	—
2027[9] Islay Brown (IRE) (49) (CWCElsey) 3-8-11b KFallon(5) (led 7f)..........................		7	14/1	50	—
1995[6] Crimson Rosella (55) (WJHaggas) 3-8-11 RMcGhin(10) (chsd ldrs over 7f)........................½		8	14/1	49	—
1654[13] Prince Zizim (53) (CADwyer) 3-8-11[3] NVarley(1) (s.i.s: hdwy 6f out: wknd 3f out)..............½		9	33/1	52	—
2251[11] Hank-a-chief (46) (BSmart) 3-9-0b[1] JStack(9) (rn wd over 4f out: a bhd).......................9		10	40/1	37	—
2158[11] Realms of Glory (IRE) (52) (PhilipMitchell) 3-9-0 JQuinn(6) (bhd fnl 4f)......................16		11	25/1	12	—

(SP 125.4%) **11 Rn**

2m 6.6 (4.10) CSF £15.58 TOTE £3.70: £1.30 £1.80 £2.00 (£9.90) Trio £72.80 OWNER Mr B. Haggas (NEWMARKET) BRED Mrs P. A. Clark

Having bolted in at Nottingham, she carried a penalty to another easy success before the Handicapper had a chance to reassess her. Three further wins in handicaps followed, two at odds-on, before the Handicapper finally caught up with her. Eleven runs, five wins. Not a bad return for a horse who has never won off a handicap mark above 75.

The cynical among you might suggest that the trainer has done something underhand by running the horse over an insufficient trip at the start of its career. The trainer's first priority must be to enable the owner to receive as much prizemoney as possible without breaking the Rules of Racing. Provided that the horse ran on its merits in its early races, I feel the trainer has done a fine job.

Punters would be well advised to look closely at the pedigrees of lightly-raced horses that they are considering supporting. A quick check can sometimes expose a fancy as likely to be suited by much further. Particularly for two-year-olds, even five furlongs is a bit of a stamina test to begin with. A horse with a middle-distance pedigree can be expected to step up in trip at regular intervals before reaching its ideal distance. A good guide is the average winning distance of sire and dam sire's progeny, as well as a bit of knowledge about the dam herself where available.

Everything worked like clockwork in the above case, but all horses are different and a similar strategy is not always rewarded. There are many things that can go wrong, some horses will simply lose heart after a few defeats. A run on ground known to be too fast or too testing can do physical damage, or horses can simply learn bad habits by running at the wrong trip. Take the case of Mua-Tab, who on pedigree might have been expected to do better once stepped up in trip. Her three maiden runs were at a maximum of a mile, but she showed a tendency not to settle as well as she could have. This is the last of them:-

857 LAVERSTOCK MAIDEN STKS (II) (3-Y.O F) (Class D)
5-00 (5-02) 1m £3,395.00 (£1,010.00: £480.00: £215.00) Stalls: High GOING minus 0.39 sec per fur (F)

			SP	RR	SF
007[2] Charlotte Corday (85) (GWragg) 3-8-11 MHills(3) (stdd s: a gng wl: led on bit 2f out: shkn up & qcknd clr ins fnl f)................	—	1	5/6 [1]	83+	34
357[5] Premier Night (SDow) 3-8-11 MRoberts(2) (a.p: rdn & ev ch over 1f out: unable qckn)............3½		2	9/1	76	27
326[5] Mua-Tab (PTWalwyn) 3-8-11 WCarson(9) (rdn & hdwy 2f out: r.o one pce fnl f)..............1¾		3	6/1 [3]	73	24
Kentucky Fall (FR) (LadyHerries) 3-8-11 PaulEddery(1) (str: scope: lw: hld up & bhd: hdwy 3f out: rdn & ev ch over 1f out: one pce)............½		4	11/2 [2]	72	23
644[7] Trilby (PFICole) 3-8-11 TQuinn(4) (prom: rdn over 3f out: one pce fnl 2f)..............3		5	8/1	66	17
614[16] Amelanchier (GBBalding) 3-8-11 SSanders(7) (hld up & plld hrd: no hdwy fnl 2f)..............nk		6	66/1	65	16
Snowpoles (MrsJCecil) 3-8-11 JReid(5) (led 6f)..............3		7	20/1	59	10
Soldier's Song (RJHodges) 3-8-11 TSprake(10) (a/like: s.s: nrst fin)..............1		8	50/1	57	8
617[9] Redskin Lady (DRCElsworth) 3-8-8[3] DaneO'Neill(11) (lw: prom over 5f)..............1¾		9	10/1	53	4
617[12] Burning Flame (RMFlower) 3-8-11 DBiggs(12) (a bhd)..............2½		10	50/1	48	—
Isla Glen (MMcCormack) 3-8-11 MFenton(6) (a bhd)..............1½		11	50/1	45	—
Persian Dawn (MajorDNChappell) 3-8-11 BThomson(8) (chsd ldr: rdn over 2f out: wknd over 2f out)..............2½		12	20/1	40	—

(SP 131.3%) **12 Rn**

n 43.53 (3.13) CSF £10.74 TOTE £2.00: £1.10 £2.80 £1.60 (£10.30) Trio £9.00 OWNER Mr A. E. Oppenheimer (NEWMARKET) BRED scombe and Valiant Studs

On this evidence, an initial handicap mark of 70 looked reasonable and Mua-Tab started favourite on her handicap debut:-

2341·CHEPSTOW (L-H) (Good to firm)
Tuesday July 2nd
WEATHER: overcast WIND: slt across

2384 MIDDLE LODGE H'CAP (0-85) (3-Y.O F) (Class D)
4-30 (4-31) **1m 2f 36y** £3,712.25 (£1,118.00: £541.50: £253.25) Stalls: Low GOING minus 0.41 sec per fur (F)

			SP	RR	
1407⁵ **Overruled (IRE) (82)** (DRLoder) 3-9-7 RHughes(2) (lw: a.p: led over 3f out: rdn & hdd 2f out: led over 1f out: r.o wl)	—	1	100/30³	86	4
2202⁵ **Classic Romance (73)** (RHarris) 3-8-12 AMackay(4) (hld up: hdwy 4f out: rdn & ev ch over 1f out: unable qckn)	¾	2	12/1	76	3
2246⁵ **Trilby (65)** (PFICole) 3-8-4 TQuinn(6) (b.off hind: led over 4f: rdn over 3f out: led 2f out: sn hdd: unable qckn)	s.h	3	3/1²	68	3
1857³ **Mua-Tab (70)** (PTWalwyn) 3-8-9 WCarson(5) (hld up & plld hrd: hdwy 4f out: hrd rdn & ev ch over 1f out: unable qckn)	s.h	4	5/2¹	73	3
1641¹⁴ **Double Up (66)** (LadyHerries) 3-8-5 DeclanO'Shea(1) (hld up: a bhd)	7	5	13/2	58	2
1775¹⁰ **Little Black Dress (USA) (69)** (RCharlton) 3-8-8 TSprake(3) (chsd ldr: led over 5f out tl over 3f out: wknd over 2f out)	3	6	6/1	56	1
			(SP 112.0%)		6

2m 8.2 (2.90) CSF £32.54 TOTE £4.80: £2.30 3.50 (£30.20) OWNER Mr E. J. Loder (NEWMARKET) BRED E. J. Loder

However, she again proves reluctant to settle after her initial races at shorter distances, and her five handicap defeats culminate in a ten-length beating off an official mark of 60. Nobody will ever know for certain, but those early runs at trips short of her likely optimum may have lost connections their chance of teaching her to settle. Although to be fair, some horses just never learn to pace themselves.

In sprint races in particular, the draw can have a decisive effect. Races are sometimes won by what appears to be the 'wrong' horse. If all the best horses find themselves racing on the slowest ground, a less-able competitor may win, especially if he or she is against a rail. Here is a result from Folkestone:-

0663·FOLKESTONE (R-H) (Firm)
Tuesday April 23rd
WEATHER: fine WIND: fresh across

758 BARHAM MEDIAN AUCTION MAIDEN STKS (3-Y.O) (Class E)
3-30 (3-32) **6f** £3,288.60 (£982.80: £470.40: £214.20) Stalls: Low GOING minus 0.53 sec per fur (F)

			SP	RR	
458¹⁴ **Spotted Eagle** (RHannon) 3-8-9(5) DaneO'Neill(3) (a.p: n.m.r on ins over 2f out: led ins fnl f: r.o wl)	—	1	14/1	78	
591³ **Watch The Fire** (JEBanks) 3-8-9 JQuinn(6) (a.p: led wl over 1f out tl ins fnl f: unable qckn)	1¾	2	Evens¹	68	
467² **Blessed Spirit (70)** (CFWall) 3-8-9 WWoods(9) (hld up: rdn over 1f out: one pce)	2½	3	100/30²	62	
648⁶ **Man of Wit (IRE) (76)** (APJarvis) 3-9-0 TQuinn(8) (led over 4f)	4	4	12/1	56	
526⁸ **Daring Venture** (TJNaughton) 3-8-2(7) TAshley(2) (hld up: hdwy over 1f out: wknd fnl f)	2½	5	12/1	44	
644¹⁴ **Never Think Twice (61)** (KTIvory) 3-8-7v(7) CScally(7) (a.s: hdwy over 2f out: wknd fnl f)	nk	6	14/1	49	
Extra Hour (IRE) (71) (WRMuir) 3-9-0 RCochrane(4) (bhd fnl 2f)	6	7	9/1³	33	
Governor's Bid (MrsLCJewell) 3-8-9 RHughes(1) (w'like: bit bkwd: a bhd)	16	8	50/1	—	
First Gallery (RMFlower) 3-8-9 DBiggs(5) (neat: bit bkwd: a bhd)	3½	9	33/1	—	
			(SP 116.7%)		9

1m 10.4 (0.10 under best) (0.20) CSF £27.81 TOTE £16.60: £2.80 1.10 1.70 (£14.00) Trio £13.10 OWNER Lord Carnarvon (MARLBOROUGH) BRED Roldvale Ltd

This maiden race contained three subsequent winners, namely Watch The Fire, Blessed Spirit and Never Think Twice. Unfortunately, they were drawn 6, 9 and 7 respectively. With the stalls on the stands' side, low numbers were much favoured this day. This enabled 14/1 shot Spotted Eagle to hug the rail throughout, and squeeze through to win. What good fortune for the connections, you may think. However, in winning on his third start, Spotted Eagle was now qualified for a handicap mark. The official Handicapper does what he has to, and takes the form at face value. In his four subsequent runs in handicaps, he beat home only seven horses. He finished the season being beaten over twenty lengths in a six-furlong sprint handicap.

An unwise choice of race early in a horse's career can have a detrimental effect on his future prospects. Wot No Fax certainly surprised punters by making a winning start to his career in this Lingfield maiden:-

1079 A A APPOINTMENTS MAIDEN STKS (3-Y.O+) (Class D)
5-15 (5-19) 1m 2f £3,980.00 (£1,190.00: £570.00: £260.00) Stalls: High GOING minus 0.51 sec per fur (F)

				SP	RR	SF
	Wot No Fax (SDow) 3-8-11 WRyan(6) (str: scope: hld up: rdn over 2f out: led 1f out: edgd lft: r.o wl) ....—	1	50/1	78	28
860[7]	**Sadler's Realm** (MRStoute) 3-8-11 JReid(2) (a.p: led over 1f out: sn hdd: unable qckn) ....¾	2	11/1	77	27
820[3]	**Spartan Heartbeat (70)** (CEBrittain) 3-8-11 BDoyle(10) (swtg: s.s: hdwy 9f out: led 6f out to 4f out: led over 3f out tl over 1f out: one pce) ....s.h	3	4/1[3]	77	27
821[6]	**Lead Him On (USA)** (PWHarris) 3-8-11 RHills(1) (hld up: rdn over 2f out: one pce) 2½	4	5/1	73	23
	Western Playboy (RHannon) 4-9-9[3] DaneO'Neill(8) (nvr nr to chal) 5	5	20/1	65	30
	Ingrina (HRACecil) 3-8-6 PatEddery(7) (unf: scope: dwlt: hdwy 9f out: rdn over 2f out: eased whn btn over 1f out) 3	6	11/4[1]	55+	5
	Bold Classic (IRE) (JLDunlop) 3-8-11 SWhitworth(12) (w'like: nvr nrr) 1½	7	25/1	58	8
820[11]	**Seventh Edition** (DBurchell) 3-8-4[7] TAshley(4) (prom over 4f) ....½	8	20/1	57	7
821[4]	**King Rufus** (JRArnold) 3-8-11 LDettori(11) (lw: led 4f: led 1f out tl over 3f out: wknd 2f out) ....s.h	9	7/2[2]	57	7
860[11]	**Ela Agapi Mou (USA)** (GLewis) 3-8-8[3] AWhelan(5) (a bhd) 1¼	10	50/1	55	5
687[9]	**Liberatrice (FR)** (EALDunlop) 3-8-6 TQuinn(9) (a bhd) 8	11	50/1	37	—
	Mannagar (IRE) (JRPoulton) 4-9-12 TIves(3) (b: dwlt: a bhd: t.o) 30	12	66/1	—	—

(SP 114.6%) **12 Rn**

2m 8.06 (3.36) CSF £447.85 TOTE £31.30: £5.20 2.80 1.60 (£116.70) Trio £532.20 OWNER Kerniquip's Racing Partnership (EPSOM) BRED D. S. Rigby
WEIGHT FOR AGE 3yo-15lb

This form did not work out very well, with only one horse from the race going on to win again that year. One of the most experienced of those behind was Spartan Heartbeat, who was beaten in a handicap next time out off a mark of 73. Wot No Fax could reasonably have been expected to get a handicap mark in the 70s until this happened on his next start:-

1790-**EPSOM** (L-H) (Good to firm, Firm patches)
Sunday June 9th
WEATHER: warm & sunny WIND: mod half against

1817 MARTIN DAWES CONDITIONS STKS (3-Y.O+) (Class B)
3-10 (3-12) 1m 2f 18y £12,486.00 (£4,674.00: £2,287.00: £985.00: £442.50: £225.50) Stalls: Low GOING minus 0.36 sec per fur (F)

				SP	RR	SF
	Bal Harbour (106) (HRACecil) 5-9-7 PatEddery(1) (lw: mde all: rdn out) ....—	1	5/2[1]	111	77
1427[6]	**Yarob (IRE) (98)** (HThomsonJones) 3-8-4 RHills(5) (lw: hdwy on ins over 3f out: chsd wnr over 1f out: unable qckn) 2	2	12/1	104	57
1079*	**Wot No Fax** (SDow) 3-8-4 SSanders(2) (lw: a.p: chsd wnr 4f out tl over 1f out: one pce) 2	3	20/1	101	54
1120[2]	**Yom Jameel (97)** (MRStoute) 3-8-4 PaulEddery(4) (lw: chsd wnr 6f: wknd over 1f out) 2½	4	9/2[2]	97	50
1015[6]	**Tawkil (USA) (102)** (BWHills) 3-8-4 MHills(7) (bhd fnl 3f) 17	5	6/1	70	23
1509[7]	**Wayne County (IRE) (110)** (RAkehurst) 6-9-5 JWeaver(3) (lw: bhd fnl 3f) 2	6	5/1[3]	69	35
	Tarte Aux Pommes (USA) (CEBrittain) 4-8-9 MRoberts(6) (hld up: rdn 4f out: sn wknd) 4	7	6/1	52	18

7 Rn

Again unconsidered in the market, he ran an exceptional race on paper, and those behind him included Wayne County, who was running off a handicap mark of 110. At first glance, Wot No Fax seemed to have shown great improvement as the time appeared to support the strength of the form, being below standard. It is only when the race is compared with one half an hour earlier that doubts set in.

1816 TALKLAND LADIES' H'CAP (0-80) (4-Y.O+) (Class D)
2-35 (2-36) 1m 2f 18y £7,197.50 (£2,180.00: £1,065.00: £507.50) Stalls: Low GOING minus 0.36 sec per fur (F)

				SP	RR	SF
1618[9]	**Rising Dough (IRE) (65)** (GLMoore) 4-10-6[5] MrsJMoore(4) (hdwy over 6f out: led over 1f out: r.o wl) 1	1	12/1	75	00
108[3]	**Hever Golf Lady (56)** (TJNaughton) 4-9-11[5] MrsJNaughton(9) (b: a.p: rdn over 2f out: r.o ins fnl f) 4	2	16/1	60	48
1102[2]	**Access Adventurer (IRE) (73)** (RBoss) 5-11-5 MissYHaynes(8) (led over 1f: led 2f out tl over 1f out: wknd fnl f) 2	3	9/2[2]	74	62
953[3]	**Carlito Brigante (75)** (MrsJRRamsden) 4-11-2[5] MissERamsden(3) (lw: hdwy over 1f out: r.o) ....¾	4	4/1[1]	74	62
	Amlah (USA) (65) (PJHobbs) 4-10-11 MrsSHobbs(2) (nvr nr to chal) ....hd	5	10/1	64	52
1449[14]	**Don't Drop Bombs (USA) (66)** (DTThom) 7-9-0v MissJFeilden(1) (lw: led over 8f out to 2f out: wknd 1f out)3½	6	9/1	34	22
1515[4]	**Norsong (53)** (RAkehurst) 4-9-13 MissJAllison(7) (b.nr fore: bhd fnl 3f) 3½	7	6/1	41	29
216[8]	**Yubralee (USA) (70)** (MCPipe) 4-11-2 MrsLPearce(6) (lw: bhd fnl 3f) 2	8	10/1	55	43
1486[8]	**Domitia (72)** (MBell) 4-11-4 MrsAPerrett(5) (lw: a bhd) 4	9	5/1[3]	51	22

(SP 110.9%) **9 Rn**

2m 8.0 (3.60) CSF £148.09 CT £873.46 TOTE £11.20: £2.60 2.30 2.00 (£60.00) Trio £111.80 OWNER Mr Bryan Pennick (BRIGHTON) BRED David John Brown
LONG HANDICAP Don't Drop Bombs (USA) 8-9

Just how truly-run was the Bal Harbour race? Wot No Fax has run to a speed figure 9lb below Rising Dough, who was winning a handicap off a mark of just 65. The Handicapper does his best for Wot No Fax as the two horses in front of him and the three behind all rated around 100. He seems to be taking a chance introducing Wot No Fax on a handicap mark of 95.

When making his handicap debut two outings later, Wot No Fax was giving weight to the well-handicapped Fahim, who had looked a potential Group horse to some observers' eyes whilst progressing through the ranks. Despite two further comprehensive defeats, Wot No Fax finished the season on a handicap mark of 88, 9lb above Frog.

Not only can the races competed in influence a horse's first Handicap Mark, but the first handicap has proved vital on occasions in the past. In 1986, a horse called Cry For The Clown landed a gamble for the Alan Bailey yard in a Ripon selling race, backed from 20/1 to 8/1. This was obviously a good result for the yard but the winning margin, five lengths, was rather annoying, given that the horse's future was intended to be nursery handicaps.

The horse was clearly better than a plater but his first nursery entry came in a seller. He got top weight of course but the mark looked more than reasonable given the regard in which the horse was held. Again heavily backed, he won a conditions race at Windsor before making his nursery debut, the race having been chosen because selling winners were not penalised. To complete his hat trick, he carried a seven pound penalty for the Windsor success to victory in a Bath nursery, backed from 2/1 to 4/5 in a twelve-runner race.

The real moral of the tale is that the most important races for a horse's handicap mark are the non-handicaps he or she runs in before a figure is awarded. This is not the ideal situation because, probably as a result, trainers are understandably loath to send inexperienced horses to compete in valuable conditions races. It is only when trainers are pretty confident that their charge is up to the task that they will run them in such races. Inevitably, these contests often end up attracting disappointingly small fields.

CHAPTER 9

THE PITFALLS AND HOW TO AVOID THEM

This section is intended to show you how to deal with some of handicapping's more tricky problems. There are a number of things that can go wrong. Let us start with the most basic. In general, there are two main reasons why horses lose. The first reason is simply a lack of sufficient speed. That is to say that the horse in question finishes the race with some 'petrol left in the tank', but quite simply can't keep up with the winner. This type of defeat becomes more common the shorter the trip of the race, and the faster the ground. The second reason for defeat is that the horse becomes tired and, irrespective of its basic speed, is a totally spent force before the end of the race. This type of defeat is the most common in jump racing, particularly as the ground gets softer.

2760-CHELTENHAM (L-H) (Good)
Thursday March 14th
Race 3: One fence omitted fnl circ
WEATHER: fine

2785   TOTE CHELTENHAM GOLD CUP CHASE (Gd 1) (5-Y.O+) (Class A)
3-30 (3-39) 3m 2f 110y (New) (21 fncs) £131,156.00 (£49,004.00: £23,902.00: £10,210.00: £4,505.00: £2,223.00) GOING: 0.59 sec per fur (S)

		SP	RR	SF
2359a* **Imperial Call (IRE)** (174) (FSutherland,Ireland) 7-12-0 CO'Dwyer (hld up: led after 16th to 17th: led 4 out: r.o wl fr 2 out) .... — 1		9/2 2	182	93
2482* **Rough Quest** (149) (TCasey) 10-12-0 MAFitzgerald (hld up & bhd: stdy hdwy 18th: chsd wnr fr 2 out: one pce) 4 2		12/1	180	91
1433F **Couldnt Be Better** (157) (CPEBrooks) 9-12-0 GBradley (lw: a.p: led 14th to 16th: led 17th to 4 out: rdn & wknd 3 out) 19 3		11/1	168	79
2482 4 **Barton Bank** (168) (DNicholson) 10-12-0 APMcCoy (prom: blnd 7th: wknd 4 out) 3 4		16/1	166	77
2482P **Young Hustler** (163) (NATwiston-Davies) 9-12-0 CMaude (chsd ldr: led briefly 16th: wknd 18th) ....nk 5		25/1	166	77
1802* **One Man** (179) (GRichards) 8-12-0 RDunwoody (lw: hld up: hdwy 16th: hit 17th: ev ch 3 out: wknd qckly appr last: fin tired) 8 6		11/8 1	161	72
2682a2 **King of the Gales** (JEKiely,Ireland) 9-12-0 CFSwan (hld up: mstke 12th: sn bhd: t.o) 17 7		50/1	151	62
2359a3 **Monsieur le Cure** (167) (JACEdwards) 10-12-0 JFTitley (lw: prom: 5th whn fell 6th: dead) .... F		14/1	—	—
1849* **Dublin Flyer** (168) (CaptTAForster) 10-12-0 BPowell (led to 14th: wknd 16th: t.o whn p.u bef 2 out) .... P		5/1 3	—	—
2373P **Lord Relic (NZ)** (147) (MCPipe) 10-12-0 DBridgwater (lw: bhd: j.slowly 5th: t.o whn p.u bef 15th) .... P		100/1	—	—

(SP 112.3%) **10 Rn**
6m 42.5 (7.50) CSF £48.90 TOTE £4.90: £1.90 £3.00 £2.30 (£47.90) Trio £84.60 OWNER Lisselan Farms Ltd (KILLINARDRISH) BRED T.A. O'Donnell in Ireland

2050-ASCOT (R-H) (Good to firm)
Thursday June 20th
WEATHER: overcast WIND: almost nil

2071   GOLD CUP STKS (Gp 1) (4-Y.O+) (Class A)
3-45 (3-46) 2m 4f £118,872.00 (£44,087.60: £20,843.80: £8,716.60) Stalls: Low GOING minus 0.25 sec per fur (GF)

		SP	RR	SF
1128* **Classic Cliche (IRE)** (120) (SbinSuroor) 4-9-0 MJKinane(7) (lw: hld up in tch: chal on bit 2f out: led wl over 1f out: drvn out) .... — 1		3/1 2	119+	66
1482* **Double Trigger (IRE)** (119) (MJohnston) 5-9-2 JWeaver (2) (lw: led tl wl over 1f out: sn hrd rdn: styd on)..1½ 2		1/2 1	118	67
1397a2 **Nononito (FR)** (JLesbordes,France) 5-9-2 SGuillot(4) (hld up: hdwy over 2f out: rdn & no ex appr fnl f) 3 3		16/1 3	115	63
1397a3 **Always Aloof (USA)** (106) (MRStoute) 5-9-2 WCarson(5) (hld up & bhd: effrt ent st: styd on u.p fnl 2f)........1½ 4		16/1 3	114	63
1428 2 **Latahaab (USA)** (87) (RAkehurst) 5-9-2 TQuinn(3) (lw: chsd ldr: hrd drvn 2f out: one pce) ....¾ 5		50/1	79 t	63
1091 5 **Upper Mount Clair** (67) (CEBrittain) 6-8-13 BDoyle(6) (hld up & bhd: pushed along 5f out: wknd ent st: t.o)..13 6		66/1	66 t	49
1482 2 **Assessor (IRE)** (105) (RHannon) 7-9-2 RHughes(1) (b: trckd ldrs: rdn over 3f out: sn btn: t.o) 5 7		20/1	65 t	48

(SP 111.6%) **7 Rn**
4m 23.2 (3.20) CSF £4.64 TOTE £3.60: £1.70 £1.30 (£1.80) OWNER Godolphin (NEWMARKET) BRED Lord Victor Matthews in Ireland

You are probably already much more of an expert in this area than you realise. Ask yourself the following question. Why did One Man not win the 1996 Cheltenham Gold Cup? If you think his defeat was due to a lack of speed, you either didn't see the race or have forgotten it. Conversely Double Trigger's defeat in the 1996 Ascot Gold Cup was due to his lack of speed once Classic Cliche challenged him. Few would argue with these assessments and they are the norm for Flat and jump racing.

Problems with Maiden Races

1998-**SANDOWN** (R-H) (Good to firm, Good patches becoming Good)
Friday July 5th
WEATHER: heavy rain races 3-4 WIND: almost nil

2505   SUN HUNG KAI SECURITIES MAIDEN STKS (3 & 4-Y.O) (Class D)
4-40 (4-55) **1m 6f** £3,582.50 (£1,085.00: £530.00: £252.50) Stalls: High GOING minus 0.25 sec per fur (GF)

		SP	RR	SF
2054[7] **Clerkenwell (USA)** (91) (MRStoute) 3-8-11 PatEddery(2) (lw: a:p: led on bit over 2f out: easily) ....— **1**		8/11[1]	81+	38
2314[2] **Warning Reef** (83) (MRChannon) 3-8-11 RHughes(8) (lw: hdwy 6f out: ev ch over 2f out: hrd rdn over 1f out: unable qckn)..6 **2**		9/2[2]	74	31
1875[4] **Belmarita (IRE)** (73) (MHTompkins) 3-8-6 PRobinson(10) (a.p: rdn over 2f out: one pce) 2½ **3**		6/1[3]	66	23
1997[6] **Rivercare (IRE)** (61) (MJPolglase) 3-8-11 JWeaver(5) (led tl over 2f out: sn wknd) 4 **4**		33/1	67	24
1769[10] **Shirley Venture** (76) (SPCWoods) 3-8-6 WWoods(4) (hld up: rdn over 3f out: sn wknd).................4 **5**		13/2	57	14
811[10] **Cypress Avenue (IRE)** (74) (RHannon) 4-9-9(3) DaneO'Neill(6) (nvr nr to chal)...............................16 **6**		33/1	44	16
2036[8] **Melomania (USA)** (TJNaughton) 4-9-12 NAdams(7) (lw: sme hdwy 5f out: wknd).............................9 **7**		50/1	34	6
1147[10] **Spread The Word** (57) (LGCottrell) 4-9-7 DHolland(1) (chsd ldr over 7f)...3½ **8**		50/1	25	—
1963[5] **Hever Golf Classic** (TJNaughton) 3-8-7 PaulEddery(9) (a bhd)...15 **9**		20/1	12	—
2205[3] **Anchor Venture** (60) (SPCWoods) 3-8-11 KFallon(11) (lw: sme hdwy 5f out: sn wknd) 1¾ **10**		25/1	10	—
Sliparis (KOCunningham-Brown) 3-7-13(7) CMunday(3) (sddle slipped s: a bhd)..........................8 **11**		66/1	—	—
		(SP 123.6%)		11 Rn

3m 5.57 (6.67) CSF £5.00 TOTE £1.80: £1.90 £1.70 £1.60 (£3.60) Trio £7.70 OWNER Sheikh Mohammed (NEWMARKET) BRED Camelot
Thoroughbreds and Michael J. Ryan   WEIGHT FOR AGE 3yo-15lb

As you can see from this maiden race, most of the competitors already have handicap marks. On the face of it, this looks a straightforward race to rate. The winner, Clerkenwell, is rated by the official Handicapper at 91. He easily beats the only other horse rated above 76 in the race into second place. The pitfall here is the running of Rivercare, the fourth horse. Rated by the official Handicapper at 61, Rivercare has beaten two horses in Shirley Venture and Cypress Avenue that he would have met on considerably worse terms in handicaps. Has he improved? With the benefit of hindsight, the answer was definitely no. The private handicap rating of 78 was well over a stone above anything he has achieved subsequently. Indeed, the official Handicapper had dropped him to 45 by the end of the year, despite the fact that all his later efforts seemed reasonably consistent.

There were a couple of clues that could have led us to doubt the value of his Sandown effort. The close-up tells us that Rivercare made the running for almost a mile and a half, and that the twelve and a half lengths he was beaten were conceded in the last two and a bit furlongs. Once you add to this the slow time of the race, he begins to look flattered in the extreme as he was clearly allowed to control a slow pace for most of the race, yet was found badly wanting once the race proper began. Horses do improve, but any improvement apparently made when setting the pace in a slowly-run race is normally bogus.

Weight on firm ground

We have all heard the adage 'back the bottom weight on soft ground'. What is not always realised is that the situation is very much reversed on firm ground. We have already discussed that there are two main reasons why horses get beaten. Firm ground goes a large way to eliminating one of these possibilities. Just watch a field of Flat horses returning to unsaddle after a race. They will give you the impression that they are still raring to go, certainly in comparison to staying chasers after returning from racing on heavy ground. Horses bred to race will go close to running until they drop, given the opportunity. Horses raced on testing ground can be a sorry sight upon their return.

We have all seen Flat races where the jockey experiences great difficulty in pulling up the winner after the winning post. To the best on my knowledge, no study of this phenomenon has ever been done, but if it had, I am certain that those who take the longest to pull up would prove to be those that won on the fastest ground. This is particularly noticeable over the shorter trips. It was my *Raceform* colleague Ivor Markham who first opened my eyes to this many years ago. Without fail, every season since has supported this theory. Essentially, with horses not getting tired, races are won by the best horse. Weight does not seem to make the difference to the performance that it ought to. Every year I encounter problems with speed figures in amateur races. This is because the weights for these races are set roughly two stone above normal handicaps to allow for the fact that many amateur riders are heavier than the professionals. You would expect this extra two stone to manifest itself in a much slower time. On fast ground, these races occasionally appear very much better on the clock than *the Form Book* says they could possibly be. The reason is that the extra weight simply hasn't had the slowing effect that all the mathematicians say it should have had.

To see just how little effect weight can have on very fast ground, take a look at this race at Musselburgh. It took place at the only Flat meeting where the going was described as firm at the course that season. The speed figure going allowance serves to confirm this. Here are the private handicap ratings for the final race:-

MUSSELBURGH- Monday 17 June

0445 WIMPEY HOMES APPRENTICE H'CAP (0-60) (3-Y.O+) (CLASS G) 1m 3f 32y

RHR	HORSE,AGE,WEIGHT	LAST THREE OUTINGS		
63d	Amnesia (IRE) *(5-8-8)*	60	46	—
61	Ambidextrous (IRE) *(4-9-7)*	60	39	57
60	Phantom Dancer (IRE) *(3-8-13)*	53	30	60
57	Funny Rose *(6-8-8)*	48	50	55
57	Teejay'n'aitch (IRE) *(4-9-4)*	49	47	57
57	Kings Cay *(5-9-10)*	38	57	51
54	Portie Sophie *(5-8-8)*	35	54	—
54	Greek Gold (IRE) *(7-9-7)*	54	42	47
53	Serious Trust *(3-9-9)*	53	40	39

It can be seen that, in this race, the lower-weighted horses look to have as good a chance as their higher-weighted rivals. However, the race result tells a different story:-

2024 WIMPEY HOMES APPRENTICE H'CAP (0-60) (3-Y.O+) (Class G)
4-45 (4-45) **1m 3f 32y** £2,332.00 (£652.00: £316.00) Stalls: High GOING minus 0.46 sec per fur (F)

				SP	RR	SF
1544⁵	**Ambidextrous (IRE)** (43) (EJAlston) 4-9-7 DWright(4) (lw: bhd & pushed along: hdwy over 3f out: styd on to ld wl ins fnl f)..................—	1	10/1	54	35
1861⁷	**Kings Cay (IRE)** (46) (THCaldwell) 5-9-5(5) SCopp(2) (chsd ldrs: led wl over 1f out: rdn & hdd wl ins fnl f)......½	2	12/1	56	37
1586³	Teejay'n'aitch (IRE) (40) (JSGoldie) 4-9-1(3) PRoberts(8) (bhd: rdn appr st: styd on fnl 2f: nrst fin) 6	3	7/1 ²	42	23
890*	Serious Trust (58) (SirMarkPrescott) 3-9-2(7) TPengkerego(3) (lw: cl up: outpcd ent st: no imp after) 1½	4	Evens ¹	58	26
1821⁵	Greek Gold (IRE) (43) (WLBarker) 7-9-2(5) JBramhill(7) (set str pce: clr ent st: hdd & wknd wl over 1f out) ...2½	5	9/1 ³	39	20
1309⁷	Funny Rose (30) (PMonteith) 6-8-3(5) IonaWands(6) (lw: bhd: sme hdwy 3f out: n.d)...3½	6	16/1	21	2
1762³	Phantom Dancer (IRE) (48) (JBerry) 3-8-8(5) CLowther(9) (chsd ldrs tl wknd fnl 3f)..................................3½	7	7/1 ²	34	2
1866⁷	Amnesia (IRE) (30) (MrsSCBradburne) 5-8-3(5) KSked(2) (b.nr fore: a rr div)...4	8	25/1	10	—
1167¹⁵	Portie Sophie (30) (MBrittain) 5-8-3(5) GParkin(5) (b: b.hind: a bhd)...nk	9	14/1	10	—
			(SP 118.2%) **9 Rn**		

2m 24.3 (4.60) CSF £107.19 CT £821.18 TOTE £8.90: £2.20 £4.20 £4.30 (£47.10) Trio £63.30 OWNER Mrs Carol McPhail (PRESTON) BRED Saeed Manana
WEIGHT FOR AGE 3yo-13lb

Despite the defeat of the hot favourite, the race proved a clean sweep for the topweights. The favourite's defeat may have been due to the inexperience of his pilot, who was the only rider in the race never to have ridden a winner previously. It does appear that weight has not had the effect that might have been expected. Look at the master ratings for the horses (exclusive of weight-for-age):-

Ambidextrous	54
Kings Cay	53
Serious Trust	48
Greek Gold	47
Teejay'n'aitch	47
Phantom Dancer	45
Amnesia	43d
Funny Rose	37
Portite Sophie	34

It can immediately be seen that this has proved a much more accurate prediction of the outcome than our weight-adjusted ratings. If compiling ratings for yourself, you might easily decide that this result has told you little you didn't already know.

Small Fields

Beware when giving ratings to horses in small fields. Even when the distances appear to indicate the merits of the horses, this is unlikely to be the case. This is the result of a maiden race:-

1697-BEVERLEY (R-H) (Good to firm)
Wednesday June 12th
WEATHER: sunny WIND: fresh half against

1863 NEW UNIVERSITY MAIDEN STKS (3-Y.O+) (Class D)
4-30 (4-30) **1m 3f 216y** £3,978.00 (£1,108.00: £534.00) Stalls: High GOING minus 0.31 sec per fur (GF)

			SP	RR
	Bequeath (HRACecil) 4-9-10 WRyan(1) (lw: hld up: qcknd to ld 1f out: r.o strly) ....—	1	4/7[1]	85+
948[2]	**Wilawander (97)** (BWHills) 3-8-4[(5)] JDSmith(2) (led: qcknd 3f out: sn rdn: hdd 1f out: no ch w wnr)...............2½	2	13/8[2]	82
1530[5]	**Baraqueta** (JLEyre) 4-9-7[(3)] OPears(3) (trckd ldrs: lost pl over 2f out: eased & sn bhd).................................16	3	20/1[3]	60
			(SP 106.5%)	3

2m 42.0 (9.60) CSF £1.73 TOTE £1.50 (£1.20) OWNER Mr K. Abdulla (NEWMARKET) BRED Juddmonte Farms
WEIGHT FOR AGE 3yo-15lb

The second horse Wilawander was a consistently useful, if rather one-paced, stayer. His defeat here suggests that the winner, Bequeath, is a very good horse to be winning this type of race. Such a view was subsequently franked when, seventeen days later, Bequeath was the impressive winner of a listed race at Newmarket. Sixteen lengths behind these two came the obviously inferior Baraqueta, who himself was eased once beaten. Should this have encouraged us to rate Baraqueta strictly on this performance? The time of the Beverley race was very slow and this resulted in Baraqueta finishing flatteringly close to his two rivals. Therefore, the answer is no. He subsequently met with decisive defeats in handicap company off official marks as low as 53.

Winning from the front

The majority of winners do not make all the running during a race, but it is not unknown. Some horses are habitual front-runners and can not be relied upon to run to their best when other front-runners are in the race. Occasionally, a horse will be allowed to establish a long lead over most or all of its rivals. Having established the lead, it will win or go very close, but the form can prove less than reliable. Take this example:-

317-NEWBURY (L-H) (Good)
Friday November 29th
WEATHER: fine

636 BRIMPTON H'CAP HURDLE (0-140) (4-Y.O+) (Class B)
2-00 (2-03) 2m 110y (8 hdls) £4,900.00 (£1,480.00: £720.00: £340.00) GOING: 0.43 sec per fur (GS)

				SP	RR	SF
	Mister Morose (IRE) (128) (NATwiston-Davies) 6-11-4 CLlewellyn (chsd ldr: led 2 out: r.o wl).....................—	1		14/1	123+	39
502*	Chai-Yo (115) (JABOld) 6-10-5 ⁵ˣ GUpton (stdy hdwy appr 2 out: r.o flat)..8	2		5/2¹	102	18
	Intermagic (110) (JCFox) 6-10-0 SFox (bit bkwd: led: clr 2nd: hdd 2 out: unable qckn)....................1¾	3		25/1	96	12
201³	Cadougold (FR) (123) (MCPipe) 5-10-13 CFSwan (rdn appr 2 out: hdwy appr last: one pce)...........3½	4		10/1	105	21
	Bolivar (IRE) (114) (RAkehurst) 4-9-13⁽⁵⁾ SRyan (prom tl appr 2 out)..18	5		8/1³	79	—
	Abbey Street (IRE) (122) (OSherwood) 4-10-12 JOsborne (hld up: rdn 3 out: sn wknd)......................6	6		15/2²	81	—
271ᶠ	Kingsfold Pet (135) (MJHaynes) 7-11-11 DSkyrme (bhd fr 3 out)...16	7		12/1	78	—
	Master Tribe (IRE) (120) (MrsJPitman) 6-10-10 WMarston (bit bkwd: bhd fr 3 out)...............................21	8		12/1	43	—
340³	Thinking Twice (USA) (138) (NJHenderson) 7-12-0 MAFitzgerald (bhd fr 4th: t.o)..........................dist	9		25/1	—	—
	Edelweis du Moulin (FR) (127) (FMurphy) 4-11-3 RDunwoody (lw: 6th whn fell 3 out)................... F			5/2¹	—	—

(SP 118.9%) **10 Rn**

Tm 3.0 (13.00) CSF £47.49 CT £808.88 TOTE £19.00: £3.40 £1.70 £4.40 (£35.10) Trio £185.80 OWNER Mrs J. Mould (CHELTENHAM)

The field set off very steadily with the exception of Intermagic and Mister Morose. By the final circuit these were the only two going at a decent racing pace and they had gone clear of their rivals, with the joint favourites content to wait at the back of the field. Chai-Yo made a lot of late ground and got past Intermagic, who did not look fit, but could never get near the easy winner. This form is misleading in the extreme. Next time out Intermagic beat only one home. Two outings later, Master Tribe, beaten out of sight, won the Ladbroke.

A slow time can often be the key to a deceptive 'made all', more notably on the Flat. The stalls will open, nobody will want to lead and the jockey who eventually ends up being the reluctant pacemaker can then control the race to his own advantage, as in this example:-

2959-CATTERICK (L-H) (Good to firm, Good patches)
Thursday July 25th
WEATHER: sunny WIND: slt across

2988 HINGE AND BRACKET H'CAP (0-70) (3-Y.O+) (Class E)
9-10 (9-11) 1m 3f 214y £3,210.00 (£960.00: £460.00: £210.00) Stalls: Low GOING minus 0.30 sec per fur (GF)

				SP	RR	SF
1696²	Contrafire (IRE) (68) (WJarvis) 4-10-0 JWeaver(1) (lw: mde all: rdn & r.o wl fnl 2f)..............................—	1		9/2²	73	29
2775²	Campaspe (42) (JGFitzGerald) 4-8-2 DaleGibson(3) (lw: trckd ldrs: effrt 3f out: swtchd & styd on appr fnl f: nt pce to chal)...1¾	2		4/5¹	45	1
2701⁸	Dr Edgar (58) (MDods) 4-9-4 JCarroll(2) (chsd ldrs: effrt 3f out: kpt on one pce).............................nk	3		14/1	60	16
2572⁹	Toulston Lady (IRE) (49) (MJCamacho) 4-8-9 LCharnock(4) (in tch: hdwy on ins over 2f out: one pce appr fnl f)...hd	4		10/1	51	7
2368³	Classic Affair (USA) (58) (RHarris) 3-8-6 DBatteate(9) (lw: plld hrd: rapid hdwy to jn ldr 7f out: hmpd & hit rails 2f out: one pce).............................½	5		25/1	60	4
2077⁹	Karaylar (IRE) (48) (WStorey) 4-8-8 JFanning(10) (hld up & bhd: effrt 4f out: no imp)...........................4	6		33/1	44	—
2519	Chantry Beath (51) (CWThornton) 5-8-11 DeanMcKeown(6) (swtg: hld up & bhd: effrt ent st: no imp).........s.h	7		9/1³	47	3
23947	Cross Talk (IRE) (68) (RHollinshead) 4-9-9⁽⁵⁾ DGriffiths(7) (lw: hld up: effrt over 2f out: rdn & no imp).............7	8		14/1	55	11
2366⁹	Baraqueta (60) (JLEyre) 4-9-3⁽³⁾ OPears(5) (chsd ldrs tl wknd fnl 3f)...½	9		16/1	46	2
2731⁵	Diamond Crown (IRE) (48) (MartynWane) 5-8-8 MBirch(8) (hld up & bhd: effrt 3f out: n.d)................1¾	10		10/1	32	—

(SP 127.9%) **10 Rn**

2m 40.4 (9.00) CSF £9.01 CT £49.10 TOTE £5.00: £2.00 £1.40 £2.30 (£3.90) Trio £26.40 OWNER Miss V. R. Jarvis (NEWMARKET) BRED Thoroughbred Trust in Ireland

Clear Margin Winners
In handicap races, horses occasionally win by a wide margin. This suggests that they are a long way in front of the Handicapper, but this is not always the case. Here is the result of a selling hurdle:-

MARKET RASEN (R-H) (Good, Good to firm patches)
Wednesday July 3rd
WEATHER: unsettled

134 'SUMMER SEASON' CONDITIONAL (S) H'CAP HURDLE (0-90) (4-Y.O+) (Class G)
2-10 (2-10) **2m 5f 110y (10 hdls)** £1,993.40 (£552.40: £264.20) GOING: 0.07 sec per fur (G)

		SP	RR
Red Jam Jar (85) (SBBell) 11-11-12 GCahill (lw: trckd ldrs: led 3 out: sn clr) ....— 1		11/1	70
North Bannister (73) (TPMcGovern) 9-11-0 TJMurphy (a chsng ldrs: kpt on fr 3 out: no imp)....27 2		11/4[1]	38
98[2] Tremble (65) (MESowersby) 7-10-6 DParker (lw: a chsng ldrs: drvn along 5th: one pce fr 3 out) 9 3		9/1	23
Nordic Crown (IRE) (80) (MCPipe) 5-11-7b EHusband (chsd ldrs: rdn 6th: wknd appr 3 out) 9 4		7/2[2]	32
101[11] Sovereign Niche (IRE) (86) (MCPipe) 8-11-13b DWalsh (led to 3 out: sn wknd) 2 5		8/1	36
100[7] Silver Bird (IRE) (67) (MJRyan) 4-10-5 KGaule (nt j.w: in tch to 7th: sn lost pl) 1¼ 6		14/1	16
95[3] Easy Over (USA) (73) (JRJenkins) 10-11-0 DFortt (bhd & drvn along 5th: t.o 3 out)..................9 7		13/2[3]	—
66[10] Classic Image (IRE) (68) (HJManners) 6-10-4[5] ADowling (hdwy 5th: wknd 7th)................20 8		7/1	—
Joli's Great (69) (MJRyan) 8-10-10b GuyLewis (hld up: effrt 6th: sn lost pl: t.o 3 out) 2½ 9		9/1	—
101[13] Cardea Castle (IRE) (59) (JAHellens) 8-10-0 STaylor (prom to 2nd: rdn 4th: t.o 6th) ....s.h 10		25/1	—
		(SP 124.7%)	

5m 24.3 (20.30) CSF £41.94 CT £274.53 TOTE £11.30: £2.20 1.40 2.50 (£11.60) Trio £135.10 OWNER Mr C. H. P. Bell (DRIFFIELD) B
Majors Racing International Ltd
LONG HANDICAP Cardea Castle (IRE) 9-11
WEIGHT FOR AGE 4yo-3lb

Red Jam Jar has taken this race by a proverbial street. The conversion table we have been using suggests the value of his superiority over the runner-up is in the order of 20lb. The logical assumption would be that he could win off something approaching a 20lb higher mark than off which he ran here. However, as so often happens, this was not the case. Although his next two completed outings were in slightly higher company, he lost them both, off marks of 95 and 93 respectively. He needed to drop to an official mark of 92 to regain winning ways.

Unexpected Results
Here is a very unlikely-looking result:-

TOWCESTER (R-H) (Good to firm)
Wednesday October 9th
WEATHER: fine

819 ASCOTE (S) HURDLE (4, 5 & 6-Y.O) (Class G)
2-20 (2-23) **2m 5f (11 hdls)** £1,989.00 (£554.00: £267.00) GOING minus 0.11 sec per fur (G)

		SP	RR
579a[8] Do Be Ware (61) (JFfitch-Heyes) 6-11-5b BFenton (chsd ldr: hit 1st: led appr last: sn rdn clr).......................— 1		16/1	41?
697[3] Parish Walk (IRE) (80) (KJDrewry) 5-10-12 AMaguire (lw: led: hit 3 out: wknd & hdd appr last: fin tired)..........9 2		4/6[1]	27
649[3] Saltis (IRE) (ALForbes) 4-10-11 TEley (lw: chsd ldrs: lost pl 3 out: kpt on appr last) ....nk 3		9/4[2]	27
634[10] Northern Law (JohnBerry) 4-10-11b[1] ILawrence (bhd fr 4th: mstke & rdn next: t.o whn p.u bef 7th).................P		4/1[3]	—
		(SP 116.7%)	

5m 20.5 (18.50) CSF £28.42 TOTE £16.30 (£10.60) OWNER Mr John Ffitch-Heyes (LEWES) BRED R. and Mrs J. Digby-Ware
WEIGHT FOR AGE 4yo-1lb

A four horse race where the favourite finishes second, the second favourite third, would suggest at first glance that the 16/1 outsider of four has improved considerably to win the race. A closer look at the competitors' history tells a slightly different tale. The favourite, Parish Walk, was sired by a miler, and was trying the longest trip he had ever run over in his life. A glance at the close up: 'Weakened and headed approaching last, finished tired', tells us that he has failed to stay. The third horse home, Saltis, had run over the distance previously, finishing third at Worcester over 3 miles. However, he is probably not a true stayer, as much of his lengthy Flat career was at distances up to a mile. The only other horse in the race pulled up lame. Do Be Ware won this race by truly staying the distance on one of the stiffest tracks in the country. The apparent considerable improvement he had made to win this race is unlikely to have really happened. To be fair, he did pick up a similar race a few months later, having not got closer than 26 lengths behind the winner, in his next three outings.

The 'Eased Down' Syndrome

The example I have picked is an extreme case, but one I saw at first hand.

675 DIDDINGTON NOVICES' HURDLE (4-Y.O+) (Class E)
3-25 (3-25) **2m 110y (8 hdls)** £2,722.50 (£760.00: £367.50) GOING minus 0.81 sec per fur (F)

		SP	RR	SF
	Mr Percy (IRE) (JTGifford) **5-10-12** PHide (lw: a.p: led 2 out: clr last: easily)................................— 1	7/2 [3]	83+	52
555*	**Courbaril (103)** (MCPipe) **4-11-3** DBridgwater (lw: chsd ldrs: led 3 out: hdd next: eased whn btn flat)...........8 2	9/4 [1]	82	49
	Nashaat (USA) (MCChapman) **8-10-12** WWorthington (lw: hdwy 4th: no imp fr 2 out).....................14 3	10/1	62	31
593[2]	**Dacelo (FR)** (OSherwood) **5-10-12** JOsborne (chsd ldrs: one pce fr 3 out).....................................4 4	100/30 [2]	58	27
416*	**Chancey Fella (91)** (HEHaynes) **5-11-12** APMcCoy (led appr 5th tl hdd 3 out: sn wknd: fin lame).........3½ 5	12/1	68	17
	Alcove (GFJohnsonHoughton) **5-10-12** AThornton (bit bkwd: in tch to 3 out)...................................9 6	10/1	46	15
	Shuttlecock (MrsNMacauley) **5-10-12** AMaguire (prom to 3 out)..1¼ 7	20/1	45	14
	Spumante (88) (MPMuggeridge) **4-10-10** BPowell (nvr nrr) 3 8	20/1	42	9
603[2]	**Caddy's First (90)** (SMellor) **4-10-10** NMann (n.d)...½ 9	12/1	41	8
	Mandys Royal Lad (JTGifford) **8-10-7**[5] LAspell (plld hrd: led tl appr 5th: sn wknd).....................nk 10	20/1	41	10
	Ferens Hall (51) (MJRoberts) **9-10-12** PMcLoughlin (plld hrd: led 3 out: sn wknd)......................1¼ 11	33/1	40	9
490[P]	**Chadleigh Walk (IRE)** (SWCampion) **4-10-7**[3] PMidgley (a bhd)..9 12	33/1	31	—
586[3]	**Genesis Four** (MrsLStubbs) **6-10-9**[3] GCahill (a bhd) ....s.h 13	20/1	31	—
634[F]	**Ragtime Song** (JRJenkins) **7-10-5**[7] DYellowlees (lw: blnd 3rd: nvr trbld ldrs: t.o fr 3 out)............dist 14	33/1	—	—
	Clifton (RCurtis) **7-10-12** DMorris (prom to 3rd: t.o whn p.u bef 2 out: dead)................................... P	33/1	—	—
	Titanium Honda (IRE) (DCO'Brien) **5-10-12** DGallagher (mstke & dropped rr 4th: t.o whn p.u bef last)............. P	33/1	—	—

(SP 143.4%) **16 Rn**

3m 36.4 (-11.60) CSF £13.05 TOTE £5.20: £2.50 £2.40 £5.30 (£17.00) Trio £142.70; £160.84 to Ayr 21/9/96 OWNER Felix Rosenstiel's Widow & Son (FINDON) BRED M. Fardy
WEIGHT FOR AGE 4yo-2lb

By the last flight of hurdles, Mr Percy was some way clear of Courbaril, who in turn was a long way clear of the remainder. With the race won, Mr Percy was eased considerably on the run-in. With second place secure, Courbaril was also eased. However, there was still a race going on for third prize, which was eventually won by Nashaat. The official distances of eight lengths and fourteen lengths do not reflect the superiority of either of the first two over the third horse. It is not always so easy to spot this type of race from the close-up, as the Racereader will only mention the easing of a horse if it is really pronounced. The moral is to always be wary of form where large distances between finishers or an eased winner are involved.

Different types of ground

Having already discussed the two reasons for losing, another piece of information is available. As they say, we should try to never look a gift-horse in the mouth. Horses get tired much more easily on soft ground. When horses are beaten, the jockey tends to stop riding flat out. When the jockey stops riding flat out, the horse slows down. The more tired the horse is, the more quickly it will lose speed.

The upshot of all of this is that horses get beaten very much further on soft and heavy ground than they would if the ground rode faster. So, be wary of any horse who has a wide-margin win in testing ground to recommend him. It is wide-margin wins in perfect conditions that should really attract the eye.

Whilst on this subject, wide-margin wins regularly occur on All-Weather tracks, mostly over longer distances. Lingfield rides fast but the phenomenon is similar at all three courses. The only theory I can offer is the resentment of kick-back, which may affect breathing. Once a horse gets clear of its field, it also gets clear of kick-back.

Monitoring races in the light of subsequent events

With all handicaps, this is one of the hardest tasks. As a beginner I ignored it completely but, until you can admit that you make mistakes and rectify them as soon as you find out, your handicapping endeavours are likely to cost you money, not make it. Here is an example of a race initially rated rather too low:-

3217-NEWMARKET (R-H) (Good to firm)
Saturday August 3rd
WEATHER: fine WIND: almost nil

3246 YE OLDE OAK H'CAP (0-80) (3-Y.O) (Class D)
3-35 (3-36) 1m (July) £4,581.00 (£1,368.00: £654.00: £297.00) Stalls: Centre GOING minus 0.55 sec per fur (F)

					SP	RR	
2621[7]	Sky Dome (IRE) (78) (MHTompkins) 3-9-7 PRobinson(8) (mde all: qcknd over 2f out: rdn & r.o wl fnl f)	—	1		9/2 [3]	88	3
1662[4]	Divine Quest (65) (HRACecil) 3-8-8 AMcGlone(3) (a.p: rdn over 1f out: r.o)	1½	2		11/2	72	2
2334[5]	Quality (IRE) (77) (WAO'Gorman) 3-9-6 EmmaO'Gorman(6) (lw: hld up: hdwy over 1f out: nrst fin)	1¾	3		14/1	81	2
3165[*]	Sylvan Princess (56) (CNAllen) 3-7-6[7] 6x PDoe(5) (trckd ldrs: rdn 2f out: one pce)	¾	4		2/1 [1]	58	
3120[*]	Smarter Charter (74) (MrsJRRamsden) 3-9-3 6x OUrbina(4) (lw: hld up: r.o fnl 2f: nvr able to chal)	1½	5		7/2 [2]	73	2
2899[*]	Disallowed (IRE) (75) (MBell) 3-8-11[7] GFaulkner(2) (trckd wnr: rdn over 2f out: sn btn)	nk	6		8/1	73	2
3063[8]	China Castle (58) (PCHaslam) 3-7-10[5] MBaird(7) (hld up: rdn over 2f out: no imp)	5	7		20/1	46	—
1119[6]	Premier Generation (IRE) (64) (DWPArbuthnot) 3-8-7 SWhitworth(1) (b: in tch 5f: sn bhd)	5	8		9/1	42	—
					(SP 121.7%)	8	

1m 39.48 (2.28) CSF £28.82 CT £303.62 TOTE £5.50: £1.70 £1.60 £3.30 (£18.30) OWNER Miss D. J. Merson (NEWMARKET) BRED Andrew Bradley

Within two days, the fourth horse Sylvan Princess had returned to winning ways at Brighton, a performance which we rated 65, 7lb above her Newmarket rating. Ten days later, Divine Quest had got off the mark at Yarmouth, gaining a rating of 78, 6lb higher than at Newmarket. The fact that both Sky Dome and Quality found improvement to win races later in the month therefore came as no surprise.

By this time, I had been back and raised the race by 4lb, which probably erred on the conservative side. Any time a horse finds improvement, it is worth checking to see how this came about. There can be any one of a number of reasons, a new trip, trainer running into form, different ground, but it is also possible that its previous performances have been under-valued.

Spotting races that you have over-rated can often be more difficult. Things that should set the alarm bells ringing are top-rated horses who get well beaten with no obvious excuse. Here is a race that I initially over-rated:-

0685-PONTEFRACT (L-H) (Good)
Tuesday April 23rd
WEATHER: overcast WIND: fresh bhd

766 CORN MARKET LIMITED STKS (0-80) (3-Y.O+) (Class D)
4-20 (4-21) 1m 2f 6y £3,566.25 (£1,080.00: £527.50: £251.25) Stalls: Low GOING: 0.08 sec per fur (G)

					SP	RR	
	Humourless (80) (LMCumani) 3-8-5 LDettori(2) (mde all: qcknd 2f out: r.o wl: eased towards fin)	—	1		7/2 [2]	98	2
580[9]	Noble Sprinter (IRE) (80) (RHannon) 4-9-8b JReid(3) (lw: a chsng wnr: rdn over 2f out: styd on one pce)	5	2		5/1 [3]	90	3
	Ladykirk (80) (JWWatts) 3-8-2 NConnorton(6) (s.i.s: hdwy 5f out: pushed along 3f out: nt pce to chal)	1½	3		5/1 [3]	85	1
	Naval Gazer (IRE) (80) (DRLoder) 3-7-13[3] DRMcCabe(4) (lw: sn prom: outpcd over 2f out: kpt on fnl f)	s.h	4		11/2	85	1
	Efharisto (71) (JWhite) 7-9-8 DaleGibson(1) (hld up: lost pl over 2f out: kpt on towards fin)	1¾	5		40/1	85	3
	Tykeyvor (IRE) (77) (LadyHerries) 6-9-8 GDuffield(5) (b.hind: chsd ldrs tl rdn & btn 2f out)	1½	6		12/1	82	3
	Sadler's Walk (80) (GWragg) 5-9-8 MHills(7) (hld up: hdwy over 3f out: rdn over 1f out: fnd nil)	7	7		7/4 [1]	71	1
					(SP 117.4%)	7	

2m 16.9 (8.60) CSF £20.36 TOTE £3.80: £2.00 £2.50 (£17.00) OWNER Sheikh Mohammed (NEWMARKET) BRED John Warren WEIGHT FOR AGE 3yo-17lb

The first to run out of this race was Noble Sprinter, who finished seventh at Ascot, running to a rating 9lb lower than the one he gained at Pontefract. Within a couple of days, Efharisto had run 11lb below his Pontefract rating in a race at Hamilton for which we had him top-rated. The ratings of the beaten horses and their next performance rating are shown below. The winner won easily and is therefore disregarded:-

94

	Pontefract Rating	Next Time Out
Noble Sprinter	90	81
Ladykirk	85	82
Naval Gazer	85	74
Efharisto	85	74
Tykeyvor	82	84
Sadler's Walk	71	33

It can be seen from this that the race is clearly over-rated, as all but Tykeyvor ran significantly worse next time out. I ended up dropping the race by 7lb.

CHAPTER 10

TIME HANDICAPPING

Despite the occasional mention of time handicapping in earlier chapters, this is not a book on the subject. What I have tried to do in the following pages is offer an insight into how time figures might be compiled without too much complicated mathematics. It should be said at the outset that the method featured here has some of the strengths of the method currently employed by *Raceform*'s "Split Second" program, but it will not produce the same results.

A well-respected official Handicapper was asked in my presence what account he took of race times in compiling his handicap. He replied "virtually none", as I recall. The value of time is not fully appreciated even in the highest handicapping circles and, as such, is a considerable weapon when trying to make winner-finding profitable.

Are our official Handicappers right to ignore race times if that is what they really do? Of course they aren't, for a falsely-run race will not only provide false distances between competitors, but may also produce a misleading finishing order for one of many reasons. The most obvious of these are that an enterprising rider can steal a race by kicking on at a critical stage and that some horses can only produce their best in truly-run contests. Some may pull too hard given a slow early pace and, for others, a normally decisive turn of speed may be nullified if the whole field is quickening at the same time.

My favourite adage for this is to tell friends that I can finish within 10 yards of Seb Coe over a mile, providing that the race is run in around eight minutes. Even so, this does not make me favourite if, on our next meeting, the Right Honourable Seb gives me 11 yards start. As with humans, so it is with horses.

Still, an awful lot of falsely-run races seem to be won by the correct horse (i.e. best at the weights). However, the finishing positions, even when correct, will give little guide to the relative merits of the participants. The edge the time Handicapper has is that punters and Bookmakers alike treat pure time ratings as just a novelty but, accurately calculated, they do have a habit of producing very good results, sometimes even in these falsely-run races.

The average punter ignores race times and, given the choice between a previous impressive winner and one who has won in a particularly fast time, they invariably support the impressive one. They are probably right more often than not, but the edge is that the weight of their money can see the fast-time horse go off at an unrealistically long price. The betting market is created by supply and demand and, whilst there are legions of punters following eyecatching performers and solid form choices, the number of punters who think time has a part to play in betting on British racing are relatively few. I have often heard normally sane, good judges saying that the nature of British racing is not suited to time figures. What they presumably mean by this, is that the participants do not always seem to set off at full stretch, as in the USA.

Having accepted the principle of handicapping by time, we have to set about establishing a method for calculating time ratings. Let us start with a few basics. *Race A* at a particular meeting is over 5 furlongs and is won in a time of one minute exactly by *Horse A*. At the same meeting *Race B*, also over five furlongs, is won by *Horse B*. Both horses carried the same weight and completed the course in a level minute. Are these performances of equal merit? Provided conditions at the track have not changed in the interim, then the answer is yes, according to a proper time handicap.

At the same meeting, *Race C*, over ten furlongs, is won by *Horse C*, again carrying the same weight, recording a winning time of two minutes and 5 seconds. Is *Horse C* automatically worse than *Horses A* and *B*, after all he did take more than twice as long to cover twice the distance? Let's go back to Seb Coe. When he held the World Records for the 800 metres and the 1500 metres, the 800 metre record was not precisely eight-fifteenths of the 1500 metre record. The further you travel, the more your average speed over the distance drops.

A time Handicapper can not just use all the races over one distance on any one day. If he does, his figures will be incomplete. Indeed, he will be lucky to be able to compare more than two races at any meeting. For this reason, it is necessary to establish a norm for the times at various distances to be judged by. These are referred to as standard times in this country, but as par times in the USA.

Now let us consider another meeting, where the five furlong race was won in a level minute by another horse carrying the same weight as A and B. Is this a performance of equal merit? Possibly, but probably not. The conditions at the other course may differ in some way. The ground may be different, the wind direction may be different, the first course might be mostly uphill on the five-furlong track and the second may be largely downhill. Even the length of the grass might have an effect.

What is a Standard Time?

A standard time is an achievable time for any particular distance at any particular course. Lists of standards are calculated and published not only by *Raceform*, but also by the trade papers. A good set of standard times is essential when calculating time ratings, as even a good method will be severely hindered by a set of dodgy standards. The 'standards' I compile for *Raceform* are set for the Flat as the time a horse rated 140 would achieve, carrying 10st on perfect ground (i.e. good).

The generally-accepted rule for standard times in this country is that each course has one for each distance used. It has been suggested that differing standards should be set for each course and distance to allow for the immaturity of the competitors. Were that the case, the standard times for the Ascot five furlong course would probably look something like this:-

Two-year-olds	April	62.3 seconds
	May	62.0 seconds
	June	61.8 seconds
	July	61.6 seconds
	August	61.3 seconds
	September	61.1 seconds
	October	61.0 seconds
Three-year-olds	April	60.6 seconds
	May	60.4 seconds
	June	60.3 seconds
	July	60.2 seconds
	August	60.1 seconds

| September | 60.1 seconds | |
| October | 60.0 seconds | and for rest of career |

Such times would assume improvement in the horses as they mature, just as the weight-for-age table does. Is this valid thinking with regard to times? In my view it is not. The advantage of a time handicap is that you can expect a horse to reproduce what it has done before and no more. Start assuming improvement and you are on dodgy ground. Another problem such a set of standard times would produce would be, how to deal with races between differing age groups? Would you use a different standard time for a three-year-old and upwards handicap, depending on whether it was won by a three-year-old or an older horse?

Calculating standard times is a complex and lengthy task. All but the most dedicated and informed speed figure compiler would be well advised to adopt one of the published sets and stick with them.

What is a Going Allowance?

A going allowance is calculated by the time Handicapper and applied to the races at a given meeting, to ensure that the level of speed ratings remains constant, although the state of the ground and therefore the times recorded, will vary day by day. Traditionally, these have been shown as seconds per furlongs or fractions thereof. Each day will be given a separate going allowance, which can even be split during a day's racing if conditions are known to have changed during the programme.

The ideal situation would be a going allowance of zero, shown as *nil sec per fur* in *the Form Book*, on any windless day when the Clerk of the Course accurately describes the ground as good.

The greater the going allowance, the slower the conditions and vice versa. A going allowance of *1.00 sec per fur* will signify very slow, probably heavy ground, whereas anything below *minus 0.50 sec per fur* will mean a firm or hard surface.

Should Time Ratings include weight-for-age?

Opinions vary, but my view is definitely not. Whereas it is almost universally accepted that collateral form handicap ratings, whether they be official or private, should include weight-for-age to enable the comparison of the generations, I take the view that the time rating is something rather different. It is a numeric expression of how fast a horse has proven it can run. As such, weight-for-age would make an unholy mess of the whole thing, assuming improvement in a horse's performance without it visiting the track, in a similar fashion to that implied by changing standard or par times discussed earlier. Some time rating compilers disagree but, although it makes comparison of time ratings with collateral form ratings more complicated, it is my contention that the weight-for-age table has no place in speed figures.

Is there one general Speed Figure Formula?

Each set of speed figures on the market is calculated to a formula, but the formulae differ. Sorting good formulae from bad is no easy task, but there are a few things I would look for. Avoid formulae with sudden breaks in pounds per length, like five and six furlongs, 4lb per length, seven and eight furlongs, 3lb per length, and so on. The formula could produce terrific ratings for the winners, only to muddle the whole thing by applying an exact number of pounds per length. Two horses carrying the same weight and completing the same course in the same time, on the same day (given no change in the ground during the afternoon) should, in theory, get the same time rating, regardless of whether they have won by two lengths or been beaten by twenty.

Is it necessary to concentrate on courses with electronic timing?

In a word, no. At most courses representatives of *Raceform* and the *Sporting Life* will take separate hand-times. Any serious discrepancy and, in these days of close-circuit television, the replay will probably be timed. A bigger problem for the time Handicapper is the moving of the running rails to preserve ground. I've even heard of one course where the stalls were moved back a few yards each race when using the 'same' start, to avoid chewing up the ground. I have no axe to grind with any of this. It is the responsibility of the Clerk of the Course and his staff to provide the best and safest racing conditions for the participants. This has to be their number one priority. However, it should be compulsory to advertise intended race distances before races are staged and announce EXACT race distances immediately after the race has been run. For those of us who compile speed figures, the information would be vital and would allow us to adjust our standard times to allow for the precise distance covered. However, the area of record times would be greyed by such a move.

Do we need sectional timing?

Only the unwise punter will ever turn down additional information. However, the paragraph above will hint at some of the difficulties we are likely to encounter when sectional times are eventually introduced, as I am sure they will be at some point. The problem is that every track in this country differs. Take for example one that is uphill, then downhill, then uphill again. Sectional times taken in isolation would suggest that the field, in a truly-run race at such a course, had run particularly quickly in the middle third of the race without this being the case.

The only way sectional times can be made useful is if a standard time is calculated for each section at each course. This sounds like an herculean task, particularly when you consider that the first furlong of a race is always slow, given that the participants begin from a standing start, and that a twelve-second last furlong is easier for a five-furlong sprinter than it would be for a two miler.

At the time of writing, Newmarket is about to begin returning sectional times. It will be interesting to see how quickly and accurately we can all begin to interpret the data.

The Logic behind my quick method for calculating Speed Figures

This was a method I devised some time ago, and one that I no longer use. The reason for its inclusion here is to demonstrate some of the key aspects of time ratings without letting the mathematics become too complicated.

The descriptions of most speed figure methods are unnecessarily complicated. A normal method is to multiply the going allowance by the number of furlongs in the race and add this to the comparison to standard for the race. For instance, the standard time for the six-furlong course at Pontefract is 1m 14.3. On 23rd April, 1996, Smart Guest completed the course in 1m 19.5. He is therefore considered to have completed the distance in 5.2 seconds outside the standard. Let us assume a going allowance of 0.2 of a second per furlong. This is what most explanations now offer. 0.2 multiplied by the six furlongs of the race gives 1.2 seconds, so this race should theoretically have been run outside the standard time by the *'standard horse'*. As the race was 5.2 outside the standard time, and not 1.2 seconds, a shortfall of 4 seconds emerges. This four seconds is turned into a number of pounds by the formula. Here we run into the problem of sudden breaks again. At five and six furlongs, a second may be considered to be worth 15lb, but at seven and eight furlongs, say 12lb. All this hard work can be undone by these assumptions. Such speed figure compilers also jump between whole pounds per length, and so a few yards difference in the race distance can make stones of difference to ratings of horses beaten 30 lengths There has to be a way of making the maths easy enough to do on a calculator, without falling prey to these artificial breaks in our formula. There is, and this is it.

The quick and easy Speed Figure Method

The key to making the maths easy is that there has to be a number of furlongs where 1lb is equal to one second. In a five furlong race, the number of lengths that can be completed in a second is regarded as being between five and six, dependant upon which publication you read. The number of pounds each of those lengths is worth varies between three and four, again depending on the source.

It follows, therefore, that the number of furlongs in the race where a pound will be the equivalent of a second, will lay somewhere between the low and high ends of the figures quoted.

The low end is 5 x 3 x 5 = 75 furlongs, the high end 5 x 4 x 6 = 120 furlongs. My quick and easy method assumes the figure to be 100. The computer program used for *Raceform's* "Split Second" ratings does not work in this manner, but it produces figures which would equate to a figure in the 80s or 90s.

At this point, the maths fall into place. By multiplying the amount a race is above or below standard by 100 and dividing the result by the number of furlongs in the race, we quickly arrive at a number of pounds the race can be considered to be fast or slow. As an example, I will use 2000 Guineas day 1996 at Newmarket. Below are listed the winners of each race, together with the race distance and the comparison to standard of the winner's time. Comparisons to standard are generally shown next to the actual race time, for instance (a1.2) means the winner has completed the course in 1.2 seconds outside or above the standard. However, (b1.2) means that the winner has run 1.2 seconds inside or below the standard. In some publications, notably *the Form Book*, the 'a' is omitted and the 'b' replaced by a minus sign.

Newmarket 4th May 1996

Dushyantor	12 furlongs	(a9.36)
Abou Zouz	5 furlongs	(a1.67)
Ball Gown	10 furlongs	(a1.37)
Mark of Esteem	8 furlongs	(a0.29)
Cool Jazz	5 furlongs	(a1.00)
Jayannpee	6 furlongs	(a1.03)
Florid	10 furlongs	(a1.30)

To establish the number of pounds slower than the theoretical standard each race is, multiply the seconds outside the standard by 100 and divide by the number of furlongs in the race giving the following:-

Dushyantor	78 slow	(i.e. 9.36 x 100 = 936 divided by 12, there being twelve furlongs in the race)
Abou Zouz	33 slow	
Ball Gown	14 slow	
Mark of Esteem	4 slow	
Cool Jazz	20 slow	
Jayannpee	17 slow	
Florid	13 slow	

The Going Allowance

All we have done so far is calculate the number of pounds each race is outside the standard, but the going allowance is the most important part of any speed figure formula. For this 'quick and easy' method, I suggest you only use the handicaps to establish the going allowance. The two handicaps on this day were the races won by Ball Gown and Jayannpee.

Ball Gown carried 8st 7lb, including the jockeys' allowance, and ran off an official handicap mark of 84, a figure which includes no element of weight-for-age. Some time ratings understandably leave out jockeys' claims, but my method allows assessment of a race before the jockeys are known.

Looking for the easiest method possible, convert all the winners' ratings to 10st. In other words, what would be the official handicap rating a fully mature horse would need to have in order to dead-heat with Ball Gown under 10st. In this case the rating would be 105 (84 + 21, for the 21lb that 8st 7lb is below 10st).

For Jayannpee, the figure is 93, given that he is a fully mature horse, carrying a weight of 9st 11lb off an official handicap mark of 90.

By subtracting their weight-adjusted official handicap marks from 140 and then subtracting the result from the actual pounds slow, these two horses now suggest a possible going allowances as follows:-

Ball Gown	140 - 105 = 35	14 slow - 35 = 21 fast

The implication here is that the Ball Gown race was a 35lb worse (slower) race than our ideal. It was only 14lb slower than the standard time, therefore the meeting must have been run on ground 21lb fast for this to have been truly-run.

Jayannpee	140 - 93 = 47	17 slow - 47 = 30 fast

(N.B. By using 140 here, we are effectively assuming that a horse officially rated 140 could achieve the standard time on good ground carrying 10st. Most speed figures are much less stringent, taking a figure of 100. If you want to make your figures their equivalent, use 100 rather than 140 in the formula above and then carry on as normal. For jump races the figure would be 135. Such a move will not alter the ratings, but will change the going allowance by 0.40 of a second per furlong, or 40lb).

Always take the most severe going allowance. The biggest minus figure is the most severe, but if no minus figures have been generated, then use the smallest plus figure. Through the race won by Jayannpee, the going allowance for this meeting would be minus 0.30 seconds per furlong, or 30lb fast if you prefer, as this is more severe than Ball Gown's race. Applying this going allowance to the pounds slow for each winner, we get the following:-

Dushyantor	78 + 30	= 108 slow
Abou Zouz	33 + 30	= 63 slow
Ball Gown	14 + 30	= 43 slow
Mark of Esteem	4 + 30	= 34 slow
Cool Jazz	20 + 30	= 50 slow
Jayannpee	17 + 30	= 47 slow
Florid	13 + 30	= 43 slow

By subtracting the figures above from 140 (175 for jump racing), we will get the speed figure for the winner, assuming that each winner has carried 10st (12st 7lb for jumps).
This gives us:-

Dushyantor	32
Abou Zouz	77
Ball Gown	97
Mark of Esteem	106
Cool Jazz	90
Jayannpee	93
Florid	97

The final process for producing weight-for-age-free speed figures is to deduct one point for each pound carried below 10st, or indeed add one point for each pound carried above 10st (as always, 12st 7lb for Jumps). In this case this gives:-

Dushyantor	carried 9st, therefore speed figure is 32 - 14 = 18
Abou Zouz	carried 9st, therefore speed figure is 77 - 14 = 63
Ball Gown	carried 8st 7lb, therefore speed figure 97 - 21 = 76
Mark of Esteem	carried 9st, therefore speed figure is 106 - 14 = 92
Cool Jazz	carried 9st 1lb, therefore speed figure is 90 - 13 = 77
Jayannpee	carried 9st 11lb, therefore speed figure is 93 - 3 = 90
Florid	carried 8st 10lb, therefore speed figure is 97 -18 = 79

Despite the fact that they are not produced using the same formula, some similarities to the "Split Second" ratings can soon be spotted. In this case, the "Split Second" figures were:-

Dushyantor	19
Abou Zouz	51
Ball Gown	62
Mark of Esteem	77
Cool Jazz	63

Jayannpee	76
Florid	66

This represents differences from our calculated figures of 1, 12, 14, 15, 14, 14 and 13lb respectively. A pretty consistent difference with the exception of Dushyantor's very slowly-run race.

Those people who require speed figures which include weight-for-age will need to refer to a weight-for-age table for each horse. Of the winners shown here, Dushyantor, Abou Zouz and Mark of Esteem all get weight-for-age in the official table that I use. The allowances are, in Dushyantor's case, 19, for Abou Zouz 38, and for Mark of Esteem 13. These figures should be added to the horses' speed figures, making Dushyantor 37, Abou Zouz 101 and Mark of Esteem 105. If you keep your speed figures with weight-for-age included, you have to remember to deduct it when assessing any race between horses of more than one age group.

For a second example, take the meeting at York on 16th May, 1996. The winners, the race distances and comparisons to standard were:-

Dr Massini	10.4 furlongs	(b0.31)
Missile	7.9 furlongs	(a1.69)
Polish Spring	7 furlongs	(a2.91)
Classic Cliche	13.9 furlongs	(b3.43)
Venture Capitalist	6 furlongs	(a0.72)
Belgravia	6 furlongs	(a2.86)
Key to My Heart	10.4 furlongs	(a0.93)

In the interests of time saving I take the race distance to one decimal point rather than any further and the above generates :-

Dr Massini	3 fast
Missile	21 slow
Polish Spring	42 slow
Classic Cliche	25 fast
Venture Capitalist	12 slow
Belgravia	48 slow
Key to My Heart	9 slow

Now establish the class of the handicaps. Missile ran off 78, carried 8st 7lb and was 12lb below full maturity from the weight-for-age table:-

Class of race is   78 + 21 - 12 = 87

Polish Spring ran off 85, carried 8st 6lb and was 11lb below full maturity:-

Class of race is   85 + 22 - 11 = 96

Key to My Heart ran off 102, carried 9st 5lb and was fully mature:-

Class of race is   102 + 9 = 111

As before, subtract these from 140 and then take the result from the number of pounds that each race was slow:-

Missile	140 - 87 = 53	21 slow - 53 = 32 fast
Polish Spring	140 - 96 = 44	42 slow - 44 = 2 fast
Key to My Heart	140 - 111 = 29	9 slow - 29 = 20 fast

This gives a going allowance of 32 fast or minus 0.32 seconds per furlong and thereby gives adjusted race speeds of:-

Dr Massini	-3 + 32 = 29 slow
Missile	21 + 32 = 53 slow
Polish Spring	42 + 32 = 74 slow
Classic Cliche	-25 + 32 = 7 slow
Venture Capitalist	12 + 32 = 44 slow
Belgravia	48 + 32 = 80 slow
Key to My Heart	9 + 32 = 41 slow

The Speed Figures for the winners assuming a weight of 10st would be:-

Dr Massini	111
Missile	87
Polish Spring	66
Classic Cliche	133
Venture Capitalist	96
Belgravia	60
Key to My Heart	99

Finally allowing for the weights carried:-

Dr Massini	carried 8st 12lb, therefore speed figure is 111 - 16 = 95
Missile	carried 8st 7lb, therefore speed figure is 87 - 21 = 66
Polish Spring	carried 8st 6lb, therefore speed figure is 66 -22 = 44
Classic Cliche	carried 9st, therefore speed figure is 133 - 14 = 119
Venture Capitalist	carried 9st, therefore speed figure is 96 - 14 = 82
Belgravia	carried 9st, therefore speed figure is 60 -14 = 46
Key to My Heart	carried 9st 5lb, therefore speed figure is 99 - 9 = 90

For those adjusting their speed figures for weight-for-age, the additions for Dr Massini, Missile, Polish Spring and Belgravia are 14, 12, 11 and 41 respectively. These produce speed figures of 109 for Dr Massini, 78 for Missile, 55 for Polish Spring and 87 for Belgravia.

We may only have figures for two meetings, but already we have learnt plenty. Mark of Esteem is a modest Guineas winner on the clock, coming out a stone below Classic Cliche's Group Two win, even after allowing weight-for-age. The races won by Dushyantor and Polish Spring were slowly-run and the form may be false. Most interesting of all, Abou Zouz and Belgravia are once-raced and unbeaten, but as a speed figure compiler we now have a view as to which is the better. In August, Abou Zouz franked our view by taking the Group Two Gimcrack Stakes, Belgravia failing to win again as a two-year-old.

To demonstrate that the method works equally well for jump racing, let us look at Cheltenham Gold Cup day, 14th March, 1996. The winners, the race distances and comparisons to standard were :-

Paddy's Return	17 furlongs	(a4.40)
Cyborgo	24.5 furlongs	(a5.30)
Imperial Call	26.5 furlongs	(a9.50)
Elegant Lord	26.5 furlongs	(a18.00)
Kibreet	16.5 furlongs	(a4.10)
Challenger du Luc	21 furlongs	(a6.70)
Star Rage	17 furlongs	(a3.80)

The above generates:-

Paddy's Return	26 slow
Cyborgo	22 slow
Imperial Call	36 slow
Elegant Lord	68 slow
Kibreet	25 slow
Challenger du Luc	32 slow
Star Rage	22 slow

Now establish the class of the handicaps.

Kibreet ran off 138, carried 10st 12lb and was fully mature. Remembering to adjust the weights to 12st 7lb and not 10st as for Flat racing:-

Class of race is   138 + 23 = 161

Star Rage ran off 117, carried 10st and was fully mature.

The class of this race is 117 + 35 = 152

For jump racing subtract these from 175, not 140 and then take the result from the number of pounds each race was slow:-

Kibreet	175 - 161 = 14	25 slow - 14 = 11 slow
Star Rage	175 - 152 = 23	22 slow - 23 = 1 fast

Giving a going allowance of 1 fast or minus 0.01 seconds per furlong and thereby adjusted race speeds of:-

Paddy's Return	26 + 1 = 27 slow
Cyborgo	22 + 1 = 23 slow
Imperial Call	36 + 1 = 37 slow
Elegant Lord	68 + 1 = 69 slow
Kibreet	25 + 1 = 26 slow
Challenger du Luc	32 + 1 = 33 slow
Star Rage	22 + 1 = 23 slow

The speed figures for the winners assuming a weight of 12st 7lb would be:-

Paddy's Return	148
Cyborgo	152
Imperial Call	138
Elegant Lord	106
Kibreet	149
Challenger du Luc	142
Star Rage	152

Finally allowing for the weights carried:-

Paddy's Return	carried 11st, therefore speed figure is 148 -21 = 127
Cyborgo	carried 11st 10lb, therefore speed figure is 152 -11 = 141
Imperial Call	carried 12st, therefore speed figure is 138 - 7 = 131
Elegant Lord	carried 12st, therefore speed figure is 106 - 7 = 99
Kibreet	carried 10st 12lb, therefore speed figure is 149 -23 = 126
Challenger du Luc	carried 11st 3lb, therefore speed figure is 142 - 18 = 124
Star Rage	carried 10st, therefore speed figure is 152 - 35 = 117

For those adjusting their speed figures for weight-for-age, the only addition required is for Paddy's Return, who was still set to receive 8lb weight-for-age and this would give him a speed figure of 135.

This method may seem neither quick nor easy at first, but just follow it through in a publication such as *Raceform Update, Form Book* or any of the racing papers, something that gives you not only a comparison to standard against the race time but also the official handicap marks of the winner. Try doing your own ratings for a meeting or two and you will quickly get the hang of it. You may well decide that using the fastest-run handicap is an inadequate way of determining the going allowance. Use your initiative and come up with something better. Could you use your old time ratings to rate the races at the meeting first and then use the fastest-run one?

Once you get going, the next logical step is to start trying to adjust the official marks of the winners before calculating the going allowance. In my experience, the average rise in weights that the winner gets from the official Handicapper is between 5 and 6lb, so allow a little more for a clear win and a little less for a close-run thing. However, do remember that a three-length win in a sprint is worth very much more than a three-length win in a staying event. Under the method detailed above, no handicap race winners can get a speed figure of more than their handicap mark, regardless of how fast they ran or by how far they won.

We have not covered the vexed question of split going allowances. A strong tail-wind can make the straight course times faster than the round course times for example. Other reasons for splitting going allowances are the differences between hurdle and chase courses at some tracks. Hurdle races are often run on the Flat course and, if there has been a lot of watering done during the summer months, this can have a marked effect, even months later. Another thing to consider is that bad weather during a meeting will almost certainly slow the times progressively through the day, as will very poor ground conditions, where the underfoot surface becomes more and more chewed up as the meeting goes on.

I hope this chapter has given you food for thought. Remember this, a slow time doesn't necessarily mean the horse has no ability (as in Dushyantor's case in our first example), it often means a slowly or falsely-run race. However, a fast time can only mislead if conditions change at the course during the meeting.

CHAPTER 11

BETTING

Andy Beyer once wrote that, to win betting horses, a handicapper should split his time 50-50 between handicapping and wagering.

The vast majority of my time is taken up with my handicapping duties (it is my job after all) and therefore my approach to betting is haphazard, at best. That, frankly, is my problem, it need not be yours.

Monday always seems to be a cracking day for betting because there is always plenty of uncompetitive racing. With cards often at the likes of Windsor and Hamilton, where an enormous draw bias can exist, betting looks easy. Unfortunately, Monday is the busiest day of the week for me. Because of my work commitments, i.e. the re-assessing of horses who ran the previous weekend, I rarely bet.

As a rule, gambling on Saturdays is not recommended. Quite simply, there is too much racing and the top races are often handicaps. The top handicaps are normally staged at the fairer tracks like Newmarket where the bias, even when it exists, is often hard to call in advance. I can normally be found racereading somewhere on a Saturday afternoon, therefore my time for prior research is very limited. All too often, however, Saturday is my heaviest betting day of the week.

Before I leave you with the impression that I am totally stupid when it comes to gambling, I do get some things right. I religiously keep a record of all bets I strike on horseracing and, for all my faults, finish in front at the end of the year as often as not. One fault of most people who gamble is that they only remember the winners. It really does pay to keep a record of all your bets, so you can see your weak points and correct them, but just as importantly exploit your strengths.

This was never intended to be a book on betting, but in the following few paragraphs I pass on a few ideas that have come to my attention over the years. That doesn't make all of them right of course, but I believe they are worthy of consideration.

I will start with one that is fact, however. I have never backed a horse in my life, but then again neither has anybody else. Virtually everyone labours under the misconception that they back horses. They do not.

A few years back I punted a horse in the Liverpool Foxhunters' who had twice run prominently for a long way in the Grand National, figuring that the experience gained of the big fences might see him forget his age and bring him back to his best.

My selection made most of the running, jumping superbly, and passed the post half a dozen lengths to the good. However, I did not get paid out, my bet being a loser. The unknown amateur rider on my selection plunged down my steed's neck at most of the early fences in a manner resembling a sack of Maris Pipers! He had succumbed to the inevitable forces of gravity before Becher's had been reached.

Understandably I was furious, but not with the pilot, with myself. Anyone who is prepared to take on the Aintree fences possessing so little in the way of riding skills commands my sincere respect. As a truly-moderate horseman myself, riding in even the local point-to-point would strike me as reckless in the extreme.

The reason for my recounting this tale is to make my point, which is that we punters do not back horses, we back horse/jockey combinations.

I have lost count of the number of times I have been at the races or in a betting shop and heard a punter halfway through a race exclaim 'who is that idiot riding so and so?'. The pilot's name varies, but among the hecklers is invariably one idiot that has backed the combination. People spend hours studying form and compiling ratings but the lesson that most need to learn is that form can be barely half the story.

I could cite numerous cases, but will only bother with a typical one. Let me take you back to 4th January 1995 and the Beech Handicap, run on the Fibresand at Wolverhampton. Two normally excellent judges in Cornelius Lysaght on Radio 5 and Frank Carter, in his guise as Augur in the Sporting Life, have given the Mark Johnston-trained Milngavie as the best bet of the day. At first glance their research seems very sound, his five runs at Wolverhampton in 1994 having yielded three wins and two seconds, with his last win coming off the same handicap mark from which he runs here. The problem is that, in the spring of 1994, the Johnston horses were being ridden with amazing success by the brilliant Jason Weaver, and today Milngavie will be partnered by Tyrone Williams. Now I have nothing against Williams as he is undoubtedly a decent pilot, but Jason Weaver he ain't.. Milngavie started a 3/1 favourite, shorter than was forecast in either trade paper, and finished a distant fifth.

Such logic might suggest that amateur and apprentice races should be avoided like the plague. This is not so. A horse with a sound form chance and an established jockey in that sphere becomes a very attractive betting proposition. My version of the old Sherlock Holmes edict of "eliminate the impossible and whatever is left will come to pass" comes in useful. All top jockeys must have ridden their first winner somewhere but that does not mean you should rush in to support a pilot who has never ridden a winner. By all means back horses ridden by apprentice, conditional or amateur riders, but only those ridden by jockeys you have noted as decent pilots.

Backing a horse to win the Grand National is a single bet. Add to this bet a selection to win the Derby and you now have two unrelated events, which you can combine in one bet, called a double. Let me explain what I mean. If two events are unrelated they are termed mutually exclusive and can be doubled. If events are not mutually exclusive, they can not be combined in multiple bets. The reasons for this are pretty obvious. For instance, wouldn't we all like to be able to back Tottenham to win 1-0, with Tottenham to lead at half-time and full-time, combined with Teddy Sheringham to score the first goal of the game, and with Teddy Sheringham to score the last goal of the game in a four-timer at full accumulated odds. Unfortunately, this is Planet Earth and not Heaven, so the Bookmakers prevent such bets, or at least they think they do.

Always be wary of tips, but never ignore them completely. Remember, if the message on a horse comes complete with the "It beat 'horse A' by five lengths in a gallop last week" suffix, check your handicap to see if 'horse A' would win this race with a five-length start. If not, you may well have found one to oppose because, if you are like me, by the time 'inside information' reaches my ears, most of the racecourse knows about it!

One point brought to my attention by Press Room colleague Tony Elves is that, as a Newmarket work-watcher, he much prefers a horse that he has 'spotted' to be running early on the card, his theory being that information circulates at the racecourse during the meeting. He is therefore happy with the common situation of having maidens at the top of the card.

If your opinion seems to differ from the norm, analyse the way your punting colleagues have reached their conclusions. If you are still entirely satisfied with your selection and the price is advantageous, increase your bet.

This ought to be obvious, but so many punters do precisely the reverse. If the horse you fancy is a 4/1 chance in your opinion but is available at only 7/2, then don't have a bet (remember it's not compulsory). If your selection is available at 5/1, have a modest bet, but if it is available at 33/1 then have a big bet.

Form your own judgements about which bets and which types of races work for you. Many people will tell you that the Grand National is a complete lottery, but on numerous occasions (courtesy of old Sherlock Holmes), it has proved to be one of my most profitable races of the entire year. For instance, the year of Ben Nevis's win, my five wagers on the race included all four finishers (before the day I discovered tricasts), an omission I put right in 1994 thanks to Miinnehoma, Just So and Moorcroft Boy. Indeed, only Ebony Jane cost me a payout from a Vernons Pools competition to name the first four in the race (an entry prompted by the insistence of my father-in-law who was staying with us at the time). I had included Mrs Henderson and Fiddlers Pike in my entry, hoping the soft ground would prevent more than four from completing the course. I was pretty confident in my own mind that the partnership would complete the course, although I wasn't quite expecting the marvellous showing they made on the first half of the second circuit.

This is one I often struggle with, but try to think positively. Most punters seem to believe they are cursed with terrible misfortune but, in the words of that great golfer Gary Player, I think, "the harder I practise, the luckier I get". Provided your energies are well channelled, this is as true in punting as in any other walk of life and, as a consequence, many successful gamblers are loners with few other interests in life. One betting shop punter I know backs horses with plenty of seconds and thirds in their form figures (last six races) but no wins. His ideal punt would appear to be a horse that has finished second on its last six outings. He, no doubt, considers himself an unlucky punter as most of his wagers run well but rarely win. I consider his problems self-inflicted. This may sound harsh, but the truth often hurts.

Information that is in everyone's possession is effectively worthless, and you will only profit from exploiting some angle or fact that is not general knowledge. By doing our own handicap, you will uncover patterns in a horse's behaviour that others may have missed. Don't be put off something just because the 'people in the know' say it can't win. After all, they are only human and can make mistakes like the rest of us.

Last and by no means least, betting is not just about working out what will win, but about working out what will not. Some of the best ways of winning revolve around establishing what will lose. It is in this area that your handicap ratings can be put to good use.

0300 STEWARDS TRIAL H'CAP (0-100) (3-Y.O+) (CLASS C) 5f 16y

RHR	HORSE,AGE,WEIGHT	LAST THREE OUTINGS		
106	Ansellman (6-8-6)	64	88	106
104	Bowden Rose (4-9-1)	—	78	104
104	Wavian (4-9-12)	104	84	97
103	Mr Bergerac (IRE) (5-8-13)	84	91	106
102	Jucea (7-8-4)	89	102	99
101	Sir Joey (USA) (7-9-4)	101	98	58
96	Crofters Ceilidh (4-9-2)	90	96	91

Supported on the back of a good fifth in the Wokingham at Royal Ascot, Sir Joey is a horse that does not win often and he is well worth opposing at a short price.

2341-CHEPSTOW (L-H) (Good to firm)
Tuesday July 2nd
WEATHER: overcast WIND: slt across

2381 STEWARDS TRIAL H'CAP (0-100) (3-Y.O+) (Class C)
3-00 (3-01) 5f 16y £5,215.00 (£1,570.00: £760.00: £355.00) Stalls: High GOING minus 0.41 sec per fur (F)

			SP	RR
1473⁸ **Ansellman (75)** (JBerry) 6-8-6v¹ GCarter(3) (chsd ldr: rdn over 1f out: led ins fnl f: r.o wl) ....—	1		10/1	83
2232⁴ **Bowden Rose (84)** (MBlanshard) 4-9-1b JQuinn(2) (lw: led tl rdn & hdd ins fnl f) ....¾	2		9/2²	90
2114⁵ **Sir Joey (USA) (87)** (PGMurphy) 7-9-1⁽³⁾ SDrowne(5) (hld up: hdwy 2f out: hrd rdn 1f out: r.o one pce) ....nk	3		6/4¹	92
1974⁷ **Crofters Ceilidh (85)** (BAMcMahon) 4-9-2 SSanders(1) (a.p: one pce fnl 2f) 2	4		12/1	83
2114¹⁹ **Mr Bergerac (IRE) (82)** (BPalling) 5-8-13 TSprake(4) (lw: rdn over 2f out: no hdwy) ....¾	5		10/1	78
1829⁸ **Jucea (73)** (JLSpearing) 7-8-4 PaulEddery(6) (lw: hld up & plld hrd: rdn over 2f out: no imp) ....s.h	6		7/1	69
2115¹³ **Wavian (95)** (RHannon) 4-9-9⁽³⁾ DaneO'Neill(7) (lw: hld up: bhd fnl 2f) ....¾	7		6/1³	89
			(SP 110.8%)	

57.6 secs (0.60) CSF £48.60 TOTE £14.10: £5.30 £2.60 (£21.30) OWNER Ansells of Watford (COCKERHAM) BRED W. L. Caley

Not only could we have backed the winner, but the forecast was staring us in the face. In a situation where you simply can not fancy the favourite to win, then consider its place prospects. If you feel from your findings that it is unlikely to make the frame, it can be well worth considering combination forecasts and tricasts, as long as the race can be narrowed down to a few possibilities.

RIPON- Monday 8 July

0850 KIRKGATE MAIDEN STKS (3-Y.O+) (CLASS D) 1m

RHR	HORSE,AGE,WEIGHT	LAST THREE OUTINGS		
90d	Dispol Gem (3-8-7)	41	90	70
87	King's Academy (IRE) (3-8-12)	87	87	43
83	Golden Thunderbolt (FR) (3-8-12)	83	80	74
79	Stellar Line (USA) (3-8-12)	67	79	72
74	Sicarian (4-9-7)	74	72	
73	Toulston Lady (IRE) (4-9-2)	73		
72	Road Racer (IRE) (3-8-12)	72		
69	Petarina (3-8-7)	55	69	
35	Haysong (IRE) (3-8-7)	35		
	Mustard (3-8-7)			
	Jeopardize (3-8-7)			
	Cameron Edge (3-8-7)			
—	Petit Flora (4-9-2)			

It is noticeable how often maiden races work out. First, check for any likely newcomers that might upset calculations. In the race shown, Jeopardize was sent off at 11/1, hardly a sign of stable confidence. The result would have rewarded trio and forecast players.

:075-RIPON (R-H) (Good)
Monday July 8th
WEATHER: fine WIND: almost nil

2572 KIRKGATE MAIDEN STKS (3-Y.O+) (Class D)
8-50 (8-54) 1m £3,680.00 (£1,115.00: £545.00: £260.00) Stalls: Low GOING minus 0.31 sec per fur (GF)

			SP	RR	SF
2135⁵	King's Academy (IRE) (81) (HRACecil) 3-8-12 WRyan(5) (lw: chsd ldrs: led over 1f out: styd on u.p) .... —	1	10/11 ¹	85	31
2124³	Golden Thunderbolt (FR) (78) (JHMGosden) 3-8-12 JLowe(6) (trckd ldrs: styd on u.p fnl f) .... ½	2	9/2 ³	84	30
1470⁸	Dispol Gem (72) (GROldroyd) 3-8-7 KFallon(14) (a chsng ldrs: styd on same pce fnl 2f) 1	3	9/1	77	23
746⁴	Stellar Line (USA) (84) (BWHills) 3-8-12 MHills(10) (trckd ldrs: led over 3f out tl over 1f out: sn wknd) 2½	4	4/1 ²	77	23
	Jeopardize (CEBrittain) 3-8-7 MBirch(1) (lengthy: unf: sn outpcd: styd on fnl 4f: nvr nr ldrs) 3	5	11/1	56	2
	Sicarian (MJHeaton-Ellis) 4-9-7 AProcter(7) (sn trckg ldrs: wknd over 2f out) 3	6	25/1	55	10
	Cameron Edge (ABMulholland) 3-8-7 JStack(2) (bit bkwd: b: s.s: bhd: sme hdwy 2f out: n.d) 5	7	25/1	40	—
2181⁸	Road Racer (IRE) (MrsJRRamsden) 3-8-12 MDeering(4) (bit bkwd: bhd & rn wd ent st: n.d) 1	8	25/1	43	—
2515³	Toulston Lady (IRE) (MJCamacho) 4-9-2 DaleGibson(3) (unruly in stalls: bhd fnl 5f) .... ½	9	33/1	37	—
2432¹²	Haysong (IRE) (JPLeigh) 3-8-7 ACulhane(12) (chsd ldrs: sn drvn along: lost pl over 3f out) 1½	10	50/1	34	—
1787⁵	Petarina (MissJFCraze) 3-8-7 NConnorton(13) (led tl over 3f out: wknd qckly over 2f out) 5	11	50/1	24	—
2515⁶	Petit Flora (GHolmes) 4-9-2 JFanning(9) (b.hind: dwlt: a in rr) .... hd	12	50/1	24	—
2079⁷	Mustard (ABMulholland) 3-8-7 TWilliams(8) (hld up & plld hrd: a bhd: virtually p.u 2f out) .... dist	13	50/1	—	—
			(SP 129.3%)	13 Rn	

1m 41.7 (4.00) CSF £6.15 TOTE £2.20: £2.20 £1.30 £1.70 (£3.60) Trio £15.50 OWNER Mr Michael Poland (NEWMARKET) BRED Michael Poland
WEIGHT FOR AGE 3yo-9lb

Some times your ratings will make picking between two horses difficult as they both appear to be clear of the rest. The bet to consider is a dual forecast or reversed straight forecasts, if you are confident about your assessments.

CHEPSTOW- Thursday 11 July

0800 REGAL H'CAP (0-95) (3-Y.O) (CLASS C) 1m 4f 23y

RHR	HORSE,AGE,WEIGHT	LAST THREE OUTINGS		
107	Spillo (3-9-3)	100	101	107
106	Nador (3-9-7)	102	106	97
103	Gumair (USA) (3-8-3)	103	76	95
101	Forza Figlio (3-9-3)	99	93	78
94	Prince Kinsky (3-8-7)	94	88	87

Getting this race down to the two favourites looks easy, picking between them doesn't.

525-CHEPSTOW (L-H) (Good to firm, Firm patches)
Thursday July 11th
WEATHER: fine WIND: almost nil

2616 REGAL RATED STKS H'CAP (0-95) (3-Y.O) (Class C)
8-00 (8-01) 1m 4f 23y £6,915.80 (£2,086.40: £1,013.20: £476.60) Stalls: Low GOING minus 0.44 sec per fur (F)

			SP	RR	SF
2074⁵	Nador (91) (DRLoder) 3-9-7 RHughes(4) (lw: hld up & bhd: stdy hdwy on bit over 1f out: rdn to ld last stride) .... —	1	9/4 ²	100	46
2006³	Spillo (87) (LMCumani) 3-9-3 PatEddery(3) (swtg: chsd ldr: led wl over 1f out: hdd last stride) .... hd	2	2/1 ¹	96	42
1798⁶	Prince Kinsky (77) (LordHuntingdon) 3-8-7 DHarrison(5) (swtg: a.p: hrd rdn over 2f out: ev ch ins fnl f: r.o) .... nk	3	9/1	86	32
1900⁴	Gumair (USA) (77) (RHannon) 3-8-4(3) (led over 10f out: one pce fnl f) 3½	4	15/2	81	27
1619³	Forza Figlio (87) (MissGayKelleway) 3-9-3 JReid(1) (b.hind: lw: hld up: rdn over 3f out: hdwy on ins 2f out: wknd over 1f out) 3	5	3/1 ³	87	33
			(SP 110.9%)	5 Rn	

1m 36.0 (3.60) CSF £6.88 TOTE £2.60: £1.10 £1.70 (£2.60) OWNER Sheikh Mohammed (NEWMARKET) BRED Sheikh Mohammed Bin Rashid Al Maktoum
LONG HANDICAP Gumair (USA) 8-3

Have a look at the dividends. The dual forecast has paid as much as a win bet and the straight forecast more than double the win odds on either.

113

So, by not making a choice between the two, we could easily have increased our profit on the race.

When looking for selections in races, do not always assume that the top-rated is the one to back. Horses normally progress through their first few runs and a handicap like the one I have described, which is based purely on form, is unlikely to top-rate the unexposed competitor. We all know from watching racing that plenty of horses of this type win. What I can tell you is that the vast majority of these winners will not be top-rated. What is, therefore, an excellent plan, is watching for unexposed horses which look better than averagely handicapped on your figures. That is to say that, in a ten-horse race, they rate in the top four. These are the ones that get me diving for *the Form Book*. I look at their earlier races to see if the official Handicapper could have been harsher on them and, if I feel he has been lenient, I get involved.

BEVERLEY- Friday 5 July

0745 WILLIAM JACKSON'S H'CAP (0-85) (4-Y.O+) (CLASS D) 1m 100y

RHR	HORSE,AGE,WEIGHT	LAST THREE OUTINGS		
97d	Percy Braithwaite (IRE) *(4-9-10)*	86	87	82
96	Second Colours (USA) *(6-8-10)*	91	101	99
93	Clifton Fox *(4-9-11)*	91	93	88
92	Sandmoor Chambray *(5-9-9)*	92	88	84
92	Bend Wavy *(4-9-10)*	92	89	66
89	Up In Flames (IRE) *(5-9-1)*	78	80	89
89	Queens Consul (IRE) *(6-10-0)*	24	82	89
88	Intendant *(4-8-5)*	88	87	84
87	Autumn Cover *(4-8-5)*	87	83	83

A race for seasoned handicappers with one exception. Bend Wavy, who looks reasonably treated for his handicap debut, is still on the upgrade. Once you realise that his previous four starts were in June '95, October '95, May '96 and late the previous month, you might easily form the conclusion that this is the first time in his career that he has stood up to serious training for any length of time.

1858-BEVERLEY (R-H) (Good to firm)
Friday July 5th
WEATHER: overcast WIND: mod half against

2483 WILLIAM JACKSON'S H'CAP (0-85) (4-Y.O+) (Class D)
7-45 (7-45) **1m 100y** £5,824.25 (£1,754.00: £849.50: £397.25) Stalls: High GOING minus 0.59 sec per fur (F)

		SP	RR
2128³ **Bend Wavy (IRE) (80)** (LMCumani) 4-9-10 PatEddery(9) (b.off hind: sn trckng ldrs: led over 1f out: r.o)........— 1		9/4¹	88	5.
2229³² **Sandmoor Chambray (79)** (TDEasterby) 5-9-9 MBirch(3) (lw: chsd ldrs: drvn along 4f out: sn outpcd: hdwy over 1f out: styd on same pce)..1¼ 2		9/2³	85	4
2218² **Second Colours (USA) (66)** (MrsMReveley) 6-8-10 ACulhane(7) (bhd: hdwy over 1f out: styd on same pce)..¾ 3		14/1	70	3
1322² **Clifton Fox (81)** (JAGlover) 4-9-11 SDWilliams(5) (s.i.s: hdwy u.p 2f out: hung rt. styd on ins fnl f)................s.h 4		4/1²	85	4
2145⁵ **Percy Braithwaite (IRE) (80)** (MJohnston) 4-9-10 TWilliams(4) (led tl over 1f out: grad wknd)........................1¼ 5		10/1	82	4
2351⁹ **Up in Flames (IRE) (71)** (MDHammond) 5-8-12⁽³⁾ FLynch(6) (sn chsng ldrs: one pce fnl 2f)........................1½ 6		11/2	70	3
2351¹⁰ **Queens Consul (IRE) (84)** (BSRothwell) 6-10-0 MFenton(1) (chsd ldrs on outside tl wknd wl over 1f out).......4 7		25/1	75	3
1650² **Intendant (61)** (JGFitzGerald) 4-8-5 WRyan(8) (hld up: hdwy 4f out: rdn over 2f out: wknd over 1f out)........nk 8		8/1	52	1
2000* **Autumn Cover (61)** (PRHedger) 4-8-5 DBiggs(2) (w ldrs: rdn 2f out: sn wknd)..4 9		11/2	44	
		(SP 130.4%)	9

1m 44.8 (0.80) CSF £14.19 CT £116.95 TOTE £4.00: £1.50 £1.80 £2.10 (£7.50) Trio £68.60 OWNER Lord Portsmouth (NEWMARKET) BRED
D. Grenfell and R. Hesketh.

The following race makes a great case for my method of keeping separate Flat and All-Weather figures.

0245 NEWBATTLE (S) H'CAP (0-60) (3-Y.O+) (CLASS G) 1m 3f 32y

RHR	HORSE, AGE, WEIGHT	LAST THREE OUTINGS		
67	Mithraic (IRE) *(4-10-0)*	65	63	54
64	Milltown Classic (IRE) *(4-8-3)*		44	47
62	No More Hassle (IRE) *(3-7-13)*	24	50	62
62	Kristal Breeze *(4-9-3)*	62	55	60
61	Portie Sophie *(5-8-1)*	37	42	61
61	Trumped(IRE) *(4-9-1)*	56	59	61
60	Greek Gold (IRE) *(7-9-2)*	24	60	51
59	Belacqua (USA) *(3-7-5)*	34		36
57	Teejay'n'aitch (IRE) *(4-8-13)*	30	42	57
55	Crystal Warrior *(3-9-3)*	34	53	55
51	Bright Pet *(3-8-8)*	46	51	46
50	Kalko *(7-7-8)*	50	41	40
41	Cottage Prince (IRE) *(3-8-5)*	30	36	31

Top-rated Mithraic looks a pretty worthy favourite, but second-top Milltown Classic is unconsidered at 40/1. The latter's recent performance ratings do not look encouraging, but the horse unseated her apprentice pilot last time out and her previous five efforts had been on Southwell's Fibresand. Her form on Turf the previous year tells of modest but consistent efforts, with her master rating having been gained on her most recent start.

2563 NEWBATTLE (S) H'CAP (0-60) (3-Y.O+) (Class G)

2-45 (2-45) **1m 3f 32y** £2,388.00 (£668.00: £324.00) Stalls: High GOING minus 0.38 sec per fur (F)

		SP	RR	SF
2366U **Milltown Classic (IRE)** (28) (JParkes) 4-8-3 JFanning(7) (chsd ldrs: chal over 1f out: styd on to ld nr fin) ....—	**1**	40/1	35	6
2394² **Mithraic (IRE)** (53) (WSCunningham) 4-10-0 ACulhane(3) (lw: led: hung lft fnl 2f: jst ct) ....hd	**2**	4/1 ¹	60	31
2175⁷ **Trumped (IRE)** (40) (PMonteith) 4-9-1 SDWilliams(9) (chsd ldrs: chal 2f out: carried lft fnl f: kpt on) ....hd	**3**	6/1 ²	47	18
2024⁹ **Portie Sophie** (26) (MBrittain) 5-8-1 JLowe(8) (b: w ldrs: rdn 3f out: hmpd over 1f out: nt qckn)....3½	**4**	20/1	28	—
2168⁹ **Belacqua (USA)** (33) (DWChapman) 3-7-10b NKennedy(13) (a chsng ldrs: rdn 3f out: one pce) .....nk	**5**	33/1	34	—
1468* **Kristal Breeze** (42) (WRMuir) 4-9-3 KFallon(11) (pushed along after 3f: hdwy & in tch ent st: nvr able chal)....½	**6**	4/1 ¹	43	14
2027⁷ **Crystal Warrior** (54) (DNicholls) 3-9-3 KDarley(5) (sme hdwy fnl 2f: nvr nr to chal) ....s.h	**7**	8/1 ³	55	14
2241⁹ **No More Hassle (IRE)** (36) (MrsMReveley) 3-7-10⁽³⁾ DWright(4) (lw: hld up & bhd: rdn & styd on fnl 3f: n.d) ...1	**8**	20/1	35	—
1544⁸ **Kalko** (21) (JSGoldie) 7-7-3⁽⁷⁾ IonaWands(2) (bhd: sme hdwy fnl 2f: n.d).........½	**9**	50/1	19	—
1160⁸ **Bright Pet** (45) (MrsSJSmith) 3-8-8 NConnorton(12) (mid div: drvn along appr st: no imp)......5	**10**	12/1	36	—
2394⁸ **Greek Gold (IRE)** (41) (DWBarker) 7-8-9⁽⁷⁾ JBramhill(6) (in tch to st)........s.h	**11**	12/1	32	3
2357⁸ **Teejay'n'aitch (IRE)** (38) (JSGoldie) 4-8-13 JWeaver(1) (a bhd).....1½	**12**	8/1 ³	27	—
1830¹¹ **Cottage Prince (IRE)** (42) (JJQuinn) 3-8-5 TWilliams(10) (hld up: effrt 3f out: sn btn) 5	**13**	4/1 ¹	24	—
		(SP 128.8%)		**13 Rn**

2m 27.1 (7.40) CSF £192.70 CT £1,052.22 TOTE £21.20: £4.80 £2.50 £2.80 (£133.80) Trio £230.80 OWNER Mrs Lynn Parkes (MALTON)

BRED Noel Finegan

LONG HANDICAP Kalko 7-8 Belacqua (USA) 7-5

WEIGHT FOR AGE 3yo-12lb

If your luck is out you will probably have had a straight win bet on Mithraic, but the Tote dual forecast is there for the taking, if nothing else is. Such races are a real boost to confidence, even when your punting skills might have let you down.

All of these examples happened within a few days and, over the course of the year, many similar opportunities will arise.

CHAPTER 12

THE WAY FORWARD

British horseracing is facing its most difficult problem - how is it going to cope in the years ahead? The British Horseracing Board have taken plenty of criticism for their perceived lack of activity in the area of competitive racing. Although some of the comments levelled against them are justified, on the whole I feel that racing has moved forward under their reign. When you take a sport, such as ours, that generates so much passion in its spectators, everyone has his own view as to how things can be improved. Unfortunately, all our views are different.

Already, racing is changing to meet the expectations of its supporters. In the last few years, we have seen the introduction of SIS, bringing live pictures to virtually every betting shop in the country. All-Weather racing is now becoming something more than a stop-gap during bad weather. With the opening of the third All-Weather track at the rebuilt Wolverhampton course came the advent of floodlit racing in this country. Although the evening and Sunday opening of betting shops may not have pleased everybody, punters turned out in their droves to attend the meetings covered, particularly in fine weather.

When the BHB have tried to increase interest in top races, such as the Derby, by moving it to a Saturday, they were criticised for the clash with other major sporting events. However, the increased flexibility which allows the addition of extra All-Weather meetings during bad weather has been a great success. There is still room for improvement though, as we lag some way behind the Irish as concerns rescheduling meetings.

As a Handicapper, I hold distinct views on Racing's ills. I believe that, in a number of ways, solutions lie in the more imaginative use of the official handicap ratings. I would be surprised if the reader finds nothing in this chapter with which he disagrees, but I hope that there are enough good points to generate some sort of debate.

Anyone who attends race meetings regularly will tell you that the average age of racegoers is gradually creeping upwards. Attempts to make it a family day out seem only to drive the regular racegoers away. However, there have been successes in recent years. Ask anyone who has queued up to get into Wolverhampton on a Saturday night if they think it's been worth it and they'll probably reply yes. Sadly, this is the exception. It is not only on-course that racing is losing ground, off-course Bookmakers are also struggling.

Some of the reasons for racing's decline have been self-inflicted. The farce of the 1993 Grand National has left a bad taste in everyone's mouth. A Bookmaker friend of mine still has over £2,000 worth of void bets to be collected, but these once-a-year punters, who feel that they lost their money without even getting a run, are unlikely to return. The often unfair stories portrayed on national TV about people not being paid out by Bookmakers, or race fixing, just add to the sleazy image of the sport.

However, it's not all racing's fault, the National Lottery has provided the country with a means of getting rich quick. To compete with the National Lottery on level terms would be hard enough, but the odds are stacked heavily against Bookmakers because of the current laws. The Lottery is allowed saturation TV advertising and you can buy a Lottery ticket at the age of sixteen, two years before you are allowed into a betting shop. Racing has to wait for the headlining stories such as Frankie's amazing seven-timer before a national TV audience is reached.

To make matters worse, racing has administrators who fail to see the difference between Bookmakers' turnover and Bookmakers' profit. The Betting Levy is paid by off-course Bookmakers as a percentage of their turnover. Given that many Betting Shop punters have only a limited amount of money to lose, such a Levy agreement makes it in the Bookmakers' interest to maximise profitability yet minimise turnover. Racing is an unwitting ally. Without horseracing, the present betting industry would collapse, yet they seem so reluctant to aid its future, turning more to other forms of gambling.

The failure to control the size of fields effectively contributes not only to an increase in Bookmakers' profitability, but also to the punter's lack of success. This only leads to the punter's natural loss of interest in the game, after all there must be a fair chance for him to win, or why should he play?

In Hong Kong for instance, no race with more than fourteen runners takes place. Whilst no such low limit could be expected here, it is my contention that ordinary handicaps should be limited to eighteen runners with a couple of reserves to ensure that proper place betting takes place.

In terms of maintaining off-course punter interest and so maximising the Levy, racing should be gearing itself to frame races with between eight and eighteen runners. Larger fields would only be allowed for the big handicap races such as the Lincoln, the Royal Hunt Cup, the Stewards' Cup, the Cambridgeshire and the Grand National. Such a tactic is bound to make these big handicaps even more of an event than they already are and heighten ante-post interest.

Fields of below eight are difficult to avoid in any hot spell during the summer months. National Hunt racing has been introduced during the summer months by only using courses which will be able to produce decent ground and the same must be considered for Flat racing. Relying on the likes of Bath and Brighton, which invariably produce very firm ground in sunny weather, is folly and must be rectified, either by limiting the fixtures available to such courses, or by installing effective watering systems.

Before taking you through my ideas for the ways races can be framed, I will address three more basic areas, course closures, All-Weather racing and balloting out.

Course Closures

Our racing industry seems in crisis and the subject of course closures is being discussed by people in the trade. From the punter's point of view, there do seem to be too many meetings. It is increasingly hard to keep abreast of the form day by day and interest is bound to wane as the workload on the amateur increases, whilst his spare time undoubtedly does not.

However, getting the industry to agree to less racing would be as difficult as getting turkeys to vote for Christmas. Fewer races would mean fewer winning horses and fewer happy owners, which would lead to fewer owners, trainers and stable staff (not to mention Journalists and Handicappers!).

Racing is at the stage where it needs to consider how it spends the money it receives from the Betting Levy, and the interest-free loans it grants courses for improvements. It strikes me that one or two of the sharper course executives have taken grants to improve facilities that were already adequate. Such investments seem strange from racing's point of view, but make good sense for the courses. After all, racing's administrators are getting enough criticism at the moment without shutting courses which have recently built new stands with the help of Betting Levy money.

When course closures are mooted, it is normally the lower-class or gaff tracks which are mentioned first, but it shouldn't be. A number of these serve large areas of this island which would have no racing otherwise, such as Perth, Bangor and Fakenham. This philosophy can be easily reversed, for instance Stratford is surrounded by five other jumping courses within reasonably easy reach for its patrons, namely Cheltenham, Hereford, Worcester, Warwick and Towcester. Has Nottingham not brought its own demise closer by abandoning National Hunt racing in favour of the modest Flat fare, also available locally at Leicester and Southwell. Do we need Sandown AND Kempton? Do we need two courses at Newmarket?

I have no doubt that all of the courses I have mentioned could make out an excellent case for their own survival. I hope they will not have to, as I do not want to see any courses close, but if they must, then it is vital that it is done without denying large areas of the country access to racing.

All-Weather Racing

Anathema is a word many in the industry would use to describe All-Weather Racing. I prefer to think of it as an enema! Trainers who bemoan their horses' handicap marks would benefit if Turf and All-Weather racing were handicapped separately with the need to qualify for handicap marks on both surfaces.

What is required is more All-Weather tracks with mixed meetings like those Lingfield stage though the summer. Less damage is done to the Turf course because there are fewer races on it, which enables the groundstaff to keep the course in a good condition. This would in turn allow them to hold more mixed meetings. Hopefully this would encourage more horses to alternate between Turf and All-Weather surfaces. If better horses can be encouraged to race on artificial surfaces then we can lead the way in Europe and give our Breeders' Cup hopefuls a proper arena in which to prepare.

Balloting Out

Owners and trainers are often complaining that their charges get balloted out once the ground becomes suitable. Normally such a problem only affects the poorer horses from the smaller stables and, in races like novice hurdles, it is hard to see a solution. Once a horse gets a handicap mark, the balloting out problem changes. There is a solution to this that would be a lot fairer than the system used at present.

In run-of-the-mill handicaps, the horses with the lowest weights are the first eliminated, which means that the same horses will tend to get removed from similar types of races. Take the case of the Thrussington Handicap at Leicester on 28th October 1996. David Chapman's sprinter Cheeky Chappy made his thirty-fourth appearance of the year in the race, but Logie Pert Lad, Northern Spruce and Siberian Rose were set too low a weight to avoid elimination and were unable to make their fourth appearance of the year.

In such races there is a need for a system that eliminates the most frequent runners and not the bottom weights.

Non-Listed Conditions Races and Handicaps

Non-listed conditions races rarely attract eight or more runners and ought to disappear. However, this will further limit the all-too-few opportunities for decent horses below the top grades.

To replace these opportunities, it is my view that no horse should ever be not qualified (NQ) for a handicap because it is too good. Handicaps should be framed with an intended maximum weight, but if a horse rated 102 is entered for a 0-90 handicap, it will simply be required to carry 12lb more than the intended maximum weight. Whilst on the subject of handicaps, why can't we have a rule that makes it a riding offence to not ride out to the line in all races whatever the position in the race. It should be possible to keep the present rule over the use of the whip on horses whose chance has gone, but still force jockeys to push their mounts out with hands and heels, unless their ride is distressed or injured. This will not only make racing more exciting, but will enable Handicappers to judge the race properly.

Horses without a Handicap Mark

We currently have a problem regarding horses who don't have a handicap mark. The possibility of replacing some maiden races with races for horses without such a mark (normally imports) needs to be considered so that such horses can be integrated into the handicap system a lot more quickly.

In some countries there is a system whereby horses can only drop into the lowest grades of handicap after competing for a full season. It has merit. Aren't we all sick of seeing a large field of moderate seasoned handicappers humbled by something with form figures of 000 who has had a handicap mark for all of a fortnight?

It would aid competitiveness no end if all horses, on qualifying for a handicap mark, were forced to race amongst themselves for a sensible period before being allowed into open handicaps.

Limited Stakes

These races were a really good idea, but for the fact that some numskull decided fillies should receive a sex allowance (normally 5lb). Consequently, if a filly rated 55 beats a colt rated 55 by a head in a 0-55 limited stakes, the official Handicapper finds it much easier to raise the second horse out of the rating band than the winner. As a result, if such a race is run again a couple of weeks later, the winner would probably still be qualified, but not the second!

The sex allowance in such races should be shelved. Alternatively, given a 5lb sex allowance, a 0-55 limited stakes should only admit fillies rated between 0 and 50.

Claiming Races

Claimers are under-used in Britain and receive a bad press. The main problem seems to be that our claims are submitted after the race, therefore an impressive victory can bring the claim forms flooding in. The simple answer is for claims to be lodged before, not after the race. If the horse returns from the race lame, tough luck.

The idea of running claimers in grades seems a good but not original one. We could have races where horses are entered to be claimed for a specific amount; 3, 5, 8, 10, 12, 15, 20, 25, 30,000 pounds.

If a horse that normally contests a £12,000 claimer turned up in a £5,000 version, prospective purchasers would have to judge whether to lodge a claim before the race is run. In such circumstances there are two possibilities, the horse could be in the race to land a gamble or it could be rapidly on the downgrade, the buyer will really need his wits about him. Any multiple claims should continue to be settled by ballot.

We need to persuade the owning and training communities to accept claims as an occupational hazard. It seems to me that the people who run horses in claimers do not often want to lose them but are running in such a race because nothing else is available. As you may have already guessed, I am no great fan of sex allowances for fillies and mares. However, if this was adopted as a policy, the most moderate of these should not be forced into such races as they might be breeder-owned with the intention of retiring them to the paddocks.

Handicap Allowance Races

This is an idea that the official Handicappers will regard as a real can of worms, but if Stewarding is up to an acceptable standard, there really shouldn't be any problem.

How many times have you heard trainers complaining that their charges never win because they are badly handicapped? It isn't always true, but they do often have a point. My view is that some handicaps should become handicap allowance races, for want of a better term.

In these races, horses would run off their current handicap mark but would receive a 7lb penalty for each handicap win in the last twelve months. However, runners would receive a 2lb allowance for each time they had finished second, third or fourth in a handicap during the same period. To demonstrate I have listed below the Girdlestone Pumps Handicap at Newmarket on 28th June, 1996.

Horse	Starting Price	Weight Carried	Record in Handicaps	Weight Adjustment
Angaar	3/1	9-1	00	nil
Dande Flyer	7/2	8-11	2401130334	+2
Stoney End	7/2	8-6	2	-2
Galine	13/2	9-0	1024	+3
Total Aloof	9/1	8-11	00	nil
Rushcutter Bay	10/1	9-7	00010	+7
Pleasure Time	12/1	8-1	012200300043	-3
Playmaker	16/1	8-10	3000	-2

In this case, the betting would not have been made more open but the result would have been closer as Galine and Rushcutter Bay had three and a half lengths in hand on the rest of the field.

Friday June 28th
WEATHER: unsettled WIND: slt across

2301 GIRDLESTONE PUMPS H'CAP (0-85) (3-Y.O) (Class D)
4-00 (4-00) 5f (July) £5,026.00 (£1,498.00: £714.00: £322.00) Stalls: Low GOING minus 0.14 sec per fur (G)

			SP	RR	S
20784 **Galine** (78) (WAO'Gorman) 3-9-0 EmmaO'Gorman(4) (swtg: hld up: rdn over 1f out: led ins fnl f: comf) ....—	1	13/2 3	90	67	
21437 **Rushcutter Bay** (85) (TTClement) 3-9-4v(3) JStack(8) (lw: trckd ldr: led over 2f out: hdd & no ex ins fnl f).....1¾	2	10/1	91	68	
16468 **Total Aloof** (75) (WJHaggas) 3-8-11 BDoyle(5) (b.off fore: chsd ldrs: outpcd 2f out: kpt on fnl f)...................3½	3	9/1	70	47	
21434 **Dande Flyer** (75) (DWPArbuthnot) 3-8-11 TQuinn(2) (b: hld up: effrt over 1f out: no imp)............................nk	4	7/2 2	69	46	
18233 **Pleasure Time** (66) (CSmith) 3-8-2v1ow1 MFenton(7) (led over 2f: rdn & btn appr fnl f) ....hd	5	12/1	60	36	
16286 **Angaar (IRE)** (79) (ACStewart) 3-9-1 MRoberts(6) (chsd ldrs: outpcd 2f out: r.o again nr fin) ....½	6	3/1 1	71	48	
18055 **Playmaker** (74) (MAJarvis) 3-8-10 PRobinson(9) (lw: b.off hind: chsd ldrs 3f)...8	7	16/1	41	18	
20212 **Stoney End (USA)** (70) (MRChannon) 3-8-6 PatEddery(3) (a bhd)...7	8	7/2 2	14	—	
		(SP 115.4%)	8 F		

59.62 secs (1.12) CSF £60.05 CT £538.29 TOTE £9.70: £2.20 £2.90 £2.70 (£61.80) Trio £425.30; £125.81 to Newcastle 29/6/96 OWNER Mr S. Fustok (NEWMARKET) BRED Deerfield Farm

Another handicap with far from open betting was the Scania Trophy at Ayr on 4th July 1996. For this, the adjustments would have been as follows:-

Desert Frolic	4/5	8-13	11	+14
Cheerful Aspect	9/2	9-7	4440	-6
Northern Motto	6/1	7-7	040004	-4
Redstella	7/1	9-6	00	nil
Home Counties	10/1	9-10	300	-2
Lord Advocate	14/1	8-10	000001031120	+17

Had such a race taken place, Desert Frolic would probably not have been an odds-on favourite, although she would probably have won. The race finished as follows:-

Thursday July 4th
WEATHER: overcast WIND: fresh against

2418 SCANIA 1996 TRUCK OF THE YEAR TROPHY H'CAP (0-85) (3-Y.O+) (Class D)
7-35 (7-35) 1m 5f 13y £4,182.00 (£1,266.00: £618.00: £294.00) Stalls: Low GOING: 0.37 sec per fur (GS)

			SP	RR
2239* **Desert Frolic (IRE)** (70) (MJohnston) 3-8-13 4x JWeaver(5) (lw: mde all: clr ent st: styd on strly) ....—	1	4/5 1	79
20564 **Northern Motto** (53) (WStorey) 3-7-7(3) NVarley(2) (rdn appr st: styd on wl fnl 3f: nvr able to chal) 3½	2	6/1 3	58
23905 **Lord Advocate** (78) (DANolan) 8-8-7b(3) SDrowne(6) (chsd wnr tl outpcd fnl 3f) 8	3	14/1	48
19775 **Redstella (USA)** (63) (RMWhitaker) 7-9-6 DeanMcKeown(1) (dwlt: sn prom: rdn 8f out: hung lft & no imp fnl 3f)...2	4	7/1	56
21646 **Cheerful Aspect (IRE)** (78) (EALDunlop) 3-9-7 KFallon(3) (chsd ldrs: rdn 4f out: sn btn) 5	5	9/2 2	64
15856 **Home Counties (IRE)** (67) (DMoffatt) 7-9-7(3) DarrenMoffatt(4) (bhd: rdn 5f out: n.d)..............................6	6	10/1	46
		(SP 116.3%)		

3m 0.1 (15.30) CSF £6.27 TOTE £1.60: £1.10 £2.10 (£4.90) OWNER Maktoum Al Maktoum (MIDDLEHAM) BRED Gainsborough Stud

It can be seen from the second example that horses with multiple wins in handicaps over the past year would not be aimed at such races. This type of race would instead offer opportunities to horses who have been knocking at the door without winning. Should the likes of Cheerful Aspect and Northern Motto fail, the fact that they have been beaten off a theoretically lower mark than intended by the official Handicapper ought to enable the horses' marks to fall more quickly than at present.

During the 1996 Flat season, the Jack Banks-trained Prince Babar had a tremendous record in the big handicaps without winning one. His only win from the season was in an Ascot apprentice race. Beaten less than two lengths in the Victoria Cup, the Wokingham, the Schweppes Golden Mile, the New Zealand Handicap, the Ayr Gold Cup and the Autumn Handicap, Prince Babar's handicap mark rose from 82 on Victoria Cup day to three figures by the end of the season. This is an extreme example but it shows how the official Handicapper has to react to quality efforts in defeat. The Prince Babars of this world deserve the odd winning outlet for their talent without the need to resort to soft conditions races. Whilst it is unlikely that handicap allowance races can be framed to attract such good horses, those lower down the scale could easily benefit.

These races would be perfect for consistent types who rarely win. Take the example of Desert Invader, who won off a Handicap Mark of 57 in an Amateur Riders' Handicap during February 1996. Below are his following runs in All-Weather Handicaps:-

Date	Handicap Mark	Finishing Position	Beaten	Odds
1/3	64	3/10	0.5	4/1
6/3	64	2/10	1.75	10/3
18/3	69	2/9	1.25	3/1
31/5	73	9/10	29	12/1
22/6	70	4/13	2.25	14/1
6/7	70	5/11	4.25	25/1
27/7	70	2/16	0.25	9/1
9/8	75	10/13	13.5	10/1
16/8	75	4/13	3.25	7/1

It can be seen from this that Desert Invader continually ran well without winning and his Handicap Mark gradually rose. Incidentally, a further thirteen runs after August 16th have failed to yield another victory at the time of writing, despite numerous placed efforts. Turf and All-Weather his losing run stands at twenty-seven and his last run in a Handicap was off a mark of 68.

Listed and Group Races

Even at the top end of the scale, it appears Britain has its problems. At the annual Horserace Writers lunch every December, we journalists proclaim the trainer who has won the most prizemoney abroad in the past year. In 1996, Michael Stoute took the honour courtesy of the exploits of Pilsudski and Singspiel in some of the world's top races, but this is not normally the case.

Pattern races in this country are just too competitive. A listed race in Germany will often attract two or three English-trained runners, yet Germany rarely supplies a competitor for a similar race over here. The problem extends right the way up the scale. Most years, four or more of the runners in the Italian Derby are trained in Britain, but rarely do we see an Italian-based horse running in a British Group One.

The most extreme view is that it is the European Pattern that is at fault and our options seem to be to either get it fixed, or pull out altogether and form our own classification system. While the situation remains whereby it is easier to win a German Group One than a British Group Two, the problem is bound to continue.

In 1995 the likes of Branston Abby and Hever Golf Rose ran regularly abroad, denying the racing industry the Levy that their participation in races here would undoubtedly have generated, as they are horses that are well known and who punters are prepared to support. Nobody in their right mind would argue against International Competition, but it needs to be a fair fight on a pretty level playing field.

If we were to persuade international racing to adopt a Pattern consisting of five levels of Group race, most of the races both here and in France could keep their current status with many races elsewhere in Europe being dropped to Group Four or Five. Being something of a realist, I accept that this is most unlikely to happen but prizemoney alone does not seem to work, as throwing money at our higher-class races appears to have done nothing to increase field sizes.

The fact that we have problems, even at the very top level of our racing, is illustrated by a look at the career of Lammtarra. His four wins came in a listed race at two and three Group Ones as a three-year-old, namely the Epsom Derby, the King George VI and Queen Elizabeth Diamond Stakes and the Prix de l'Arc de Triomphe. To win the big three on his only starts as a three-year-old understandably drew great plaudits from Journalists, but Handicappers struggled to put an exalted rating on the colt.

However, the fault lies with the whole system and not with Handicappers. Indeed, it can be easily argued that the International Classifications over-rated Lammtarra in relation to both Pentire and Freedom Cry, with whom he shared tight finishes at Epsom and Longchamp respectively and who themselves had a close-run thing when they met in the Irish Champion Stakes. A Pattern system set up to facilitate the improvement of the breed had patently failed to establish the true merits of one of our shining lights. In his four-race career, Lammtarra was asked to concede weight to just two horses, admittedly both Classic winners, yet received weight from eighteen of the forty opponents he ever faced.

Such a reading of events questions the very existence of a weight-for-age scale, and how we can address such a problem is a real conundrum. Obviously, the top races should not be handicaps or have conditions which require the carrying of penalties. The nearest I can offer to a solution is that Group One races after the Derby should be run at level weights. In this way only an exceptional three-year-old could be retired as an Arc and King George winner and, in order to win these races, rather more than do at present would be forced to stay in training.

CHAPTER 13

GLOSSARY OF TERMS

Term	Definition
Adjusted ratings	Master and performance ratings adjusted to the weights and conditions of a particular race, allowing direct comparison of the competitors.
Balloting out	The system by which horses are eliminated from races where too many horses have been declared to run. Currently, in handicap races the horses allotted the lowest weight are the first to be eliminated.
Banker	A selection considered so certain of victory that a punter's entire betting bank can be placed on it. In reality, there is no such thing.
BHB (British Horseracing Board)	The BHB is the body that runs racing on a day to day basis in Great Britain.
Box race	A Flat race in which the stall number drawn appears to have had a significant bearing on the outcome.
Card	A word used to describe the races being held at a particular course on a particular day.
Class (of race)	All racing is split into seven classes, by importance. Class A representing the top-quality races, down to Class G the poorest.
Close-up	Describes the running of each horse in a race.
Computer Raceform	A personal Computer-based *Form Book* using Microsoft Windows, launched in 1991. This allows fast access to the next day's declarations, previous form and statistics, as well as a *Note-Book* and own rating facility.
Full maturity	When a horse is considered to have achieved its optimum ability at a particular distance, judged by the official weight-for-age table.
Fully exposed	A horse which has sufficient form for the onlooker to know its ability.
Furlong	220 yards, or one-eighth of a mile.
Gaff tracks	The lower-grade tracks, normally in country locations, which stage a large proportion of the more modest races.

Handicap race	A race in which the competitors are given a weight according to their known ability for the purpose of ensuring a close race and open betting.
Handicap mark	A rating given by the BHB handicapper's which is used in allotting weights to be carried in handicap races.
International Classifications	An annual set of ratings, on the best horses from various countries, allowing comparisons to be made between each country's best horses and between years.
Jockey Club	The organization which deals with rules and discipline within racing
Lengths in hand	The superiority one competitor appears to have over a rival.
Made all	When the winning horse has led for the entire distance of the race.
Master ratings	A master rating is one figure which identifies a horse's ability under any particular code. A horse can therefore have separate master ratings for chase, hurdle, Turf Flat and All-Weather Flat.
Minimum trip	The rules of racing state that no Flat race can be run over a distance of less than five furlongs, and that no hurdle or chase race over a distance below two miles.
NQ	A horse that is Not Qualified to run in a particular race as it does not satisfy the conditions of the contest.
Off course Bookmakers	High Street Betting Shops and Credit Offices.
On course Bookmakers	The individuals or representatives of firms who attend race meetings for the purposes of laying bets.
Par times	The American expression for a standard time.
Pattern race	The best Flat races, divided into Group One, Two and Three.
Pedigree	A word used to describe a horse's parentage. Normally shown as its sire (father), followed by a dash, then its dam (mother) and finally its dam's sire, normally shown within parenthesis.
Performance ratings	A performance rating is a numeric assessment of the level of ability that a horse has shown in a specific race.

Pounds (lb)	Weights carried by horses are expressed in stones and pounds (14lb equal one stone).
Private handicap	A term used to describe ratings compiled by people other than the official Handicapper.
Punters	People who place bets.
RPH	*Raceform Private Handicap.*
SIS	Satellite Information Services, the organisation which beams live pictures from racecourses into British Betting Shops.
Slowly-run race	A race with an unduly slow early pace, as none of the competitors wanted to force a stronger gallop.
"Split Second" time ratings	The time ratings compiled by *Raceform* and shown in their publications, on a scale of 0-100.
Standard times	A benchmark against which to judge race times. As courses and distances vary, each distance at each course has its own standard time.
Talking horse	One whose reputation greatly exceeds what it has so far achieved.
Time ratings	An assessment of the horse's performance in a race, based on the time taken to complete the course.
Weight-for-age table	A table which shows in pounds the average lack of maturity of any age group, over any particular distance, at any time of year.
Wins-to-runs ratio	The number of times a horse has won, judged against its overall number of outings.

RACEFORM GOING ALLOWANCE PER RACE

STARTING PRICE AND FAVOURITE INDICATOR

RACEFORM RATING AWARDED FOR THIS PERFORMANCE

SPEED FIGURE AWARDED FOR THIS PERFORMANCE

TRAINER/AGE/WEIGHT/HEADGEAR/JOCKEY/ALLOWANCE/OVERWEIGHT/DRAW

TOTAL STARTING PRICE PERCENTAGE

OWNER/TRAINER LOCATION/BREEDER

STALLS PER RACE

TOTE DIVIDENDS

RACE TITLE

RACE DISTANCE

RACE CONDITIONS

VALUE TO FIRST SIX

EXCLUSIVE NOTE-BOOK COMMENT

RACE TIME AND OFF TIME

RACE NUMBER TO WHICH THE INDEX WILL REFER

OFFICIAL HANDICAP RATING

TIME TAKEN 0.08 QUICKER THAN RACEFORM STANDARD TIME

LONG HANDICAP WEIGHT

OFFICIAL WEIGHT-FOR-AGE

LAST RACE IN WHICH HORSE WARRANTED A NOTE-BOOK COMMENT

IN-FOCUS COMMENT HIGHLIGHTS FACTORS AFFECTING THE RACE

STARTING PRICE AND RELEVANT MARKET MOVES

1148-**NEWMARKET** (R-H) **(Good to firm)**
Saturday June 1st
WEATHER: overcast. WIND: fresh half bhd

1630 NGK SPARK PLUGS H'CAP (0-100) (3-Y-O +) (Class C)
4-45 (4-46) 5f (Rowley) £5,848.00 (£1,744.00: £832.00: £376.00) Stalls: Centre GOING minus 0.40 sec per fur (F)

				SP	RB	SF
11073	Top Banana (91) (HCandy) 5-9-5 CRutter(4) (lw: hdwy over 1f out: qcknd to ld wl ins fnl f: rdn out)	—	1	3/11	101	70
11784	Bowden Rose (83) (MBlanshard) 4-8-11b JQuinn(9) (chsd ldrs: led ins fnl f: sn hdd & unable qckn)	1/2	2	7/13	91	60
13217	Croft Pool (100) (JAGlover) 5-10-0 SDWilliams(10) (a.p: led 1f out: sn hdd & no ex)	1/2	3	25/1	107	76
117810	Tart and a Half (79) (BJMeehan) 4-8-7b LDettori(12) (chsd ldrs: ev ch over 1f out: no ex ins fnl f)	hd	4	6/12	86	55
1149?	Sweet Magic (84) (PHowling) 5-8-12 FNorton(2) (chsd ldrs: rdn & no ex appr fnl f)	3/4	5	6/12	88	57
11494	Cyrano's Lad (IRE) (89) (CADwyer) 7-9-3 CDwyer(1) (led 4f: one pce)	s.h	6	12/1	93	62
111313	Pride of Brixton (88) (GLewis) 3-8-9 PatEddery(3) (dwlt: nvr nr)	nk	7	8/1	91	53
13213	Takadou (IRE) (95)MissLCSiddall) 5-9-9 JWeaver(6) (lw: nvr trbld ldrs)	3/4	8	12/1	96	65
11138	Laurel Delight (83) (JBerry) 6-8-11 JCarroll(7) (b: nr fore: chsd ldrs over 3f)	2	9	20/1	77	46
14469	Ashtina (68) (BAPearce) 11-7-5(5) MartinDwyer(8) (lw: outpcd)	5	10	50/1	46	15
11867	Master of Passion (83) (JMPEustace) 7-8-11 MTebbutt(5) (b: prom: stumbled after 2f: no ch after)	21/2	11	9/1	53 ++	22
1430*	Sailormate (85) (SRBowring) 5-8-13b DeanMcKeown (11) (ref to r: t.n.p.)	R		7/13	—	—

(SP 125.6%) **12 Rn**

58.62 secs (-0.08) CSF £24.45 CT £428.80 TOTE £3.40: £1.60 £2.30 £7.50 (£25.50) Trio £205.90 OWNER Major M. G. Wyatt (WANTAGE)
BRED Dunchurch Lodge Stud Co.
LONG HANDICAP Ashtina 7-8
WEIGHT FOR AGE 3yo-7lb

IN-FOCUS: **The stalls were placed in the centre for both sprints on the card, but were dominated by horses racing closer to either rail.**
1107 **Top Banana** found a fine turn of speed to pass the field in the last couple of furlongs and goes to Royal Ascot with every chance, although it must be remembered that he finished second in last year's Stewards' Cup off just 79. (3/1)
1178 **Bowden Rose**, who ran a cracker from a bad draw last time, went to post really well. Racing wide apart from the winner, she is having no luck and must surely win soon. (7/1: op 11/1)
Croft Pool, off a 2lb higher mark than he has ever won, ran a terrific race and would have prospects in listed company over this trip. (25/1)
1064 **Tart and a Half** is in good form at present but does not exactly make a habit of winning. (6/1)
1113 **Sweet Magic**, lightly-raced for a five-year-old, ran well and should soon find an opportunity. (6/1)
1149 **Cyrano's Lad** (IRE) ran well but found this trip too short. (12/1)
1186 **Master of Passion** lost all chance when clipping the heels of a rival and pulling off a front shoe. (9/1)